T0369011

J-Management

Fresh Perspectives on the Japanese Firm in the 21st Century

Edited by Parissa Haghirian

Sophia University, Tokyo

iUniverse, Inc.
New York Bloomington

J-Management
Fresh Perspectives on the Japanese Firm in the 21st Century

iUniverse books may be ordered through booksellers or by contacting:

iUniverse
1663 Liberty Drive
Bloomington, IN 47403
www.iuniverse.com
1-800-Authors (1-800-288-4677)

ISBN: 978-1-4401-2537-9 (sc)
ISBN: 978-1-4401-2540-9 (dj)
ISBN: 978-1-4401-2538-6 (e-book)

Printed in the United States of America

iUniverse rev. date: 4/27/2009

Contents

1. Introduction

Why a students' book on Japanese management? The idea for this book comes from a class on Japanese management, which I teach every autumn term at the Faculty of Liberal Arts at Sophia University in Tokyo, Japan. This class comprises a mix of Japanese students, of whom many are bilingual, and international students from countries all over the world. In the class I present theories on traditional Japanese management styles and compare them with international management styles. As the Japanese economy is in transition we naturally discuss students' every day observations and their impressions of Japanese management.

The class provides time for discussion in which international students pose many questions on the topics that interest them. These questions allow the Japanese students to explain the background of Japanese management processes, which furthers the understanding of their international colleagues as well as deepening and clarifying their understanding of their own culture and society.

We are not judgmental in this class. Rather I try to help students to develop two management skill sets based on their knowledge of Western and Japanese management styles.

However, there is a lot of knowledge created in these classes and at some point we decided that it would be a good idea to make the content of these discussions available to a wider audience. Though the end product may not meet the criteria of rigorous academic research–this is not the object of the book–the materials are sufficiently interesting that we felt the need to bring them to the attention of and to benefit a wider audience. We hope that this book might stimulate other student-centered work in the future.

Most chapters provide a synthesis of ideas and were researched and written by cross-cultural teams. The main objective is to give insights into the current situation of Japanese management and to explain the Japanese views. The chapters therefore not only contain an overview of relevant sources on the topics, but also include the personal experiences and opinions of the writers.

This book will appeal to anybody who is interested in learning about the latest trends and developments and who wishes to gain fresh insights into Japanese management, culture and society. Undergraduates, both of Japanese universities as well as universities worldwide, but also researchers and international managers will find this a useful overview of the current situation in Japan.

The book is divided into four parts. The first part explains the development of Japanese management after the war (Baktash Muhammadi) and the reasons for the bubble economy (Hitomi Kakishima, Hayaka Kawamura, Saaya Konishi, Aya Yoshida). In the second part, we describe which new developments Japanese society and Japanese corporations have to deal with. Here structural and economic changes (Manuel Lukas and Miho

Saito), demographic changes (Aaron Schiffer and Yui Inada) and cultural and social changes (Rolf Madrid, Yuka Tanaka and Greg Taylor) are discussed.

The main part of the book deals with the changes which can be observed in Japanese management today. Here the students discuss different management disciplines such as Human Resource Management (Akihiro Kayama and Momoko Kusayanagi), Distribution (Matthew Cabuloy and Megumi Aoki), Production Management (Natsuki Hayakawa, Pascal Kalbermatten and Mari Okachi), Marketing (Jun Nishida and Anna Sanga), Knowledge Management (Alison Onishi) and Entrepreneurship in Japan (Jeffrey Honma, Kotaro Kinoshita and Ayano Sakuragi).

The final part of the book deals with diversity issues in the Japanese firm. Here Yuuko Shimizu and Asako Washizu write about the employment conditions of Japanese women and Nodoka Kobayashi, Kaoru Miki and Delphine Pilate discuss the Japanese firm as a multicultural workplace.

This book was supported by friends and colleagues at Sophia University. Prof. Emmanuel Cheron, Prof. Keisuke Otsu and Prof. Linda Grove, all of Sophia University, were very supportive during the writing process. Many thanks also to Neale Cunningham for his efforts on proof-reading the manuscripts and for his valuable feedback. The cover photograph was taken by Michael Tiffany, who is also a student at our faculty.

Dr. Parissa Haghirian

Faculty of Liberal Arts

Sophia University, Tokyo, Japan

August 2008

2. Post-War Economy

By Baktash Muhammad

Japan after World War II

After the Japanese defeat in the Second World War, on August 14, 1945, when Emperor Hirohito accepted the terms of the Potsdam Declaration, Japan was officially occupied by the Allied forces, which consisted of Britain, the former Soviet Union, and above all the United States of America. Besides these three main players, Australia, India and a couple of other countries also played a very important role in occupying Japan and were part of the Allied forces. The Americans started controlling Japan behind the scenes. In front a so-called government was established to implement the reforms set by the Supreme Commander of the Allied Power (SCAP), with General Douglas McArthur at its head. The American occupation officially ended on April 28, 1952, on the basis of a peace treaty which was signed in San Francisco on September 8, 1951 (Pyle 1995).

At the beginning of the occupation the American policy towards Japan was not the same as Europe. This policy saw Japan as important but secondary compared to Europe. Immediately after the defeat, Japan was facing many economic and social problems because the economy had been totally destroyed during the war. The total estimate of loss in national wealth by the end of the war was about five times as high as the damage caused by the great earthquake of 1923 (Adams and Hoshii 1972).

After the occupation, the very first thing that America attempted to do was to dismantle Japan's military system (Pyle 1995). The implementation of this policy led to high unemployment caused by the demobilization of the military forces, the closure of military production sites and the repatriation of Japanese from abroad. The unemployment figure peaked at 13.1 million people of whom 750,000 were women (Nakamura 1995).

The second problem that Japan and its economy faced was a power shortage. At that time, coal and hydropower were the two main sources of power generation. The big drop in coal output due to a Chinese and Korean refusal to work in coal mines was another problem that the economy faced. The Chinese and Korean workers refused as they were no longer afraid of Japanese power. Another problem was starvation, which was caused by the food shortage as the Japanese rice crop output fell in 1945 (Adams and Hoshii 1972). Therefore there was a fear of starvation due to the bleak food supply situation (Nakamura 1995).

On the monetary side, inflation was a big dilemma for the government and the Allied forces. The first cause of this problem was the issuance of the saving funds by the former government, which had secured its income from savings and public bonds, etc. Because of its compulsory saving policy, the government did not pay out these bonds during World War II, but once the air raids intensified the government had no choice but to release the funds fearing public unrest. The second reason for inflation was unwanted provisional military funds, which started surfacing in the market. These funds were basically used to provide the salaries of demobilized troops, payments for completed orders of military goods, compensation for losses, etc. This caused inflation of about 50% to 365% during the years 1945-1949. The increased supply of money at the root of inflation forced the common man in Japan to start hoarding commodities in anticipation of day by day price rises (Lincoln 2004). This led to a rapid decline in bank deposits in December 1945 (Nakamura 1995; Adams and Hoshii 1972).

The situation right after the defeat led to a number of economic measures and many changes were undertaken by the government and the Allied forces. As mentioned above, demobilization of the Army was the very first measure that the Allied forces implemented in Japan. That action created inflation during the early period of the occupation. Therefore, the Americans were eager to stabilize the economy and to initiate supportive measures. SCAP introduced a number of reforms such as "the dissolution of the combines (*zaibatsu*) and the democratization of agriculture and labor." (Adams and Hoshii 1972) SCAP did this to accomplish a wider distribution of income and ownership of the means of production (Pyle 1995). In December 1945, the Diet passed a trade union act under pressure from SCAP. This act guaranteed the right of workers to strike, negotiate collectively and also to organize other activities. Land reform forced absent landlords to sell land cultivated by tenants to the government, and also farmers who cultivated their own fields could only keep 2.451 acres. As a result of this reform, about 80% of the tenant cultivated land was released (Adam and Hoshii 1972), and the portion of tenant cultivated agricultural land was reduced from 50% to 10% (Nakamura 1995). Therefore, land reform was a further economic measure which was engineered by the Americans. In 1947, the Diet pressed into passage legislation modeled on American anti-trust laws that formed a Fair Trade commission for policing businesses and to eliminate monopoly practice.

To curb inflation, the government and SCAP took numerous measures, including a limitation on withdrawing money, which was limited to 500 yen per month per household. This limitation had two purposes: one was to hold money in banks and second to control the circulation of money in the market. Despite these measures taken by the government to stop inflation, the rise in prices and the expansion in note issues continued (Adams and Hoshii 1972). Therefore, the government and SCAP had to wait for the implementation of the Dodge Plan to combat inflation (Nakamura 1995).

Besides economic reforms, the government and SCAP also introduced social reforms. Women's right to vote was one of them. It was also one of the main goals for the Americans. After this reform, in the first general election in April 1946, more than 13 million women voted for the first time and thirty-nine women were elected to the Diet. On the education side, after a tour of Japan, twenty-seven American educators recommended a full change in the Japanese education system and full adoption of the American education system and its philosophy. The reform introduced a single educational track of 6+3+3 schooling: six years of primary school, three years of secondary and another 3 years of high school, and 4 years of college education (Hamada and Kasuya 1993). The SCAP education reform aimed to root out the nationalist orientation of schools and replace it with a democratic and individualist philosophy (Pyle 1995).

To deal with the issue of inflation, the Dodge Plan was implemented. The Dodge Plan was an extensive fiscal and monetary policy developed under the leadership of the Detroit Bank president Joseph Dodge (Adam and Hoshii 1972). Mr. Dodge, a believer in the free-market economy, completely rejected the role of the government. Rather, he gave importance to the efforts of the people themselves in the rehabilitation of industry. He advanced three basic policies for the Japanese economy. The first was a balanced budget. The issuing of long term-bonds was banned under the Finance Act of 1947, but the government issued short-term bonds with maturities of one year to cover its deficits and continually rolled them over. Second, new loans for the Reconstruction Bank were suspended. According to Nakamura (1995), this action was aimed at cutting off the sources of supply of new currency, which were seen as the fundamental cause of inflation. The third policy was to decrease and eliminate subsidies. These policies were followed by the establishment of an exchange rate of 360 yen to 1 dollar in April of 1949, which was maintained for 22 years. The above mentioned policies forced businesses to be more efficient in their production, supply and distribution and to rely less on government subsidies. On the other hand, the yen to dollar exchange rate provided a good grounding for the export of Japanese goods as they were cheaper than products from European countries.

One should not forget the role America played in promoting the export of Japanese goods. Besides the cheap yen-dollar exchange rate, as the main occupying force, America provided special rights for the import of Japanese goods through the 1950s as a matter of national policy (Tabb 1995), or simply opened its markets to Japanese business and Japanese goods. The Americans played an important role in developing Japan's post-war economy (Olsen 1978).

But one should remember that America only played the role of a catalyst. The other factor behind Japan's postwar economy and its success were the Japanese themselves. This effect became evident during the Korean War of 1950-53 and during the Japanese economic boom between 1960 and the first half of the 1980s.

Japan's Economic Recovery

The turning point for the recovery of the Japanese economy came during the Korean war of 1950-53. At the end of World War II, the Korean Peninsula was divided into two parts: north and south. The North was controlled mainly by the Soviet Union and the South by the U.S. After the invasion of South Korea by North Korean troops, America, under the flag of the United Nations, entered the Korean War to support the South Koreans. America committed its troops, as well other resources available in Japan, to the Korean War.

Owing to the yen-dollar exchange rate and the low wage system, Japanese goods were the cheapest. On the other hand, Japan still had expertise to produce military equipment. These two factors helped the country export its goods outside, especially to supply American servicemen in Korea. The action was strongly encouraged by the U.S. government, which wanted Japan to recover so it could use its economy and military in the Cold War. "The massive American demand for supplies during the Korean War kept the growth rate high during the early post war period, probably until about the 1960s." (Minami 1986, p. 52)

Owing to the ideal location that Japan had, it was very easy for the Americans to supply equipment from Japan to the Korean peninsula. These special procurement orders and exports gave the Japanese economy, which was facing problems with inventories and unemployment, a very good start. As a result of the implementation of the Dodge Plan, the Japanese economy was facing a deflationary crisis (Kosai 1981). Therefore, the outbreak of the Korean War changed the Japanese situation and Japan became a supply base for America. Japan had also gained a lot of expertise in manufacturing before the war, which made the country a favorable supplier for the American war effort in Korea.

From 1950-1953, the export of supplies to American servicemen, or special U.S. procurement, reached over 1.5 billion U.S. dollars, "whereas normal exports in 1949 had been 0.5 billion U.S. dollars." (Tabb 1995, p. 92) Almost at the same time, the export of other goods rose tremendously, but due to a rise in prices imports did not increase.

This changed the import-export trade balance very favorably out of the red in the latter half of the 1950s. The moment the Korean War broke out, SCAP removed the ceiling on the export of cotton that had previously been set to 4 million spindles (Adams and Hoshii 1972). As a result, the industry expanded at a very fast rate. In 1951, Japan became the number one exporter of cotton fabrics, with little over half of the production compared to the pre-war period.

In 1951, the boom leveled off because the Americans suspended purchases of strategic materials. Because exports peaked during the boom, once purchases were suspended, all export materials turned to inventory. Owing to export cancellations, the problem of inventories also extended to export commodities, with textiles at the top of the list. As the economy was recovering, some trading firms became insolvent and banks began to advance relief funds to rescue these firms. Despite these problems, the Japanese economy did not slow down and it maintained its high level of growth thanks to increased investment in equipment and increased personal consumption.

As mentioned above, the Korean War had an important effect on equipment and plant. With the income from exports, companies started to invest in equipment, plant and technological innovation. The government supported companies fully by providing them with loans. American measures, such as democratization, land reforms, the dissolution of *zaibatsu* and the creation of trade unions, helped companies improve their competitiveness and also helped increase the purchasing power of the people. Having lost its military power due to demobilization, the Japanese made economic growth their new national objective in order to face and regain their international position. Many industries, such as electric power, steel, shipping and coal, were the main focus of the government, with further strong support from the business community. The government could provide this support only because of the reduction in defense spending. Basically, the security of the country was totally left to America. Article 9 of the 1947 constitution prohibited Japan from waging war against other nations and also from having military capability for waging war. In this way, the government could focus fully on "rich nation" rather than "strong military."

The Japanese attempted to keep up with international competition. Of course, this was not a new ideology for the Japanese government; which had been following this ideology since the Meiji Restoration. The low interest rate encouraged key businesses to invest in equipment and plant. In this way, the government wanted to address the need to catch up with Western technology. At the same time, importing new technologies from outside was also another way for Japan to catch up with the West. America played a very important role in this regard, too. Private companies sold technologies to Japanese firms at a very small profit (Reischauer and Jansen 1995). As a result of investment in plant and equipment and importing the new technologies, Japan was able to close the technological gap and become a strong competitor with outstanding business and marketing techniques.

After World War II and during the Korean War, it was the exchange rate, the positive attitude of the Japanese people toward a bright future, along with the policies of the government that helped Japan regain its per capita level of wealth of the pre-war level by 1955. Because of this, Japanese exports kept on increasing from the 1950s, while the key import was oil. According to Nakamura (1995), until the 1950s, the main source of energy for Japan was coal, but oil replaced it at a very rapid rate by the mid 1950s. The coal shortage of 1950-51 and the miners' strike in 1952 shifted demand to electric power and oil as a source of energy (Kosai 1981). Oil constituted roughly 80% of energy imports by the beginning of the 1970s (Koshiro 2000). The Korean War boom was not the only boom. Japan has had a number of other booms, that is, in 1953, the investment boom, from 1956-57, the "*Jimmu* boom," and the plant and equipment investment expansion of 1959-61, the "*Iwato* boom." From 1950 to the mid-1960s, Japanese GDP grew at a rate of 5% (Nakamura 1995).

These booms came along with changes at the governmental level as well. With American support, Japan became a member of four international organizations: the IMF, the World Bank, the General Agreement on Tariffs and Trade (GATT) and the United Nations, in 1952, 1955 and 1956 respectively. Thus Japan took its first steps into the international environment.

At that time, demographic changes could also be observed. The Japanese population grew rapidly from the 1950s until the early 1960s. "The unprecedented rapid population increase during the first half of the 1960s was a result of the baby boom of 1947 until 1949." (Minami 1986, p. 267) The effect of the increase in the labor supply by the mid-1960s was canceled out by rapidly growing exports. As exports grew, the labor market kept on supplying labor to maintain production. Thus companies could keep up with growing exports. On the other hand, increased productivity and exports had a very important effect on wage increases, which equaled those in the United States (Reischauer and Jansen 1995). Companies grew profits and, as is the Japanese tradition, companies started to take care of employees more effectively. With an increase in wages, people had more disposable income. This triggered a rise in domestic consumption that helped Japanese factories to develop at a faster rate.

The 1960s

The 1960s were years full of political turbulence and economic progress. On the political side, in 1960 the Japan-U.S. Security Treaty was due for revision. The old treaty contained a number of unequal clauses. The government faced a lot of difficulties in revising the treaty and passing it through the Diet. It faced numerous, large-scale, daily demonstrations. Finally the government passed the revised treaty on May 19, 1960. Even after passing the treaty, the reaction among the Japanese public was strong and on June 15, 1960, college student Michiko Kamba died in the fighting that followed the radical students' invasion of the Diet (Kosai 1981).

Soon after these events, Minister of Economy, Trade and Industry (METI) Hayato Ikeda became prime minister. The very first thing he did was implement the ten-year "income-doubling plan." His policies focused on active promotion of economic growth. This plan was another step towards the recovery of the Japanese economy and at the same time a successful step to place Japan on the path of progress. According to Takatoshi Itô (1992), the goal was achieved in seven years instead of ten.

1960 was also the year of trade liberalization, which means important quotas were removed, foreign exchange transactions were liberalized, foreign capital was admitted to industries which produced one third of manufactures, and foreign technology was welcomed. The government faced many questions regarding the outcome of this policy: whether it would work or not, and would there be continuing rapid growth of gross national product to fulfill the requirements of the economic plan (Ho 1973). In fact, the policy effectively increased the Japanese GNP. In 1968, the Japanese GNP in U.S. dollar terms ranked third in the world after the United States and the Soviet Union (Nakamura 1995). These steps helped Japan increase its production and exports during the 1960s. It is important to mention that throughout the American government had an open market policy toward Japan, meaning Japan could export its goods tax-free to the United States and, on the other hand, the United States asked Japan to place restrictions on imports (Reischauer and Jansen 1995).

In 1964, there were three events which most baby boomers in Japan would remember: the Olympics, the launch of the Tokaido bullet train from Tokyo to Osaka, and the opening of the Shutoko Tokyo Metropolitan Expressway. These events, especially the Olympics, which were held for the first time in Asia, had a significant effect on Japan. Japan's cities were thoroughly modernized prior to the Olympics, a number of expressways were built, and a monorail linking Haneda Airport to the center of Tokyo was opened. These events, especially the Olympics, brought Japan back into the spotlight, and these events showed that Japan was on the road to prosperity (Chiba 2007).

Many leading economists argue about the causes of high growth during the 1950s and 1960s. Some argue in favor of high investment, others say it was because of the high export rate, while some Keynesian economists believe it was due to strong consumption. One would not argue who is right and who is wrong, but, seeing the social impact of the economic growth of the 1950s and the 1960s, all consumers wanted the "Three Cs": car, color TV, and cooler. Thanks to the market and the scale of production, which generated demand and reduced prices, these items were affordable to the new blue collar workers. However, other factors such as capital accumulation, technological upgrading, or production and organizational innovations must also be considered when discussing the rapid development of the Japanese economy at that time.

The 1960s also saw strong investment in different sectors, especially manufacturing and plant and equipment, the "*Iwato* boom." (Nakamura 1995) In the second half of the 1960s, Japanese companies, with the help of the government and strong consumption, completely closed the technological gap between Japan and the West. As a result, the competitive strength of Japanese industries increased. This helped exports to grow on average by 18.4 percent per year during the 1960s.

The other factor which played a very important role during the growth of the 60s and 70s was the increase in the number of Japanese who started living in cities. According to Japan Fact Sheet (2008), the percentage of Japanese living in cities rose from 38% to 72% from 1950 to 1970. This helped swell the workforce. As the same source states, by the end of 1968, national income had doubled, reaching an average annual growth rate of 10%. Also, in terms of GNP, Japan moved quickly and joined the ranks of the most industrialized nations of the world.

In the late 1960s, demand for cars increased, which lead to the establishment of Japan Automobile Manufacturers Association (JAMA 2008). Car production increased dramatically at the start of 1965. In relation to other car manufacturers, Japan ranked 6th in the world in 1962.

As demand in domestic and international markets increased, as from 1965, the use of new technologies and efficient methods of production became the top priority for car manufacturers. The use of robots in factories became more frequent. As exports increased, Japanese automobile companies started to invest outside Japan. Investment increased during the late 1970s and early 1980s.

Before moving to the events of 1970s, one should consider the figures, which clearly show the fast growth of the Japanese economy, together with the time-line and the stated objectives. In December 1955, the Hatoyama cabinet planned a 4.9% growth in GNP, but achieved 8.8%. Its object was economic independence and full employment. In December 1957, the Kishi cabinet planned a 6.5% GNP growth rate, but achieved 9.7%. The objective at this time was to achieve maximum growth, high living standards and full employment. In December 1960, Ikeda's cabinet planned 7.8% GNP growth, but achieved 10.0%. The objective of this plan was for maximum stable growth toward full employment and higher living standards. In January 1965, the Sato cabinet planned 8.1% GNP growth, but achieved 10.1%. Again, in the second term, the Sato cabinet planned for 8.2% GNP growth, but this time achieved 9.8%.

The growth in GNP during these periods is very clear evidence of how Japan rose from the ashes and changed its status to the world's second biggest economy. This growth did not stop after the 1960s, but during the 1970s it did slow.

The 1970s

During these years, the Japanese economy grew rapidly by an average of 10% (Nakamura 1995), until the oil shock of 1973. The oil shock caused decline, especially in the manufacturing industries, as the cost of transportation as well as the prices of raw materials increased dramatically. According to Kosai (1981), the oil crisis not only affected Japan, but also the global economy. Although The Japanese Ministry of Economy, Trade and Industry (METI) announced that Japan possessed a 79-day crude oil reserve, it could not prevent panic among the Japanese people. The price of crude oil kept on climbing. The increase in the price of crude oil caused price increases across a range of other goods such as toilet paper. During the panic, one person was seriously injured in a supermarket stampede (Nakamura 1995).

At this time, suppliers withheld supplies from the market because of the cost increase in raw materials and labor. This action widened the gap between supply and demand further, causing prices to climb steeply. This was not only the case for consumer goods, but also for many other items. Nakamura calls this time "crazy price" inflation (*kyoran bukka*). (Nakamura 1995, p. 213)

After the oil crisis, Japanese industries faced recession during 1973-74 because operating profits in many firms dropped. Besides the oil crisis, another important reason was wage increases. Most unions organized chains of strikes, demanding an increase in wages. The increase in prices of raw materials and increases in fuel prices stopped firms from covering their outlays by increasing product prices, so profit margins fell. Moreover, firms had to pay interest on the funds that they had borrowed during the growth period, further deepening the recession of 1973-74.

Government executed further changes: during the second half of the 1960s until 1973, because of the increase in exports, the Bank of Japan (BoJ) raised the official discount rate from 5.84% to 6.25% in September 1969 (Adams and Hoshii 1973). Also, by means of window guidance, the supply of funds in the market was directly limited. After maintaining an exchange rate of 360 yen for 22 years, in December 1971, after the Nixon shock, the Japanese government and the BoJ decided to switch to a floating exchange rate, and the new rate was set to 308 yen to the dollar (Kosai 1986). During 1973, the yen rose again against the dollar to 265 yen, and briefly reached the 170 yen mark in October 1978. Despite the hike in the yen against the dollar, Japanese exports did not decline, and, on the contrary, increased. This phenomenon can be explained with the help of *J-curve*. As the exchange rate increases, exports denominated in foreign currencies increase for some time as well. The reason behind this is that exports are subject to pre-existing contracts, so there is a certain time-lag before the new contracts become effective and the old contracts close, thus decreasing exports (Nakamura 1995). But, after the Nixon shock of 1971, the era of rapid growth in Japan ended and Japan would not enjoy the same growth again.

The period from the second half of the 1970s through to the early 1980s was the time of worldwide inflation, slow production, and rising unemployment. The maintenance of trade deficits by other nations and the growth in Japanese exports targeted Japan for international criticism. Under the pressure of the U.S, Japan once again raised the yen exchange rate. As a result, the yen-based export growth rate declined, due to the difficulty of raising dollar-based export prices, the net yen income of export industries decreased, and business profits also declined. Meanwhile, government expenditure increased not solely due to rising prices. The administration adopted the social security system in 1973, plus a number of other social reforms, such as index-linked old-age pensions and free medical care for elderly, all of which increased fiscal expenditure. Japan was under continuous pressure from the U.S to increase government spending. This also caused a budget deficit. To cover the growing budget deficit, in the 1978 fiscal year budget, to float the economy, the government issued deficit-covering bonds. The government deficit kept on increasing, and, as a result, the government had no choice but to issue more deficit-covering bonds. Of course, this led to increased bond expenditure due to repayments of principle and interest, putting further pressure on the treasury (Adams and Hoshii 1972; Nakamura 1995; Kosai 1981).

Increasing Competitiveness

By the latter half of the 1960s and the beginning of the 1970s, Japan achieved its competitiveness goals and had a strong voice in international affairs. Many authors believe that Japan followed a mercantilism policy, which means exports and only exports. Looking at historical developments, it becomes clear that Japanese government policy was to facilitate exports. On the other hand, the Japanese Ministry of Economy, Trade and Industry (METI) tried to reduce competition inside the Japanese market and urged companies with the same product lines to merge and compete globally. As Abegglen (1985) argues in his book *Kaisha*, it was METI which tried to restructure the auto industry to reduce the number of participants to make it more competitive. At that time, Nissan absorbed Prince and Minsei Diesel and also took over Fuji Heavy Industries' domestic production. Toyota and Hino formed an affiliation to facilitate the rationalization of the truck business. Of course, in the long run, this worked in favor of Japan in such a way that it reduced the number of competitors in the domestic market and strengthened them in international competition.

Along with government policy, the "*Iwato* boom" of 1959-61, which was basically a boom in investment on plant and equipment, also helped Japan gain a competitive edge, which it was missing in technology. Thus Japanese export businesses enhanced their international competitiveness. They gained competitiveness as regards "software," such as product quality, performance, and functions. Typical examples of highly competitive Japanese products are high end steel items, machine tools equipped with numerical control features, and highly advanced construction machinery that takes advantage of new technologies in mechanical, electric, controlling, and hydraulic engineering. Other examples are automobiles and other machinery with the most advanced, environmentally-friendly and energy-saving functions, and extremely small-sized computer chips and various electronic parts. Japanese manufacturers began including these technological achievements in their export goods. Japanese companies added value to products throughout this era.

Successive technical innovation reinforced international competitiveness, therefore Japanese GNP and exports increased. Thus, Japan achieved economic independence as a technical and industrial nation, and then returned as a member of international society. Besides the automobile industry, all other industries in Japan, such as textiles, steel, optics, shipping, etc., also enjoyed rapid growth and all contributed to the Japanese economic miracle. In fact, these industries were among the first to receive the full attention of the government.

In this part of the chapter, it is very important to mention the part that human power played in rapid growth. As mentioned above, the baby boom of 1947-49 was the biggest factor behind the labor supply during the 1960s; without it rapid growth would not have been possible. Furthermore, various policies of companies, such as life-time employment, seniority-based promotion and personnel training, were some other initiatives which motivated the workforce to work harder. Of course, one would also not rule out the cultural aspect that Japanese in general tend to work hard. Life-time employment is not something that is mentioned or enforced by law, but, during the high growth period, it was very cheap for companies to hire workers for a lifetime. In this way, companies achieved two things: the loyalty of the employee and second the guaranty of not losing the worker. Joining a firm established a life-long relationship, similar to being in a family or an alumni association member (Sano 1995). In many cases, workers did not change jobs and stayed with the same company until retirement. Although salaries in companies were low, when we consider seniority-based promotions and the associated rise in salaries, it cancels out the effect of initial low wages. This is another reason why Japanese workers did not readily change jobs during the 60s and the 70s.

Japanese companies place strong emphasis on training employees. In this way, companies ensure transfer of all knowledge and help make work more efficient. Thus the three aspects of the Japanese management system played a very important role during the high growth period of the 60s and the 70s. It is important to state that, during the period of the 50s and 60s, Japanese industries also faced labor shortages. To deal with this problem, a lot of companies hired part-timers and temporary employees, both of whom consisted of women. The first advantage was that it made up for the shortage in labor and, second, companies paid a lot less in return for their labor.

But, of course, as the saying goes "nothing is permanent but change," during the recession period, especially after the oil crisis, most companies switched to more cost effective alternatives, which Nakamura calls an "operation scale-down." (1995, p. 222) Companies mainly focused at this time on reducing the cost of labor, thus precipitating personnel cuts. The very first thing that firms did was dismiss temporary female workers and part-time workers. Of course, it was against the Japanese tradition and the principle of life-time employment to dismiss workers on a large scale. Therefore, companies avoided reducing personnel on a large scale like in Western countries.

Since then, most companies have switched to hiring more females and more part-time workers. The number of part-time workers rose from 700,000 in 1975 to 1.46 million in 1980, to 2.3 million in 1985 and to 4.67 million in 1991. They comprised 2.9 percent, 5.8 percent, 8.6 percent and 12.6 percent of the labor force in 1975, 1980, 1985, and 1991 respectively. In this way, the Japanese labor force played a role in the rapid growth period and suffered after the recession and the oil shock in the first half of the 1970s (Nakamura 1995).

With all the progress and achievements, Japan paid a heavy price in the form of air, water and noise pollution. After the word *kôgai*, or environmental pollution, came into use in the first half of the 1960s, the subject became a social issue in Japan. According to Jun Ui (2008), environmental pollution was mainly *Minamata* disease, *Itai-Itai* disease, and *Yokkaichi* asthma. Of course, the sources vary from industry, to automobiles and cities, down to agricultural chemicals (Nakamura 1995). These were all well known phenomena and posed a serious threat to life and health. The government and the business community took bold steps to solve the problem of pollution. One example comprised the launching of the Pollution Prevention Association (*Kôgai Boshi Jigyo Dan)* in 1965. In following years, the government passed some strict measures to curb pollution. Exhaust gas restrictions for new cars were implemented in 1966. The Pollution Prevention Law went into effect in 1967. In 1971, a law preventing air, water and noise pollution was also passed. A year before this law passed, in 1970, the government rectified the basic law and deleted the clause "harmony with economic development" and reinforced the goal of preventing environmental pollution. By deleting the clause, the government also strengthened regulations to prevent overall pollution. One of the big projects that the government and the business community took on was cleaning Tokyo Bay. The outcomes of all these measures were clean water and air, as well as the control of noise pollution.

Conclusion

In conclusion, I would say that rapid growth in Japan would have not been possible without combining government policies, the efforts of the people and the contribution of the business community. We have seen above that during the 1950s, especially in the first half of the decade, the Korean War provided a stimulus for the economy. At the same time, American policies, which were basically in favor of Japan, allowed Japan to export to the U.S. market. One also saw that the 1960s were politically not a good decade, but economically it was the decade of fast growth.

The 1964 Olympic Games were another event which baby boomers would always remember (Chiba 2007). One reason is the variety of games and the participation of athletes from all over the world in Japan, and the opportunity for people to meet them and admire them. Another reason was the opening of the bullet train and the expressways. On the economic side, the income-doubling plan of Prime Minister Ikeda which provided people with a disposable income, also helped the domestic market grow. Of course, the 1960s also opened people's eyes to pollution, which forced the government to take drastic measures to remedy the problem. The active participation of the business community in social issues was also ensured at this time.

The 1970s were years of a slow-down in the economy and the Nixon shock and two oil shocks. These forced the government to rethink its financial and monetary policies. The floating of the yen against the dollar came during the 1970s. The 1970s also witnessed the adoption of a social security system and a number of other social reforms such as old-age pensions and free medical care for the elderly. It was also the decade of panic caused by the oil crisis, leading to shortages in other commodities, even in toilet paper.

The two decades of the 60s and 70s as a whole helped Japan reach its goal of catching up with the technical advantage that the West had. With its high exports, it gained enough foreign exchange reserves so that it could change its status from a debtor nation to a creditor nation, and, by 1985, it replaced the United States as the world's leading creditor.

The 1970s also saw big changes in the human resource management situation in Japan. Owing to the recession, many companies laid off a large number of part-timers and temporary employees, of whom many were female workers. At the same time, learning from their mistake of hiring life-time employees, many companies switched to hiring part-timers on short-term contracts, so they could lay them off any time they wanted.

At the start of the 1980s, the government kept interest rates low, which allowed people to borrow more. This made money extremely cheap and with excess money people and individual investors started to invest in real estate and stocks. This action caused the price of real estate to sky rocket.

Bibliography

Abegglen, J. and Stalk, G. (1985): *Kaisha; the Japanese corporation*. New York: Basic Books.

Adam, T.F.M and Hoshii, I. (1972): *A financial history of the new Japan*. Tokyo: Kodansha International.

Chiba, H. (2007): *Milestones 1964: An Olympic year*. The Japan Journal, August 2005. Downloaded from http://www.japanjournal.jp on December 29, 2007.

Hamada, K. and Kasuya M. (1993): *The reconstruction and stabilization of the postwar Japanese economy: Possible Lessons for Eastern Europe?* Research Paper 672. Yale – Economic Growth Center Paper Series, Yale University.

Ho, A. K. (1973): *Japan's trade liberalization in the 1960s*. International Arts and Sciences Press.

Itô, T. (1992): *The Japanese economy*. Massachusetts: The MIT Press Cambridge.

JAMA, Japan Automobile Manufacturers Association (2007): *The rapid expansion of motorization (1965-1975)*. Downloaded from www.jama.org on December 28, 2007.

Japan Fact Sheet (2008): Downloaded from http://web-japan.org/factsheet/ on January 29, 2008.

Kahn, H. (1970): *The emerging Japanese superstate: Challenge and response.* Englewood Cliffs: Prentice-Hall.

Kosai, Y. (1981): *The era of high-speed growth note on the postwar Japanese economy.* Tokyo: University of Tokyo Press.

Koshiro, K. (2000): *A fifty year history of industry and labor in postwar Japan.* Tokyo: The Japan Institute of Labour, 2000.

Lincoln, E. J. (2004): Interview. Downloaded from www.japanreview.net/japan_price_index_history.html on December 23, 2007.

Minami, R. (1986): *The economic development of Japan.* New York: St. Martin's Press.

Nakamura, T. (1995): *The postwar Japanese economy.* Tokyo: University of Tokyo Press.

Olsen, E. A. (1978): *Japan: Economic growth, resources scarcity, and environmental constraints.* Boulder: Westview Press.

Pyle, K. B. (1995): *The making of modern Japan.* DC Heath & Co Publishing.

Reischauer, E. O. and Jansen, M. B. (1995): *The Japanese today.* The Belknap Press.

Sano, Y. (1995): *Human resource management in Japan.* Tokyo: Keio University Press.

Tabb, W. K. (1995): *The postwar Japanese system cultural economy and economic transformation.* Oxford: Oxford University Press.

Ui, J. (2008): *Industrial pollution in Japan*. Downloaded from http://www.unu.edu on January 4, 2008.

Watanuki, J. (1992): *Japan in the 1960s and after: The politics of high economic growth*. Research Paper. Tokyo: Sophia University.

3. Bubble-era Economy and the Burst of the Bubble

By Hitoshi Kakishima, Hayaka Kawamura, Saaya Konishi, and Aya Yoshida

The Plaza Accord

The Plaza Accord agreement, which was signed in 1985, is considered to have led to the bubble boom. During the bubble boom period, which started at the end of the 1980s, the United States was concerned with its trade deficit due to the appreciation in the dollar and announced in a joint statement that is was to cooperate and intervene with the G5 nations: Japan, the U.S., France, Germany and the United Kingdom. As a result, the yen continued to appreciate sharply. The exchange rate, which had been about 240 yen per dollar, rose rapidly to 150 yen a dollar within a year (Itami 1990).

There are thought to be two fundamental reasons for the dollar's devaluation. First, to reduce the U.S. current account deficit, which had reached 3.5% of GDP at that time. Second, to help the U.S. economy emerge from the serious recession that had begun in the early 1980s. The U.S. Federal Reserve System, which is the central bank of the U.S. and provides the nation with a safe, flexible, and stable monetary and financial system, had overvalued the dollar to make industries in the United States, especially the automobile industry, less competitive in the global market. Devaluing the dollar made U.S. exports cheaper compared to its trading partners, which encouraged other countries to buy more American-made goods and services. The Plaza Accord succeeded in reducing the U.S. trade deficit with European countries, but failed to fulfill its primary objective of alleviating the trade deficit with Japan. This is because the deficit was caused by structural conditions rather than monetary conditions. U.S. manufactured goods and services became more competitive in the export market, but were still largely unsuccessful in the domestic Japanese market because Japan had structural restrictions on imports. The recessionary effects of the strengthened yen in Japan's export-dependent economy created an incentive for the expansionary monetary policies that led to the Japanese asset price bubble of the late 1980s.

On February 22, 1987, the G7 nations (G5 nations + Italy and Canada) gathered at the Palais du Louvre (Louvre Palace) in Paris to put a brake on the increasingly weak dollar following the Plaza Accord. The Louvre Accord was concluded by the seven nations in an attempt to halt the downward slide in the value of the dollar and to stabilize the exchange rate, and stated that each country should cooperate and intervene to this end (Kondo 1999).

There have been many arguments and discussions concerning the Plaza Accord. Exports are a big prop in Japan, thus to arbitrarily adjust the exchange rate is very risky. The export industry suffered a relative loss of competitive edge as there was an artificial appreciation in the yen through concerted intervention. This unfavorable agreement is thought to have had its roots in the Japan-U.S. trade conflict.

The Bubble Economy

Following the 1985 Plaza Accord, the yen gained sharply in value, reaching 120 yen to the U.S. dollar in 1988, three times its value in 1971 under the fixed exchange rate system. Under the Plaza Accord, Japan accepted a large appreciation in the yen, and compensated for slow export growth through an expansionary monetary policy. Easy money triggered the speculative bubble economy, with rising real estate and stock prices. A consequent increase in the price of Japanese export goods reduced their competitiveness in overseas markets, but government financial measures contributed to growth in domestic demand. During the bubble era, the Japanese government relaxed monetary policies to aid export industries, which were suffering under a strong yen.

The term "bubble economy" that Japan experienced in the 1980s and the 1990s is defined as stock inflation caused by surplus monetary capital (Matsumoto 2001). The characteristic of a bubble economy is always the same regardless of the country. In each case, optimism about stock or land prices increases, and investment continues. According to Kinugawa (2002), the bubble economy can be classified as a "stock bubble" and a "land price bubble."

Stock Bubble

In a stock bubble, investors assume that stock prices will continue to rise. Since the yen appreciated sharply due to the Plaza Accord in 1985, and a high-yen recession followed in 1986, the Bank of Japan (BoJ) cut the bank rate from 5% to 4.5% on January 30, 1986, and it fell to 3% on November 1 of the same year. Moreover, after the Louvre Accord in 1987, the bank rate was cut further to 2.5%, which was the lowest rate in history. The BoJ kept the rate at 2.5% for more than two years. This was a critical mistake. Even though Japan was on the road to a gradual recovery in 1987, as declared by The Economic Planning Agency, the BoJ eased the monetary supply over the long term. This mistake inflated the bubble at an amazing speed. There are the two main reasons why the BoJ could not reverse its policy. First, Japan was expected to stop the world-wide slump in stock prices caused by Black Monday on the New York Market. Second, the BoJ focused on the "stability of stock prices" by easing the monetary supply. Japan was actually showing signs of recovery from 1987, and stable stock prices could be observed without symptoms of inflation. Consequently, the BoJ was unable to reverse policy and tighten the monetary supply at that time (Kinugawa 2002).

Land Price Bubble

One of the key effects on Japanese society in the bubble era—from December 1986 to February 1991—was soaring land prices. Soaring land prices, which started in the commercial areas of city centers, not only influenced Japanese real estate, but real estate world-wide. According to the "capital city remodeling plan," which was made public in May 1985 by the National Land Agency, it was estimated that the demand for offices in Tokyo by 2000 would be 8000 hectares. By "the fourth national generalization plan" in 1987, the estimation was lowered to a demand of 4000 hectares of office space. This estimation by the National Land Agency is considered proof that land prices in commercial areas in Tokyo had started to rise.

In Tokyo, around 1985, land prices in city center commercial areas started to rise first, and then in the south-west, followed by the north-west and finally in the entire area of Tokyo. One key aspect is that soaring land prices started from the city center commercial area. This is because the urban economic structure had changed with the rise of an information society and internationalization. The accumulation of operational and central administration functions in central Tokyo resulted in a rapid demand for offices and consequently land prices in central commercial areas rose sharply.

Leading companies in the Kansai area and local companies moved their headquarters to Tokyo. This was accompanied by an influx of foreign financial companies and brokerage firms, all swelling the demand for office space. A large number of foreign financial firms moved to Arkhills Akasaka in Tokyo. This resulted in an immediate drop in the rate of vacancies. The steep increase in demand for offices tilted supply and demand out of balance. Though it was true that office demand increased sharply, it was also true that the National Land Agency overestimated the number of offices required. This prediction focused attention on office space.

According to the National Land Agency, in a land price public notification on January 1, 1986, land prices rose for the year in central Tokyo by some 20 to 30%. However, in adjoining prefectures, land prices rose by only some 5 to 10%.

Residential land prices in Tokyo within five kilometers of Tokyo Station rose by 22.7%, within 10 kilometers by 12.3%, within 15 kilometers by 7.7%. For instance, Chiyoda ward in Tokyo used to have values of 4.5 million yen per square meter in the bubble era, but now prices are at only 1.5 million yen per square meter. Residential land prices more than 20 kilometers from Tokyo Station, however, increased at just an average rate.

One of our relatives purchased a house in Hatsukaichi City in Hiroshima during the bubble era. First, he had to draw lots to get the land. He drew a losing number twice, but finally he drew a winning number. Owing to the high demand for land at that time, it was very difficult even to obtain a piece of land. He thought it was better to get land as soon as possible because it was said that land prices would increase over time. He built his own home in Hatsukaichi City in 1990. The land cost 19 million yen and the house 21 million yen. Unfortunately, however, land prices peaked when he made the purchase. Since then, land prices in Hatsukaichi City have fallen gradually. He thought he would continue to lose money if he held his house any longer; therefore he sold it three years ago. He could sell it for only 19 million yen in total. He said, "There were many people like me who lost a lot of money due to bubble-era land prices."

Bubble Dream Resorts

During the bubble era, from 1986 to 1990, a resort development boom started in Japan. Owing to the money glut, the low interest rates and the five-day week, people had more leisure time. This meant people were interested in spending their spare time fruitfully—a desire which was catered for by new resort spots.

The largest example of new resort development is a European-style resort called Huis Ten Bosch, located in Saseboshi in Nagasaki prefecture (http://english.huistenbosch.co.jp/). The theme park is full of streets just as you would find them in the Netherlands. Theme park president, Yoshikuni Kamichika, was granted permission to develop the area on the condition that he would re-create the exterior appearance faithfully. The resort is both Dutch and European in style. There are restaurants, hotels, amusement parks, museums and beautiful forests.

At the far end of Huis Ten Bosch, there is a residential district called "Wassenaa," which was also built during the bubble era. Wassenaar is an area for leisure homes modeled on traditional Dutch homes. Wassenaa is off-limits to the public. HTB (Huis Ten Bosch) constructed 249 houses, including condominiums. Each house or unit was priced at from 80 million to over 160 million yen. In fact, during the bubble era, almost all the houses were reserved, but it was ill-timed. Immediately after the Wassenaa foundation was established, the Japanese bubble economy burst. Some 65% of bookings were cancelled. By 1999, more than 130 houses had ended up on the shelf.

In 2001, HTB finally cut prices by half, from 60 to 30 million yen. In October 2001, HTB entrusted sales to a major real-estate company and advertised in the Tokyo metropolitan district. As a result, they sold 15 houses, but still have some 110 houses unsold. According to HTB, through the price reduction and the affiliation with the major real-estate company, they received many inquires and requests for viewings. Many viewers said that they wanted to spend a night there sometime. Therefore, HTB obtained a hotel permit for part of Wassenaa and has an "accommodation experience plan," which it hopes will lead to further sales.

Another typical bubble-era land development was One Hundred Hills, called Chibari Hills, which is located in Chiba City in Chiba prefecture. It is of course a pun on Beverly Hills in Los Angeles—Chibari Hills conjures up images of Beverly Hills. It takes one and a half hours from Tokyo Station to reach, and then requires a further 25 minute walk from the nearest station, Toke. Each house built for sale was priced at from 500 million to 1.5 billion yen in 1989. There were more than 500 applications for 60 structures. But soon after Tokyo Real Estate commenced sales the bubble economy burst. Tokyo Real Estate built 49 houses, while 11 plots remain undeveloped, and sold only 24 houses. The houses were located too far away from the central city and were also too expensively priced, even during the bubble era. Monthly utilities alone were 300,000 yen. Until recently, there were rows of "For Sale" signs in front of unsold houses, but even those signs have been removed as there is no prospect of a sale. A city real estate agent says, "We do not know the exact value of the houses, but there is little possibility that people would buy even if prices dropped to around 100 million yen." Within 20 years, the value of the properties has declined by one-fifth to one-fifteenth. Ironically, Chibari Hills is called a very exclusive ghost town or bubble monument. On the front of gate of Chibari Hills, a sign reads, "No Visitors Allowed." No one lives there anymore.

Bubble Lifestyle

From the end of the 1980s, the Japanese spent as much money as they wanted, and a large number of people were to be seen in all cities at midnight. Also, as property values rose ever upwards, people thought that the bubble would never burst. Thus, the Japanese convinced themselves that the bubble economy was a distinct and separate phenomenon from the real economy and therefore could not damage it (Wood 1992). Many male salaried Japanese workers still remember those days, such as Mr. Sato, one of our relatives, who was interviewed for this chapter. During the bubble economy, office trips known as *shain ryokô*, where companies paid full traveling expenses for a trip, usually abroad with fellow workers, were very popular events. Some other events during the "golden ages," as he states, were the regular so-called *nomikais* (drinking parties) and company golf tournaments—and of course full expenses were paid by the company. Moreover, the amount of money he received as a bonus increased strongly during the bubble era but decreased again after the bubble burst.

The Burst of the Bubble

In the late 1980s, the Japanese bubble expanded rapidly and it looked unlikely to stop. Stock prices and land prices boomed. The Nikkei Index reached its highest level ever at 38,915 yen by the end of 1989, and stock prices were expected to rise even further. It seemed only a matter of time before it would exceed 40,000 yen. However, in 1990, stock prices suddenly started to fall and have fallen ever since. Yet in 1990 land prices were still high and the Japanese economy was still in good shape (Kinugawa 2002). These facts may have led to wrong decisions that caused the bubble economy to burst. There are two causes that led to the bursting of the bubble economy: first, the tight money policy on the part of the Bank of Japan, and, second, the control of land prices by the government.

A tight money policy was achieved by the Bank of Japan by increasing the bank rate to stop or slow down inflation. The first hike was on May 31, 1989. Before the first rise, the bank rate in Japan was 2.5%. This was the lowest bank rate ever in Japan, and this rate was maintained for 2 years and 3 months. Tanaka (2002) says in his book that the Bank of Japan was too slow in enforcing a tight money policy. The Bank of Japan should have increased the bank rate much earlier. First, the Bank of Japan increased the bank rate from 2.5% to 3.25%. At this point, stock prices were very high already and were rapidly increasing. The first rate hike had no effect. On October 11, 1989, the Bank of Japan decided to raise the bank rate for the second time, from 3.25% to 3.75%, and then on December 25 the bank rate was increased again for the third time to 4.25%. At this point, stock prices were still increasing and most people expected them to continue rising the next year too. Unfortunately, stock prices suddenly fell at the beginning of 1990. Many people involved in the Japanese market did not realize that the bubble was starting to burst. Stock prices were expected to rebound soon.

The Bank of Japan thought so too and raised the bank rate two more times during the year: 1% on March 20 to 5.25% and up a further 0.75% on August 30 to 6%. Effectively, the bank rate increased from 2.5% to 6% within a year and a half. This increase in the bank rate was a little too high. The Bank of Japan maintained this high rate of 6% even when the bubble was starting to burst. By the time the bank rate was lowered, it was already too late. A bank rate of 6% was maintained for almost a year until the Bank of Japan announced a decrease to 5.5% on January 1, 1991 (Tanaka 2002).

Control of land prices was obviously aimed at halting the increase in land prices. During the bubble, land prices were very high, so it was becoming difficult for people to buy houses. The Japanese government enforced a number of different policies to control prices. First, land transactions were regulated by the National Land Agency. This measure was introduced in 1986 as a system to monitor land prices. Whenever land was bought or sold, a report was filed with the prefectural governor, and, if the transaction was considered overpriced, the governor could advise on a price correction. Second, in 1990, regulation by the Ministry of Finance was introduced. This regulation restrained bank loans to real estate businesses. Also, when banks made loans to real estate businesses, construction businesses, and non-banks, they had to file a report. This regulation was applied to all banks and insurance companies. Third, the Ministry of Finance reformed land taxes. Land possession, land transfer profit and land income taxes were all increased. Increases in these taxes made it more expensive to buy or sell land, and reduced the speculative holding of land, and allowed land to be used more effectively. Fourth, the Ministry of Construction regulated land use. In 1992, this regulation was strengthened in the New Town Planning and Zoning Act. Some land could only be used to build houses. Among these policies, particularly the regulation of loans to real estate businesses had a great effect on decreasing land prices, since the capital used to buy or sell land, which had supported the sharp rise in land prices, was being regulated. These policies were put into place from 1986 to 1991. It is clear that both the tight money and land price control policies caused the bubble economy to collapse, since stock prices started to fall at the beginning of 1990, followed by the fall of land prices in 1991, just after policies were changed (Tanaka 2002).

The Nikkei Index peaked at 38,915 yen at the end of 1989. Stock prices started to fall from the beginning of 1990 and by March 22 they had fallen below thirty thousand yen. Stock prices fell by as much as 20% during the first three months of 1990. This represents the beginning of the bursting of the bubble. At the time, however, few people realized it. Both financial institutions and the financial authorities that supervised them ignored the initial signs. Despite the sharp fall in stock prices, the Bank of Japan continued to raise the bank rate. On October 1, stock prices fell to 20,221 yen—almost half of peak prices. However, land prices remained high. Stock prices started to fall again from the end of 1991 and by August 1992 stock prices were 14,309 yen. During this time, a series of financial scandals caused stock prices to fall further. In June 1991, Nomura Securities was reported for loss compensation. At the end of July, four major brokerage firms released lists of clients they had compensated for losses. These problems caused private investors to refrain from investing in stocks. Enormous amounts of illegal investments by banks were also a big problem. The famous Itoman fraud case in the spring of 1991 was the first of many such scandals. Sumietsu Itô, an officer at the Institute for Kyowa Development Corporation, and Ho Yong Chung, owner of several real estate companies, approached Yoshihiko Kawamura, former officer at the Sumitomo Bank and President of Itoman Corporation at that time, and Ichiri Isoda, the president of Sumitomo Bank, to obtain financing through Itoman Corporation. Itô, Ho and Kawamura used the money for their own benefit, not for the company, and the Itoman Group was left with a large number of debts. The Sumitomo Bank ended up lending an enormous amount of money to the Itoman Group, which Itoman could not repay. Other loan problems were uncovered at the Fuji Bank, the Kyowa-Saitama Bank and the Tokai Bank at the end of July, 1991. These problems had been masked by the bubble, but came to light once the bubble started to burst. These problems were not unique, but, as the bubble burst, they occurred on an exceptional scale and created distrust in financial institutions and the Ministry of Finance (Kinugawa 2002; Tanaka 2002).

On July 1, 1991, the Bank of Japan decided to lower the bank rate to 5.5% from 6%. In October, the government announced that the economy was in recession, and the Bank of Japan lowered the bank rate to 5% on November 14, and on December 30, the bank rate was lowered again to 4.5%. The Bank of Japan lowered the bank rate twice in 1992, once in 1993 and by 1994 the bank rate was just 0.5% (Kinugawa 2002).

The Lost Decade

People say that 1990s were the lost decade. During this decade, the Japanese economy suffered and showed an extremely low growth rate because of the after-effects of the bubble economy. Japan was in recession during the 1990s. The key word for this period is *furyo saiken*, which is translated as "bad credit." Before going into any details about the Japanese economy in the 1990s, let's look at *furyo saiken*. It is a loan that can no longer be collected due to, for example, the bankruptcy of the company that received the loan. Obviously, many companies could not pay back loans after the bubble burst. During the bubble, many companies borrowed money from banks against assets such as stocks and land. Because the price of assets was skyrocketing, people thought the more assets one bought, the more money one made. Investments were made in many assets by borrowing money for short-term operative means. This was called *zaiteku*, which can be translated as "money management activities." Many companies were doing this more than their main business. As the bubble burst, the price of assets fell sharply. Companies were left with large debts with assets that were of low value. Companies could not pay back the money they owed even if they sold the assets they had bought. Banks could not get back the money that they had invested. Thus "bad credits" became a nation-wide problem.

Bad credit clearly had a negative effect on the Japanese economy and is held as the principle reason for the slump in the Japanese economy. Bad credits were negative in different ways. First, in the process of disposing of bad credits, companies and borrowers often went bankrupt. Even when companies did not go bankrupt, they had to restructure the company by cutting expenditures. Firing workers was one of the solutions. A lot of companies had to fire workers in the 1990s and this came as a big shock to the Japanese people. In Japan, life-time employment was a natural thing and usually ordinary workers were never fired. Many people struggled to find new jobs. Unemployment increased and investment in plant and equipment fell. Moreover, banks were more reluctant to grant loans. Banks were saddled with bad credits. Banks raise money through deposits and loan this money. However, they could not collect interest income because most loans became bad credit. Also, even if a promising opportunity to loan money arose, it was difficult to raise more money to invest. This damaged the banks. In the process of disposing of bad credits, some banks went bankrupt and others merged to survive. The first failure of a financial institution was that of Tôyo Shinyo Kinko in 1991. In 1996, bank failures were in full swing. This caused a finance shortage in the Japanese economy. As mentioned above, many banks went bankrupt and surviving banks were weakened and thus reluctant to grant loans. The money supply in the Japanese market shrank and market activity fell.

Bad credit had a very negative effect on the economy, however, it could not be dealt with too quickly, otherwise too many companies and banks would have gone bankrupt. It had to be done gradually. Yet, there were a large number of bad credits, so it was a long process. The recovery of the Japanese economy depended on the elimination of all bad credit and this is why the depression in Japan has been so long (Kinugawa 2002; Tanaka 2002).

Bibliography

Galbraith, K. J. (1991): *Baburu no monogatari*. Tokyo: Diamondosha.

Itami, H. (1990): *En ga yureru kigyô wa ugoku*. Tokyo: NTT Shuppansha.

Japan Times (1999): *Itoman execs sentenced to prison*. Downloaded from http://www.japantimes.co.jp/ on September 9, 1999.

Kondo, T. (1999): *Baburu gôi no kenkyû*. Tokyo: Toyo Keizai Shinhôsha.

Kinugawa, M. (2002): *Nihon no baburu*. Tokyo: Nihon Keizai Hyoronsha.

Kuroki, S. (2002): *Baburu fukyô kara no dakkyaku*. Tokyo: Gakubunsha.

Matsumoto, K. (1993): *Keiko to kabuki wa dô ugoku*. Tokyo: Diamondosha.

Matsumoto, A. (2001): *Endaka—enyasu to baburu keizai no kenkyû*. Tokyo: Surugadai Shuppansha.

Nikkei Bijinesu (1990): *Chika geraku de sengohatsu kiki, tôsan ni migamaeru ôraku—nichigin*. Nikkei Bijinesu November 19, 1990, p. 14 – 17.

Nikkei Bijinesu (1992): *Shuyaku fuzai, zero seichô mo.* Nikkei Bijinesu, March 9, 1992, p. 20-24.

Tanaka, T. (2002): *Gendai nihon keizai baburu to posuto—baburu no kiseki.* Tokyo: Nihon Hyoronsha.

Wood, C. (1992): *The bubble economy*. New York: The Atlantic Monthly Press.

4. Structural and Economic Changes

By Manuel Lukas and Miho Saito

The success of the Japanese economy until the 1990s has been puzzling to many observers. Despite fundamental deviations from the model of a liberal economic system, Japan has grown at a stunning rate. Japan developed a unique system of institutions, based on long-term relations in employment and businesses, and with the strong involvement of politics and bureaucracy in private business decisions. This allowed for an astonishing social equality and the relations of competitors seemed harmonious rather than hostile (Vogel 2006a).

Until the end of the 1980s, the Japanese economy was seen as the most successful economic model in the world. One major aspect influencing economic success was the strong connection between government and economy. Unlike in other industrialized countries, cooperation between policy and the business world is considered to have had a positive impact on the economic development of Japan. Stability was one of the main goals behind this cooperation and it supported the technological and innovation processes.

The ruling party of Japan, the Liberal Democratic Party (LDP), has stayed in power for more than 50 years since its foundation in 1954, except for one alternation of power, which occurred in 1993, when the LDP lost its majority in the Lower House election. The third player is the Japanese bureaucracy, which, compared to Western industrialized countries, plays a very dominant, important role. This constellation of LDP, bureaucrats and business provided a lot of stability for Japanese businesses, and also created trust among the Japanese population. During the bubble economy, this successful model suddenly became problematic. First, the close cooperation between these three players blocked radical changes. Another major problem was the loss of trust among the Japanese population in this model. Japan and its economic model suddenly seemed to be out of date. Frustration increased during the 1990s. The need for radical changes became evident. Calls for political change have been heard for decades. In 1995, finally, the government seemed to make moves towards market deregulation.

After the bubble burst and the economic crisis hit, many institutions were brought into question and the demand for reforms became louder. The Japanese system seemed to have become dysfunctional for a mature economy in a global environment and stronger international competition. However, even if the need for reforms was acknowledged, many obstacles had to be overcome. One reason is that the alliance of bureaucracy, LDP party members and vested interests has the power to block reforms whenever their interests are at stake (Kwan 2000). Therefore, the political dimension of the economy is especially relevant in Japan.

As the economy developed, many industries rose and sunk again as comparative advantages shifted. This brought changes to corporate, employment and industrial structures. However, structural change is not limited to these aspects of the economy. The structure also includes the relevant economic, political and social institutions (Sakakibara 2003). Not only is a formal organization part of institutions, but also all the rules, norms and expectations, which guide human behavior (La Croix and Kawaura 2006). Such institutions in Japan are life-time employment, with in-company labor markets, the bank-loan centered financial system and the guidance of industries by the bureaucracy and the LDP (Vogel 2006a). The institutions have benefits, but also create costs. Whether these institutions are efficient depends on the industry. Therefore, change in a particular institution does not impact the whole Japanese economy in a uniform way. There is no general convergence towards an U.S.-like model of a liberal market economy. Adjustments of institutions and business practices differ considerably between companies and industries. Adjustments are not just a result of government sponsored reforms, but also come from the independent renegotiation of relationships.

Structural Particularities of the Japanese Economy

Every market economy experiences ups and downs as part of the normal business cycle. But the stunning length of the Japanese recession in the 90s indicated that this was more than a cyclical recession. Weak growth is the key feature of every recession, but the stagnation in Japan has been very long lasting, resulting in what is called the "lost decade." The normal instruments to deal with a recession, easing the monetary supply and public spending, both failed, although they were applied on a very large scale. The government was rather slow in taking monetary and fiscal countermeasures, but they would have been appropriate to cope with a normal recession (Sakakibara 2003). In fact, the government's policy failures have worsened and protracted the crisis, even though they are not the cause of it (Hall 2007).

Japan's economic system is a product of its complex history. During the rebuilding of the economy after the war, and during the periods of high growth, the state always took an important role in the coordination of industrial development. Businesses, bureaucracy and government were highly connected, sharing the same goals. The officials selected key industries and provided financing and a sound environment. The system was therefore not a market economy in a pure sense, as some important allocation decisions were not left to the market, but became political issues. The virtual one-party rule and the power of non-government politicians and vested interests are very exceptional for a modern market economy (Sakakibara 2003).

A particularity of Japan's financial industry is the so-called "convoy system." Under this system, market participants do not act like rivals, but rather like a naval convoy, which means that no one is left behind. Strong competitors have to bail out the ones in trouble. Therefore, inefficient firms are not forced to leave the market (Kwan 2000). The emphasis is on stability and equality, rather than on competition and efficiency. Not only were industries provided with resources, but also many protective measures and regulations were implemented for the benefit of certain industries. This protectionism also included competition-eliminating regulations to protect possible losers of economic developments. Part of the concept was to give export-oriented companies a safe environment in the domestic market in order to make them competitive in the global market. Economic growth has been highly dependent on exports since the late 1960s, although Japan remained a closed economy to the rest of the world (Sakakibara 2003).

This system worked very well as long as there were enough cost-efficient investment opportunities. In the beginning, the economy benefited on a grand scale from infrastructure projects such as transportation or utilities. The close relationships between major players such as the LDP, the bureaucrats and the business world were a major factor that led to Japan's economic success in the 80s. This system worked very well in times of prosperity, but it was not able to counter the economic crisis appropriately. Although Japan has adapted very well to conditions after the war, it seems to have had major difficulties with the new challenges. The question is why Japan's economy is not able to transform itself and adapt to the new environment. To answer this question it is crucial to recognize that Japan has developed a unique economic system, fundamentally different from the ideal of a liberal market economy. Companies are protected from failure, so the inefficient ones do not leave the market. This is to secure stability for the employees. As stability, harmony and equality are highly valued in Japanese society, the domestic Japanese economy has some socialist features, with the allocation mechanism far away from a pure market allocation. In strong contrast, the export-oriented industries compete in the competitive global market under international rules. The key element of most institutions is a long-term orientation and conflict avoidance. These institutions worked very well for manufacturing companies in the "catch-up" period (Vogel 2006a).

However, after the bubble burst (see previous chapter), harmony-loving, risk-avoiding and egalitarian Japanese society seems to have problems taking the necessary steps to adapt to the new environment. Conservative forces within the bureaucracy, the LDP and the government are able to block reforms and preserve the current situation through excessive regulation (Sakakibara 2003).

Political Reforms

From 1996 to 1998, both the 82nd and the 83rd Prime Minister, Ryutaro Hashimoto, promoted financial reforms to bring about a sustained recovery. This had temporary success in leading to a short-lived recovery in the economy in 1996. However, the economy went back down along with the world due to financial crises in Asia, Russia and Latin America.

Everything seemed to change when Junichiro Koizumi became prime minister and started to introduce structural reforms. Koizumi himself is one of the most unique politicians Japan has ever seen. Japanese politics are said to be faction-oriented. Koizumi, however, did not stick to traditional ways; hence, he was called the "maverick leader of Japan." Ironically, he attracted the public by criticizing his party, the LDP, for its money politics, which eventually led to victory in the Upper House election in 2001.

Koizumi's structural reform was intended to boost Japan's economic growth rate, which had stagnated after the crisis. These reforms started in 2001 with the rhetorical slogan, "Structural Reform without Sanctuaries," under the basic stance of "no growth without reform."

Koizumi, as a reformer, had to face criticism from a group of LDP conservatives. His reforms placed a great deal of emphasis on the special public corporations, the postal system, and regional reform zones, with the privatization of the post office being the best known reform and Koizumi's core target. Because by privatizing the postal services, the tax that was supposed to be paid to the post offices would go to the government. This is based on the fact that the government does not need to pay tax to the private sector. Furthermore, reformers were afraid that Japan's market-based financial system would never develop unless they privatized the postal system (Vogel 2006b).

The government also carried out more Koizumi-centered structural reforms concerned with private sector demand and employment and adopted the "Basic Policies for Economic and

Fiscal Policy Management and Structural Reform 2002." This bill included tax reform, economic revitalization strategies, and government expenditure reform. Based on these guidelines, the economy in Japan steadily recovered. Thus, Koizumi's structural reforms played a significant role in turning around the once depressed economy in Japan.

Political Decentralization

The purpose of decentralization reform is to radically change the basic structures of politics and the administration system. Hence, it is called the "third reform," following the Meiji Restoration (the first reform) and the alliance occupation in the postwar period (the second reform). Decentralization began in 1995 in reality, following the approval of both the Upper and Lower House in 1993 (Ogata 2007).

As previously stated, people lost trust in the central government. This triggered moves to transfer some decision-making power to local offices in order to balance the power distribution in terms of financial decisions, mainly concerned with budgets. In addition, decentralization from the government has the potential to maximize the power that each regional citizen holds in the establishment of a localized government (The Daily Yomiuri 2007). Fiscal decentralization has been carried out as one of the decentralization policies for over a decade. Nevertheless, various obstacles have remained, and there are difficulties ahead, and decentralization has not yet seemed to bring the hoped for success (The Daily Yomiuri 2006). Many local law makers have their own tasks to tackle before they attempt to cope with the decentralized budget and power. Many cities are still facing crushing debts (The Daily Yomiuri 2007). Regional tasks and problems ought to be solved before a decentralization of power is realized. As stated above, decentralization will not show successes for some years due to the current problems; however, on the other hand, it will eventually be possible to devolve more responsibility to local governors when citizens are ready for it.

Market Deregulation

One of the most important tasks in overcoming the crisis was to increase competition in the domestic sector in order to make it more efficient and profitable. This can be done by removing administrative control over market entry and exit, which was thought to help balance supply and demand (OECD 2004). This function of supply and demand balancing should be carried out by the market and is not a sphere of activity for the bureaucracy and politics in a market economy.

The government has introduced various policies to promote competition, but progress has not been very striking (Vogel 2006a). In some sectors, the reforms successfully removed market distorting regulations of supply-and-demand balancing. The sectors where deregulation was most successful are telecommunication, trucking, distribution and financial services. Also many utilities such as mobile communication, electric power and gas were affected by the reform. Although the reforms affected only one part of the economy, consumers already benefit greatly and save trillions of yen each year thanks to lower prices. The Free Trade Commission (FTC) has become more independent and has more resources to investigate and enforce the competition law. Price fixing and bid rigging agreements have been successfully eliminated. As another measure to increase competition, the number of exemptions from the anti-monopoly law (AMA) was reduced significantly. However, measures regarding large companies with substantial market power are still quite feeble.

Financial Deregulation

One of the major changes was undertaken in the financial sector. The financial sector has been reformed in a comprehensive way.

Plans for the deregulation of foreign exchange and financial markets were initiated by the Hashimoto government in 1996 (Craig 1998a). The need for reforms became urgent due to the danger of the bankruptcy of major banks with huge non-performing loan problems, the declining importance of Tokyo as a financial center and the credit crunch, which was a burden for the whole economy. Bank lending was falling, which was a bad sign for a bank-centered economy. As there was no lobby in favor of such a development, the political process for the reform was not jeopardized by vested interests like many other reform plans (Bosse and Köllner 2001).

In order to understand the problems of the financial sector, it is crucial to know its past. In Japan, the banks have historically played a very prominent role in this system. They carried out the function of financial intermediates and had close relations with the funded companies. The relationship with the financial intermediary was often exclusive, forming the so-called main bank system, which means that one bank is in charge of providing the financial resources and also has monitoring, advisory and intervention functions. This system is a legacy from the war, during which the government had assigned companies to a specific bank, which then provided financial resources (Sakakibara 2003). Most heavy industry and military production was involved in the deal and these are the companies that became the backbone of early-post war industry due to their facilities, technological know-how and skilled workers. After the Second World War, companies started taking huge credits from the banks. On the other hand, the banks held stocks of companies they were lending to (Flath 2005).

The banking system basically had the task of providing cheap capital to industry. The profitability of the financial institutions and the returns for the saver were not goals in this system. This cheap capital helped rebuild the economy after the war and develop a strong export sector. But on the downside, the financial institutions could not develop properly (Craig 1998a).

To maintain this system, the government protected the banks by not allowing new market entries and by splitting up the market into city banks, regional banks, long-term credit banks and trust banks (Sakakibara, 2003). Bank competed in terms of size. They tried to attract as many deposits as possible and lent to even questionable borrowers due to a lack of monitoring by the Ministry of Finance. As the banks could not receive an adequate return for the risk, the government and the convoy system provided implicit insurance in case of serious problems. The administration also took an active part through the Bank of Japan and the Ministry of Finance, which were in close contact with the banks and had a control and guidance function (Craig 1998a).

With the opening of the bond market in the mid-1980s, the high profit margin of the cartelized banking sector, which was high because of the size of the banks but not very high per unit, came under pressure. Profits shrank, but the banks refrained from downsizing and restructuring, which was the cause of overcapacity and thus low profitability (Flath 2005). The problems of Japanese banks were originally caused by protective regulation. In this environment, the financial market remained underdeveloped and institutions were inefficient and noncompetitive. This fact caused the financial sector to be highly underdeveloped, even though Japan is the world's biggest creditor nation (Craig 1998a).

The burst of the bubble created major problems for the financial industry. Many banks got into trouble as their assets, especially stocks and real estate, lost value on a big scale. Many mortgages became partially unsecured. This created major problems for banks and caused immense losses. Moreover, creditors were in trouble and were not able to pay interest, or even failed. Many of the credits that the banks had extended during the bubble became non-performing loans (NPLs). These "bad credits" are especially problematic in combination with deflation. The burden of debt increases and debtors become even more likely to fail (The Economist 2006). The inefficient distribution of credits and the artificially low interest rates can be identified as the causes of non-performing loans. Loans were not only distributed under economic but also political criteria. Many risky and unprofitable projects were funded. Rising real estate prices made mortgages very attractive and the loans were sometimes even higher than the collateral (Iwamoto 2006).

For many banks, NPLs became a crucial issue. The relationship of NPLs to assets became critical in the late 1990s and much higher than in the U.S. during the financial crisis of the 1980s. Owing to the very low profitability of Japanese banks, they did not have sufficient resources to deal with the situation. As the whole industry was in trouble, the convoy system did not work, as there were not enough strong banks to rescue the large number of struggling banks. This suddenly became clear when the large Hokkaido Takushoku Bank failed in 1997 (Craig 1998b).

However, non-performing loans are not only an indicator of the situation of the banking sector. Because the debtors of these credits come from the struggling domestic manufacturing and service industries, NPLs point to structural problems in these sectors. Almost all the debtors are small- and medium-sized enterprises and not the mostly export-orientated large companies (Sakakibara 2003). Loss of asset value forces banks to cut lending.

The reforms were labeled as making financial institutions "free, fair and global." The old system was the very opposite of this. The goal was to increase the competitiveness and efficiency of the financial institutions, and also the diversity of products and thereby the choice for investors and borrowers. The reforms focused on deregulation. Foreign exchange transactions became less regulated. Liberalization of the domestic insurance and banking business was also part of the plan (Craig 1998a).

The reforms that were announced by Hashimoto in 1996 were implemented from 1998 to 2000. The first step was the removal of restrictions on foreign exchange markets in April 1998, which completely liberalized international transactions. Further steps were the liberalizing of asset management, derivative dealing and over-the-counter sales. The supervising system for securities companies was switched from licensing to registration and regulations for many activities were abandoned (MoF 2000).

As a result, companies in the financial industry obtained more freedom. The old restrictions, which restricted each company to one specific business area, were abolished. Banks could participate in activities they had been excluded from before. Mergers and acquisitions with overseas involvement helped restructure the Japanese financial market (Kwan 2000).

As the Japanese government took Britain's "Big Bang" reforms as a model, the achievements have to be compared with the effect of the British financial deregulations. The reforms of the Thatcher government allowed London to become the world's main financial center. However, Japan's Big Bang has been less successful than its British counterpart in every way. Some of the domestic problems have been solved, and competition and efficiency have certainly increased. The transition in the financial sector continues and the new regulatory environment is likely to create more efficient and competitive structures in the financial sector. But the reforms failed to increase Tokyo's importance as a financial center (Minier 2006). The importance of Tokyo's Stock Exchange has been falling since the bubble burst. The Big Bang failed to stop this decline. Tokyo has even lost is position as the financial center of Asia and has to compete with Hong Kong and Singapore. Shanghai and Shenzhen will be the next challengers and they are likely to become more important than Tokyo as a financial center in Asia (Craig 1998a).

Legal Reforms

Since the late 1990s, Nippon Keidanren and the ministries have pushed for reforms that provide businesses with more options, and these reforms are considered to be shareholder-centered (Vogel 2006a). Moreover, after 1997, deregulation of reorganizing corporate groups proceeded very rapidly, and as result shareholders were able to invest in these corporations.

As the liberalization or deregulation of markets proceeded, more corporations have attempted mergers and acquisitions. In 1997, merger and acquisition procedures were made easier; so-called "meetings for reporting to shareholders," where half of the shareholder meeting was used to require the approval of a merger beforehand, were abolished. If the acquiring company had the approval of its shareholders, short-form mergers became possible (Shishido 2007). The number of mergers and acquisitions has increased year by year, and in 2006 about two thousand M&A transactions occurred in Japan (Matsuda 2005).

In 1993, the government also started to expand certain shareholder rights. One of the most noticeable legal changes was cross-shareholding, which even now is increasing although it was introduced more than 10 years ago. In cross-shareholding, two different companies can swap equity shares, which can promote business stability between the two companies. Liberalization of Japan's markets has inevitably had a great effect. Cross-shareholdings represent less than a quarter of the market today (The Economist 2006). Furthermore, since the beginning of the 1990s, foreign shareholders have been playing an increasingly significant role in the Japanese stock market (Learmount 2002), dominated by Japanese corporations, as foreign capital companies have started to move into the market.

As for other significant corporate law changes focused on shareholder accountability, in May, 2000, the government adopted the Corporate Spin-off Law, so that corporations could easily spin off and sell divisions to new subsidiaries. Thanks to this law, companies can now split without shareholder approval if they meet the required criteria. In 2001, the government passed another reform bill; moreover, in 2002, the government finally allowed large firms to adopt a committee style board, which had been widely used in the United States. Those changes were considered to be shareholder-centered, but at the same time they were required in a liberalized economic market. Thus, the government is likely to continue to move forwards so that corporations will have more freedoms and flexibility in the open market (Vogel 2006a).

Until very recently, the employment rate was relatively low due to the collapse of the bubble. According to OECD (2006) research, the employment rate in Japan was 68% as of 2003. Japan was ranked 12th in the world, although, in the same year, in terms of GDP Japan was ranked second behind the United States. The Japanese government exercises its power to the minimum because changes in the employment system should be embedded in norms and practices. Nonetheless, it is indeed true that the government has the goal of maintaining employment and offering more freedom (Vogel 2006a).

One of the most remarkable legal reforms is the Equal Employment Opportunities Law adopted in May, 1985 (Flath

2005). Since then few major labor laws have been adopted; however, there have been some changes in labor laws since the mid-1990s. Legal working hours were cut to 40 hours per week in 1994.

The biggest legal change that impacted the labor market, however, was the Old Persons' Stabilization Law in 1994. The background to the law was the problem of Japan's declining population and an aging society. The percentage of elderly persons is increasing and that of younger persons is decreasing. Thus, the law provided employed workers with the opportunity to retire at 65 instead of 60. Subsequently, the age of payment of a public pension was raised from 60 to 65 (Sugeno 2002).

In 1995, a law was introduced for workers who have to change jobs due to unavoidable industrial structural changes: "Special Measures Law Concerning Employment Stabilization of Workers in Specified Depressed Industries." This law has a lot to do with the wave of globalization. In addition to depressed industries, the yen's appreciation has emerged as a problematic issue. Thanks to this law, however, workers are able to change jobs without having an unemployed period and they can obtain benefits as well (Ministry of Health, Labor and Welfare 2007).

In terms of childcare, the Childcare Leave Payments system was revised to make the 1991 Childcare Leave Law more effective. Based on the law, 25% of wages are paid when a worker takes childcare leave. As can be seen above, labor laws keep changing as they provide Japanese workers with more comfortable working conditions, in keeping with the government's goal (Sugeno 2002).

As far as changes allowing more part-time work are concerned, the government revised the Working Dispatching Law and the Employment Security Law in July, 1999. These revisions increased legal security for those who are unemployed and seeking jobs, which enabled employers to hire dispatch workers (*haken*) with greater flexibility. Moreover, by adopting this law, firms could successfully reduce labor costs. Hence, Japan's labor market gained a greater amount of flexibility. The most recent revisions of the Working Dispatching Law were carried out in June, 2003, and introduced in March, 2004. These revisions allowed extended maximum contract periods for firms to hire dispatch workers. By placing emphasis on non-regular workers, including dispatch workers, the labor market could benefit from a reduction in labor costs, flexibility, and lower wage costs (Vogel 2006).

In Japan, retail activities have stagnated since 1990. This was not just due to the post-bubble economic situation, but also changes in customer behavior. In order to boost retail activities, the Ministry of Economy, Trade and Industry (METI) introduced the Law Concerning the Adjustment of Retail Activities by Large Scale Retail Sectors and the Law of Large-Scale Retail Store Location in 2000 (Hirata 2002).

Effects of Reforms

Thanks to the various reforms, legal changes and external factors, there have been different changes in Japanese companies and the economy as a whole. Policy and legal reforms have changed the environment, but they cannot directly change business behavior. The system has changed in a unique Japanese way. Some aspects have been liberalized, but this does not mean that Japan is heading for a U.S.-like economic system. Companies have changed the conditions of some of their long-term relations, but have not abandoned them. The opportunities for companies to switch to more Western business practices have increased, but in many industries companies have maintained old practices (Vogel 2006a).

The motivation behind all reforms was to overcome economic stagnation and to allow the economy to flourish again. Therefore, the success of all reforms has to be assessed by looking at the economic results.

After a decade of poor growth, the growth rate picked up in 2001. The growth level is still well behind the high rates achieved in the 70s and 80s, but seems acceptable in international comparison. Japan's potential growth will be around 1.5% in the near future. Japan has left behind the economic catch-up period that brought high growth rates. Such growth rates are not feasible anymore as the Japanese economy has matured. Growth will not be driven by capital accumulation, but rather by technological progress and efficiency gains. The fall in potential growth is also due partially to a shrinking labor force. New growth is not only export driven, but meanwhile also comes from domestic demand (OECD 2006). This permits one to be optimistic for the future of the Japanese economy.

Behind this growth are the first steps taken to restructure the Japanese economy. Legal changes have allowed for new dynamic developments. Domestic and international mergers and acquisitions as well as corporate reorganizations are helping restructure companies (Kwan 2000). Recently, companies started attaching more importance to profitability. Many managed to increase their return on assets (ROA) significantly compared with the 1990s. The corporate reorganization demanded by the capital markets has become easier to realize due to changes in the law and the tax code (Nippon Ginkô Chôsa Kihô 2005).

Corporate restructuring in recent years has taken various forms. As Japanese companies do not want to lay off people, they have tried to decrease labor costs and increase productivity. New employees are more likely to be hired as temporary workers. Workforce reduction has been achieved through the normal fluctuation of employees.

Companies have also changed their financing sources. The main bank is still an important partner for many companies, but relationships have changes. Strong companies have shifted more towards direct financing, while financially-stricken companies become more dependent on main banks (Vogel 2006a).

By way of example, in the retail industry structural changes have become very visible. The old Japanese retail distribution system was very complicated and expensive. Thanks to the easing of regulations under the Large-Scale Retail Location Law, many discount store chains have entered the market, offering a wide range of goods at discount prices. New drug stores are following a more American-style shop concept and offer almost everything except fresh food. These big discount stores have captured a substantial share of the market and have changed the structure of the retail market (Iwamoto 2003). This can be explained by the fact that traditional institutions and business practices do not seem very beneficial for the retail industry. For example, as it is not a knowledge-based business, life-time employment is not a great benefit, but significantly hampers flexibility and imposes high costs. Other industries have maintained some institutions and business practices, as they equipped companies with a comparative advantage, also against global competition.

Pressure on the domestic market has come from low-wage countries, to which a lot of manufacturing was relocated. Part of production has been moved to China or India (Sakakibara 2003). This has led to shifts in industrial and employment structures, which appear threatening to many Japanese, as the manufacturing industry is associated with the rise of the Japanese economy. But this development has forced companies to increase competitiveness by internationalizing and restructuring.

Pending Problems for the Japanese Economy

In addition to the positive developments after reforms, there are still many problem areas in the Japanese economy. The main issues are high public debt, the fragile banking industry and the unproductive domestic sector.

Public Debt

As a classic instrument of countercyclical policy, public spending was expanded during the economic crisis in the 1990s. Because the crisis lasted much longer than expected, public debt kept on accumulating. A major portion of current debts was caused by spending after 1992. Before, Japan had run a budget surplus and had had a sound debt situation (OECD 2006). Public spending was used to keep the unemployment rate down and as an instrument of regional income redistribution. A major goal of public works was to create jobs in the construction industry (Kwan 2000). In the 1990s, employment in the construction sector grew significantly, while productivity in the construction industry actually fell (Sakakibara 2003). In many examples, public funds were used very inefficiently.

Even though Japan's debt ratio peaked in 2002, the amount of debt is still significant. In 2006, the debt equaled roughly 170% of GDP. This was the highest ratio among all OECD countries. Even if the huge assets of the Japanese state are included, in 2006, net debt was still almost 90% of GDP. As regards fiscal income, tax cuts and slow growth have hurt tax revenues. The tax base narrowed, as many companies made losses and could thus avoid paying taxes. As a consequence, the primary deficit grew. There is a structural gap between income and expenditures, which is not sustainable in the long run (OECD, 2006, p.65). The share of government expenditure of

GDP is still low compared to most European countries, but has risen steadily during the crisis.

In order to deal with the huge debts, the Japanese government will have to turn the primary deficit into a surplus (Waldenberger 2001). Tax hikes, especially by broadening the tax base, will be necessary in the future and are a potential threat to economic growth Some fiscal consolidation has been achieved. Spending has been reduced in recent years. But future cuts will become more difficult as expenditures for health care and pensions will have a negative impact on the national budget. This is aggravated by Japan's demographic problems, especially an aging population. Even so, Japan will be able to run a primary budget surplus over the medium term (OECD 2006). But the surplus needs to be significant in order to reduce the debt ratio on a grand scale.

The high level of debt, together with the public income situation, makes Japan's public debt a serious problem (Waldenberger 2001). Fiscal discipline has to improve in the future to prevent the debt from becoming a threat to the financial stability of the Japanese state. This restricts the government's ability to provide further economic stimulation through public spending or tax cuts. Rather the state has to increase revenues by reforming the taxation system and broadening the tax base. The current personal income tax system is very complicated and distorting. Fundamental reforms are needed. Income tax is much lower than in other industrialized countries and the amounts transferred to the fiscal authorities are rather humble by international standards.

Banking and Bad Loans

The Big Bang reforms bringing financial deregulation have caused some changes in Japanese banking. Besides other measures, it has helped face up to the problem of non-performing loans (NPLs). However, otherwise, success has been patchy. Although Tokyo's importance as a financial center has not grown, the domestic market has become more competitive, versatile and even international. The NPL problem has been largely solved. Most banks were able to generate profits again in recent years, but profitability remains low (Hall 2007). The problem of overcapacity has not been seriously addressed (La Croix and Kawaura 2006). More than a decade after the bubble burst, Japanese banks still have NPLs in their portfolios. But the size of the NPLs in the portfolio of the banks is diminishing rapidly. The portion of bad loans in the overall credit market is steadily decreasing (OECD 2006). The problem is now under control due to better policy and a stronger economic environment (OECD 2006). Another problem for the banks is a sizable overcapacity, which also impairs performance. A radical downsizing is necessary to improve profitability and competitiveness. Attempts to reduce overcapacity have not been as successful as dealing with NPLs (La Croix and Kawaura 2006).

A big problem after the bubble was the credit crunch. Bank lending declined during the decade between 1996 and 2006. Just recently, bank lending began to recover at a very modest speed (OECD 2006). The problem seems to be that investment demand is still growing quite slowly due to a lack of profitable business opportunities (Hall 2007).

The main bank system is still important in Japan, although it has lost its predominance. Large companies use alternative ways of financing, such as the equity or corporate bond markets. Most small- and medium-sized companies finance themselves indirectly with one bank in a leading position (Vogel 2006a). Liberalization has revitalized the financial sector. There are still some problems, such as low profitability and overcapacity. Mergers and acquisitions, also with foreign involvement, have helped to kick-start the restructuring of the banking and insurance industry (Kwan 2000).

Domestic Sector

The Japanese economy comprises a dual structure with two very unequal sectors. One is the sector consisting of highly competitive and technology-based, export-oriented industries. Companies like Toyota and Sony have gained worldwide reputations. Many companies sell their products successfully all over the world and are market leaders. These success stories have projected a positive image of Japanese companies around the world. But the competitive export sector is only a small fraction of the economy. The unproductive domestic sector still dominates the ratio of value added activities and accounts for most employment. Sectors such as retail, food, and construction are uncompetitive, resulting in high prices for consumers. This sector has remained unchanged despite the low productivity due to protective regulations and subsidies. The lack of productivity also creates a wage and income gap between the two sectors (Sakakibara 2003). The dual structure of the economy is also reflected in the exchange rate. On one hand, the yen is historically low and seems undervalued against the dollar, as Japan runs a current account surplus, thanks to strong exports. Reasons behind this weakness are high savings, low interest rates, and very high liquidity (Global Insight 2007). Furthermore, speculative carry trades, investing cheap yen credits abroad, put downwards pressure on the Japanese currency.

The problems of productivity become clear in a comparison with the United States. Japanese labor is about 30% less productive than American labor. The income gap is only smaller because Japanese employees work more. Japan's productivity level is also very weak compared to other major industrialized countries (OECD 2006). The productivity gap comes only from the domestic sector, which makes for the lion's share of GDP. In fact, the export-oriented industries are even more productive than the U.S. average (Sakakibara 2003).

Despite these constraints, there has been some change. Export industries have moved their production sites abroad because exporting was not profitable at current exchange rates. More and more imported products compete in the domestic market. This has led to so-called "deindustrialization," a shift from the manufacturing to the service industry, with a reallocation of capital from Japan to production sites overseas (Matsuba 2001). Rising productivity driven by structural change and more efficient labor use are a great opportunity for Japan to boost the economy. A wider spread of the application of information technology will also help to catch up with the productivity levels of other industrialized countries.

Conclusion

The changes in laws, regulations, politics, and economic structure are complex. Some reforms are based on a liberal model, while others continue Japanese traditions. However, these reforms have influenced companies and management practices.

Within Japanese companies, considerations about cost-effectiveness and return on investments have become more important decision criteria (Kwan 2000). Old business practices and relations are reconsidered under these aspects. This does not mean that Japanese companies will become Westernized. But the options for managers in Japan have increased. And Western management practices and corporate governance would be legal and feasible. Japanese companies have hesitated to relinquish their strong relationships; however, they have restructured them. Other aspects have changed, such as the introduction of more performance- rather than seniority-linked salary systems (Vogel 2006a).

In some sectors, having a long-term orientation and strong relationship with employees is still a comparative advantage. In other sectors, such as retail or construction, the costs are higher than the benefits and more cost-effective business practices will be implemented. China has been considered a threat because it attracts manufacturing from Japan. But the growing Chinese market is also a huge opportunity for Japanese companies as an export market. As productivity is still well behind other major industrialized countries, there is also large potential for improvement (Sakakibara 2003).

Although the effects of globalization are also influencing Japan, it is still very isolated from the world economy. Imports are still at a very low level and the ratio of foreign workers in the workforce is low. Integration into the global economy is a big challenge for Japan, but is necessary for further economic development as it offers tremendous opportunities. Another promising opportunity would be an increase in the participation of women in the labor force. There is a huge, latent potential among the female population waiting to be tapped for the labor market and to increase the output of the Japanese economy (OECD 2006).

Structural changes in Japan are not isolated events; there is also some continuity beside novel changes. Although some of the most severe economic problems seem to have been solved, Japan's economy is still in a transformation process. This process of adaptation to new global and technological developments will take decades rather than years (Sakakibara 2003).

Bibliography

Bosse, F. and P. Köllner (2001): *Reformen in Japan – Einführung in die Thematik.* In Bosse, F. and P. Köllner (Eds.): Reformen in Japan. Hamburg: Institut für Asienkunde.

Craig, V. V. (1998a): *Financial Deregulation in Japan. FDIC Banking Review, 1998.* Downloaded from www.fdic.gov on November 11, 2007

Craig, V. V. (1998b): *Japanese Banking: A time of Crisis.* FDIC Banking Review, 1998. Downloaded from www.fdic.gov on November 11, 2007.

The Daily Yomiuri (2006): *Decentralization drives still falling short.* The Daily Yomiuri, October 30, 2006

The Daily Yomiuri (2007a): *Local lawmakers must budget wisely.* The Daily Yomiuri, April 27, 2007.

The Economist (1997): *Tax reform runs late.* The Economist, November 6, 1997, p. 77.

The Economist (2006): *From hero to zero.* The Economist, February 4, 2006, p. 61-63.

Flath, D. (2005): *The Japanese economy*. Oxford: Oxford University Press.

Global Insight (2007): *Report Japan: Country Intelligence – Global Insight Database*. Downloaded from www.globalinsight.com on November 9, 2007.

Hall, M. (2007): *Recent banking sector reforms in Japan: An assessment*. Asian Business & Management 6, p. 57–74.

Hirata, J. (2002): *Changes in retail commerce activities in Japan by prefecture and 13 big cities: An Analysis by Post-1985 the Japanese Census of Commerce*. Downloaded from www.ci.nii.ac.jp on January 30, 2008.

Hoshi, T. and Kashyap, A. K. (2004): *Japan's economic and financial crisis: An overview*. The Journal of Economic Perspectives, Winter 2004.

Iwamoto, Y. (2006): *Japan on the upswing*. New York: Algora.

Kwan, C. H. (2000): *Revitalizing the Japanese economy*. Downloaded from http://www.brookings.edu/papers/2000/06globaleconomics_kwan.aspx on December 22, 2008.

La Croix, S. and Kawaura, A. (2006): *Institutional change in Japan – Theories, evidence, and reflections*. In: Blomström and La Croix (Eds.): Institutional change in Japan. London: Routledge.

Learmount, S. (2002): *Corporate governance*. Oxford: Oxford University Press.

Matsuba, M. (2001): *The contemporary Japanese economy: Between civil society and corporation-centered society*. Tokyo: Springer.

Matsuda, N. (2005): *Raifudoa sôdô mondai teiki*. Kokuminkaikan, August 22, 2005, p. 1-2.

Minier, J.-F. (2006): *Japan's big bang: Too little, too late?* Far Eastern Economic Review, December 2006, p. 17.

Ministry of Finance Japan (MoF) (2000): *Japanese big bang.* Ministry of Finance Japan. Downloaded from http://www.mof.go.jp/english/big-bang/ebb37.htm on January 6, 2000.

Ministry of Health, Labor and Welfare (2007): *Jizoku kanô na shakai hoshô seido to sasaeru junkan.* White Paper.

Nippon Ginko Chôsa Kihô (2005): *The state of the Japanese economy: From the perspective of employment and income.* Bank of Japan Research Bulletin. Downloaded from www.boj.or.jp on January 20, 2008.

Ogata, T. (2007): 2006 *Chihô bunken kaikaku suishin no tenkai.* The Kagawa University Economic Review, March 2007.

OECD (2004): *OECD reviews of regulatory reform: Japan – Progress in Implementing Regulatory Reform 1999.* OECD Publishing. Downloaded on www.sourceoecd.org on November 9, 2007.

OECD (2006): *Economic Surveys: Japan (July 2006).* OECD Publishing. Downloaded on www.sourceoecd.org on November 9, 2007.

Sakakibara, E. (2003): *Structural reform in Japan.* Washington: Brookings Institution Press.

Shishido, Z. (2007): *Changes in Japanese corporate law and governance; corporate governance in Japan.* Oxford: Oxford University Press.

Sugeno, K. (2002): *Japanese employment and labor law.* Carolina Academic Press.

Vogel, S. (2006a): *Japan Remodeled: How government and industry are reforming Japanese capitalism.* Cornell University Press.

Vogel, S. (2006b): *Japan After Koizumi: The Abe opportunity.* Downloaded from http://www.brookings.edu/opinions/2006/10china_vogel.aspx on December 22, 2007.

Waldenberger, F. (2001): *Japan an der Schwelle zum dritten Jahrtausend: Mit Reformen aus der Krise.* In: Bosse, F. and P. Köllner (Eds.): Reformen in Japan. Hamburg: Institut für Asienkunde, p. 193-199.

5. Demographic Changes

By Aaron Schiffer and Yui Inada

Besides attempting to revive the economy, Japan faces numerous other problems. On top of major structural transformation, demographic changes are taking place in Japanese society. This chapter explores Japan's demographic changes and their implications for business management. The rapid aging of Japan's population and the fall in the fertility rate have been accompanied by a huge change in household structures. These changes have had a major influence on the Japanese economy and, in turn, Japanese management practices, the Japanese pension system, and the development of new consumer groups within the population. Another very interesting aspect of Japan's situation is the increasing importance of women in the workplace.

Japan's Aging Society

After the Second World War, Japan's birth rates shot up because of the promise of safety that came with peace. Japan's crude birth rate for 1947 was 34.3%, the highest it ever reached in the post-war period. There were some 2.7 million babies born in 1947, and the next two years saw numbers almost as high. The concentration of population in one small age group, which arose from the large number of babies being born in a short period of time following the war, is captured by the phrase "baby boomers." A "baby boom" signifies a period when many more babies are born than usual. America shared the same phenomenon, although Japan differs in that the boom really only lasted three years. After the boom, the birth rate slowed again in Japan. By 1960, Japan's birth rate was 17.2%, nearly half the rate of some 10 to 13 years earlier. The birth rate was still healthy enough that the population was growing in size as a whole, though not rapidly. In the early 1970s, the birth rate rose to a steady 19% for a few years (Ishikawa et al. 2006). This is considered the second baby boom in Japan. Needless to say, the second boom was not as large as the first because the 19% birth rate was substantially smaller than that in the late 40s and early 50s. Although the second boom was not of the same magnitude as the first, it was still significant as it created a further segment of high density population in one small age group.

At the beginning of the 21st century, the first wave of baby boomers is around 55 to 60 years old, and the second wave of baby boomers is around the age of 30 to 35. This means that Japan's society is considered to be rapidly aging because there is a large concentration of population around the age of 60, with another large segment moving into their 40s. Beside the booms, the overall high birth rate in Japan that followed the war created a large number of people in the 30-65 age brackets. "In 1990, Japan had the same percentage of those over 65, a little over 12%, as the United States did. Today, while the rate has changed little in the United States, decreasing childbirth rates, longer life expectancy, and no immigration have pushed up Japan's rate." (Ohnishi 2006) The point is that there are a large number of older people living in Japan, which makes it an aging society.

Falling Birth Rate

Besides aging, Japan is also facing a falling fertility rate that has had positive and negative effects. "Japan's fertility decline was both the earliest to occur in the post-war period and the greatest in magnitude. Moreover, its fast mortality transition (change in the mortality rate) over the past few decades has given the country the highest level of longevity in the contemporary world." (Ogawa 2005)

To evaluate how the fertility rate has affected the country, it is necessary to investigate how much it has changed. The first wave occurred from 1947 to 1950. The three years following the war were unique. The fertility rate was above 4% in the three-year, post-war baby boom. It is interesting how quickly the fertility rate dropped after three years, marking the end of the first boom. It is also noteworthy that, over the past 50 years, the fertility rate in Japan has fallen steadily, apart from in a few exceptional years.

There are multiple reasons why Japan's total fertility rate fell after the war and has kept doing so ever since. Japan's post-war drop in the fertility rate was caused by reasons that changed over time. The leading cause of the decline in the total fertility rate before the first major oil crisis was the decreasing number of births within each single family. At that time, the number of third and fourth children born dropped significantly. After the oil crisis hit Japan, other reasons become more significant. Since the 1980s, the number of marriages has also decreased. By the end of the 1980s, Japan was no longer a "universal marriage society." There were more and more people who broke the mold and never married. The journal also asserts that rising educational attainment among women and rising female employment are two socioeconomic factors that have been playing a major role in affecting Japan's marriage market. Women who are better educated and have better job opportunities have alternative lifestyles to rearing children. Simply, the argument goes that women's priorities have shifted from having children to becoming educated and working (Ogawa 2005).

Although the fertility rate continued to fall through the 1990s, the reasons behind the decline changed. In the early 1990s, the leading cause was no longer the reduced chance of first marriage (getting married for the first time), but the lower probability of having a first birth. In the latter half of the 1990s, the leading cause behind Japan's falling fertility rate was once again a reduced chance of first marriage. A reduction in second births (having a second baby) was the second leading cause for the falling fertility rate in the latter 1990s. It would appear that Japan's poor economic performance in the 1990s was a huge contributing factor to the fall in the fertility rate in more recent years. These years were post bubble years in which Japan experienced a dramatic loss of economic power and growth. When the economy suffers from a depression, people instinctually become more money conscious. Thus, the fertility rate was affected negatively as rearing children is an additional financial burden. Maruo (2006) states that, "According to a Japanese survey, some 70% of the respondents said public aid was crucial in increasing the fertility rate." Therefore, it can be inferred that people in Japan generally feel that the government needs to help more financially in order for people to start having more children. Also, the rise in the costs of child rearing has naturally had an adverse effect on the total fertility rate. However, "…the Japanese economy has been showing signs of recovery, and the nation's fertility rate is likely to rise a bit. It is reported that the number of children that single Japanese women eventually hope to have has increased." (Maruo 2006)

The high economic growth that Japan experienced after the war can be attributed to factors related to the falling fertility rate and its effects on Japan's population. These factors are: a high savings rate and high allocation of savings to productive investment that caused substantial investment in public and private infrastructure, good use of advanced technology imported from industrialized countries, a calm political situation, and the availability of well educated and trained workers. The claim is made that, "most of these factors are closely linked to population." (Ogawa 2005)

Changing Household Structures in Japan

Japan's rapidly aging society and falling fertility rate have coincided with a large change in the overall population of Japan. Together with that change, economic transitions have also occurred. One rapidly changing and key element of Japan's demographic structure is the Japanese household. The total number of households, household size, household type, and distribution are changing very significantly (Hakuhodo Institute 2007). According to census statistics, one-person households will outnumber all other households in 2007. According to Ishikawa et al. (2006), Japan's total population is decreasing, the number of households is increasing, the size of households is decreasing, and the number of one person households is rapidly increasing. The standard Japanese household is definitely no longer three generations living together as one person households now outnumber all other types. Boasting one of the longest life spans on the planet, Japanese people are now spending more of their time living alone than living with someone else (Hakuhodo Institute 2007). Because there are such a significant number of Japanese people living alone, the fate of the country's stability rests on its ability to accommodate their lifestyle.

Effects of Demographic Changes

The drastic changes described above confront the Japanese government with similar problems to those faced by Western governments, such as problems with the pension system and an explosion in medical costs.

Strains on the Pension System

In terms of financial security, huge problems have arisen with the pension system. Brooke (2004) claims that, "In 1950, when the national pension system started to take shape, 35% of Japan's population was 15 years or younger and 4.9% of Japanese were 65 or older. Since 1970, the number of workers supporting a pensioner has dropped from 8.5 to about 3.5." Married couples' fertility decisions at reproductive age have definitely been affected by the financial uncertainty that came with Japan's management reforms (Ogawa 2005). The Japanese pension system is based on a rating system by means of which the insurance young people pay now is provided to older people as their pension. With a continually declining birth rate and an increasing number of older people, who are becoming an ever larger portion of Japan's total population, it is becoming difficult for the Japanese government to manage this system.

The Japanese government now has to adjust this system as young people are required to make ever higher payments as the number of retired people increases (Nikkei Business 2004). Moreover, young workers highly distrust the present pension system and are refusing to make their pension contributions. The Japanese pension system has two different types of pension: the national pension and the social security pension. Full-time workers usually have deductions made automatically from their salaries for the social security pension and the national pension, while others have to pay national pension contributions by themselves. The national pension system states that all people living in Japan between the ages of 20 and 60, including students, the unemployed, and business owners, have to pay insurance contributions for the national pension. However, the ratio of unpaid insurance for the national pension reached 37.2% in 2002, which means some 40% of potential applicants are not paying the insurance (Nikkei Business Associe 2004). The payment ratio for the national pension system among people under 24 is 47.4% and 49.4% for people between 25 to 29. Moreover, the effective payment rate for people in their 20s is about 33% if the data is recalculated to include people who are omitted from the data or students who are exempted during university (Mainichi Shimbun 2003). This situation arose due to the fact that the government can not force those who are not full-time workers, such as students and *freeters*, to pay national pension contributions. As they do not belong to a specific company as a full-time worker, there are no automatic insurance deductions and, therefore, the decision to pay contributions is completely a matter of ethics. In February 2004, the ruling party in Japan introduced a bill to reform the pension system. The bill consisted of raising pension contributions and cutting pension payments. The maximum employee pension contribution was fixed at 18.3% of annual income and at 16,900 yen per month for the national pension, to be effective by 2017. The bill also includes a cut in benefits from employee pension insurance from 59.3% in 2006 to 50.2% by 2023. The bill was approved in June 2004, but was strongly opposed because the birth rate predictions announced later were below the estimated number upon which the changes to the pension system were based (Nikkei Business Associe 2004).

Another strain on the Japanese pension system is the standard family structure, which is based on the ideal that the husband works as a salaried company employee and the wife becomes a housewife, even though actual household structures have been changing rapidly, and the system doesn't fit the situation on the ground anymore. In the Japanese pension system, if housewives have an annual income below 1.3 million yen, they are exempted from paying insurance contributions. This system might be preventing women from being independent because the system itself is favorable for housewives and less so for working women. It virtually provides a free pension to about 11 million housewives. Furthermore, the system limits housewives from working as they can not earn more than 1.3 million yen a year. Some argue that the barrier of 1.3 million yen should be removed (Haruka 2004) in order to let housewives work freely and pay their own insurance contributions. The government should improve childcare and nursing care support instead of exempting housewives from insurance contributions since a key reason why working women leave their job is that they can not work and take care of their children and elderly parents at the same time. Therefore, if the government and companies establish a support system for those who want to work, but have to take care of their children and parents, these women would not have to leave their jobs. The pension burden and the declining birth rate problem will not be solved unless the Japanese government stops privileges for housewives, otherwise, working women will work even harder worrying about a unstable future, distrusting the pension system, while being unable to afford having children (Haruka 2004).

Explosion in Medical Costs

The rapidly growing number of elderly people has caused an explosion in medical costs. In 2006, the government decided to raise the ratio of payment for medical costs from 20 to 30% for people over 70 years old with incomes of over 6.2 million yen for a couple or 4.8 million yen for single persons. After 2008, the ratio will be raised from 10 to 20% for people between the ages of 70 to 74 whose incomes are below the stated amounts. Only the ratio for people over 75 remains the same. Government is trying to reduce expanding medical insurance costs and is shifting costs on to patients who might then be reluctant to see a doctor. Similar to the pension problem, medical costs will go up as the number of older people increases over the next decades, and the government will struggle to minimize payments by young people and adjust the appropriate ratio of medical costs for older people (Nikkei Health Care 2006).

Labor Shortages in the Near Future

In addition to the problems caused by an older population, there is a further serious problem that Japan will have to deal with in the near future: labor force shortages. On November 22, 2007, the Ministry of Health, Labor and Welfare announced that the labor force in Japan will decrease from 66.6 million in 2006 to 55.8 million in 2030 if the percentage of people working remains the same. Moreover, although the total population in Japan peaked in 2006 and decreased afterwards, the male population already started declining in 2005. According to data from the Ministry of Public Management, in March 2005, the overall population was 0.04% higher than the year before; however, the total male population was 0.02% down on the previous year—the first decrease since records began. Now, Japan is facing a serious labor shortage problem due to the declining birth rate and an aging society. This problem forces Japanese companies to seek potential workers such as *freeters*, married and unmarried women, and elderly people over the age of 65. It is predicted that, if the number of working women and older people increases, the labor force will only decrease by 480,000, while the labor force will shrink by 1.7 million if employment rates among these groups do not change (Nihon Keizai Shimbun 2007c).

Higher Integration of Women in the Japanese Workforce

Japanese companies are especially eager to bring women into the workforce because 70% of women leave work after they have children. There are some 3.5 million potential workers in the population of married women if the working environment is changed properly for their needs (Nihon Keizai Shimbun 2007d). However, there are many obstacles that women face. The Japanese employment system is based on the traditional Japanese family structure in which the husband works outside the house and the housewife does chores at home. This concept discourages women from working as full-time workers for two important reasons. First, the family support system states that dependants may not have an income exceeding 1.3 million yen a year. Many housewives simply try to keep their income below this amount to be a dependant of their husband as it is easier than paying taxes and insurance by themselves, and, therefore, their working hours are restricted. Second, generally, the working environment is not flexible enough for women. Once they become full-time workers, they would generally be required to work 5 days straight, from Monday through Friday, from early in the morning until late at night. This is why women leave work after marriage or childbirth as they would not be able to do chores and care for a child while they work full-time. Japanese women used to have only two alternatives in life due the barriers explained above: work or family. Furthermore, if women have to choose between work and family, they would not be willing to get married or have children, and this would lead to a further decline in the birth rate. However, Japanese companies are gradually adapting to make both work and life compatible. Now, Japanese women have a third alternative: to work flexibly and care for the family at the same time. This work-life balance has attracted people who are willing to work in a flexible style.

Recently, many companies have started to integrate more women into the workplace and are accepting working styles which suit women employees. For many working women, child and nursing care are a very important issue. To bring more women into the workplace, companies started to improve the working environment in respect of child and nursing care, especially companies in the IT and software fields. IT and software companies are very concerned about a lack of human resources because of the declining birth rate and due to the unpopularity of these fields among new graduates. Therefore, many IT vendors have measures to combat the declining birth rate, such as the extension of maternity leave, and the establishment of a child care system through shorter working hours. They are attempting to improve the working environment and attract new employees. In August 2006, groupware vendor, Cybozu Corporation, introduced a key reform of employment conditions: 6 years maximum maternity and nursing-care leave. Following in the footsteps of Cybozu, many IT service and software firms are changing working conditions for women employees. NEC Corporation has decided to allow women to take leave for infertility treatment. These changes in working conditions have been motivated by the *jisedai-hô* law, which obliges companies to create a mother- and child-friendly environment in order to nurture the children who constitute the next generation in society. One of the stipulations of this law is the assurance of one and half years of maternity leave. Although the number of companies offering leave of more than 3 years, such as Cybozu, remains low at 2%, 18% of all companies offer 1.5 to 2 years leave, and 11% offer 2 to 3 years leave, while 69% of companies offer 1.5 years leave (Nikkei Computer 2006a). Companies must accommodate the needs of women as regards childbirth and childcare because of the increasing labor shortages. Recently, non-IT companies have started to actively recruit women, and, therefore, the lead held by IT companies in respect of a positive attitude towards the employment of women has been eroded by non-IT companies. IT companies will have to provide excellent support to attract more women employees in the future. Furthermore, companies also have to consider supporting women workers when they return from maternity leave. Only a few IT companies provide return support, such as holding training courses and education programs during maternity leave, and paying baby-sitting fees. Some companies offer e-learning services so that employees can brush up their skills at home. However, such support is not yet widespread in different industries. In particular, IT companies need to establish such supports systems for returning employees because in the IT industry technology changes constantly, and it is very difficult to catch up with other workers after an absence of a year or more. Moreover, a large number of workers in the IT industry place a lot of importance on flexible working styles such as teleworking. If companies offer maternity leave for men as they do for women employees, it would be easier for women to work and arrange childcare because of the support from the husband and it will make caring for the child easier. Traditionally, men do not take childcare leave and this tendency is still strong in many companies. Managers in traditional Japanese companies are often reluctant to have male employees take childcare leave. However, they should be aware of the importance of men's participation in childcare. Creating a positive attitude toward maternity leave and allowing flexibility in working styles will be the most effective solutions to retaining women and securing the company's future workforce.

Mitsubishi Heavy Industries announced that it will have introduced a new system for employee's childcare from

November 2007. This "career return system" allows employees, who have quit because of childbirth, to return to work. Moreover, the company will pay 5,000 yen per month for pre-schooling. The company expects to recruit talented women by offering this system. Furthermore, if retired employees register the reason for their retirement, for example, marriage or childcare, they may rejoin the company more easily. Some 100 working women take maternity leave every year at Mitsubishi Heavy Industries, while about 40 women quit to have children and to get married. Using the system, the company is trying to provide experienced working women with the opportunity to return to work.

Other attempts have been made to encourage especially married women to work as part-timers to boost the workforce. Many temporary employment agencies are tying to provide jobs for married women and women on maternity leave. B-style Corporation established a system called "maternity mama employment," which provides opportunities for women to work in a stress-free manner by sharing work with others. If a worker is not feeling too well, others can support her. The system actually increases job efficiency. The company also offers telecommuting, and it is planning to set up a day nursery for workers who have small children.

Developing a New Attitude towards Work

Mr. Itô from The Japan Institute for Labor Policy and Training explained that Japanese companies improved their products and services through teamwork and *gambarism* (a compound of *gambaru* and "ism"), not clearly defining functions or responsibilities for individuals (Nihon Keizai Shimbun 2007b). *Gambaru* is the traditional Japanese work ethic. According to the Genius Japanese-English dictionary, *gambaru* is defined as trying one's best, working hard, keeping up, holding on, etc. It has been considered that working very hard for a long time with the *gambaru* spirit is the ideal attitude for workers and it is deeply related to the Japanese working style in the real world. With the concept of *gambaru*, workers are often evaluated not on the basis of results, but on the number of hours they work, their effort, and attitude. One of the most remarkable traits of Japanese working behavior, working overtime, stems from this traditional ethic. Nevertheless, Mr. Itô addresses the problem of this time-oriented working style. He is concerned that this working style can be misunderstood even though many companies are currently trying to cut overtime work to improve the work environment. In fact, it is actually very difficult to change these customs, which have been passed on from generation to generation. However, some companies have already started to break with their old corporate identity and are trying to work efficiently. Below, some examples of pioneering companies that are changing their working styles are presented.

Uniqlo is a clothing brand of Fast Retailing Corporation. It is a successful retail company which, emulating GAP, offers basic quality clothing at a very low price. Uniqlo was a forerunner in reworking the company image. Its rapid growth was supported by workers who are eager to work from when the store opens until it closes and to solve problems through effort and time. This image benefits the company, but, on the other hand, many workers are exhausted due to the hard work involved. Thus some female managers, who wanted to work after they got married tried to change the working conditions. The president of Uniqlo, Mr. Yanai, declared that "overtime is wrong" and supported the realization of 8 hours work and 2 days off. They listed unnecessary work and transferred authority at the store level. In the end, they accomplished their plans without a fall in sales.

The company Ryohin Keikaku is a further example in the drive to reduce overtime working. This company is famous for Mujirushi Ryohin, which is a brand offering a variety of products including food, clothing, and stationery. Overtime was prohibited after 7 at the head office in 2007. The president, Mr. Matsui, said that the work atmosphere, which encouraged workers to stay at the office until the last train, was not appropriate for a company that sells household goods. He believes that workers, who place more importance on their private lives, will be more likely to have good ideas for household goods.

Looking at these examples, we can see how demands for better working conditions and more choices in working styles have been increasing. How companies react to these demands will be the key to improving the situation.

Conclusion

In conclusion, the change in Japan's demography has dramatically affected both household structures and the working environment in Japan over the decades. The main aspects of the changes include the increasing number of older people and the declining birth rate. The first and second baby boomers are getting older, turning "the population pyramid" upside-down, which means the number of older people is exceeding the number of younger people. Consequently, Japan will face serious problems such as workforce shortages in the near future and bankruptcy of the pension system. Moreover, the problems caused by demographic changes affect people's working styles. Owing to the declining birth rate, companies are trying to integrate women into the workforce to secure future labor supplies and have started to improve the working environment to make it more attractive for female employees. To prevent further decline in the fertility rate and greater labor shortages, Japanese companies need to change working environments and attitudes toward work since traditional "time-conscious working styles" discourage those who wish to work and have their own life at the same time. Changes in working styles, caused by transforming demographic and household structures, have just started in Japan, and Japan is still in the middle of shifting working styles to fit workers' needs. By focusing on more time-efficient working styles and the productivity of each worker, rather than making everyone work for a long time, Japan should be able to mitigate the effects of the shortage of labor expected in the near future.

Bibliography

Brooke, J. (2004): *A Tough Sell: Japanese social security.* New York Times, May 6, 2004.

Hakuhodo Institute (2007): *The dynamics of Japanese seikatsu-sha 2007.* Research Report.

Haruka, Y. (2004): *Kekkon no merito o hakudatsu seyo.* Nikkei Bijinesu, March 15, 2004.

Howard, D. (2007): *Japanese consumers: From homogeneity to diversity.* The Nikkei Weekly, June 4, 2007

Ishikawa, A., Beppu, M. and Sato, R. (2006): *Population statistics of Japan 2006.* Tokyo: National Institute of Population and Social Security Research, Department of Information Collection and Analysis, 2006.

Maruo, N. (2006): *Birth rate born of optimism.* Japan Times, November 6, 2006.

Nihon Keizai Shimbun (2007a): *Seichô unagasu hatarakikata – jikan atari no kôritsu takame seikatsu to no chôwa o.* Nihon Keizai Shimbun, August 20, 2007.

Nihon Keizai Shimbun (2007b): *Shuyô kigyô jidan chôwa kara (ue) shafû kaete hayagaeri (shigoto watashi katei).* Nihon Keizai Shimbun, November 12, 2007.

Nihon Keizai Shimbun (2007c): *Rodôsha jinkô 2030 nen ni 1070 man ningen, kôreisha josei no shûrô sokushin nara 480 man ningen.* Nihon Keizai Shimbun, November 23, 2007.

Nihon Keizai Shimbun (2007d): *Rodôkyoku jinkô, 2030 nen ni 1000 man ningen, hataraku shikumi henkaku hitsuyô ni.* Nihon Keizai Shimbun, November 27, 2007.

Nikkei Business (2007): *Katsuyô nakereba nihon shizumu.* Nikkei Bijinesu, May 17, 2004.

Nikkei Business Associe (2004): *Nenkin mondai.* Nikkei Bijinesu Associe, September 7, 2004.

Nikkei Business Associe (2006): *Jinkô genshô.* Nikkei Business Associe, February 7, 2006.

Nikkei Computer (2006a): *Shussan ikuji shien de jinzai rzûshutsu o tomeru – tayô na hatarakikata to shigoto no mieruka ga gaki.* Nikkei Computer, December 25, 2006.

Nikkei Health Care (2006): *Iryô hoken seido kaikaku.* Nikkei Health Care, February 2006.

Nikkei Sangyô Shimbun (2007): *Shussan taisha shain o saikoyô mitsubishi jûkô hoikusho hiyô hojo mo.* Nikkei Sangyô Shimbun, November 30, 2007.

Ogawa, N. (2005): *Japan`s transition from the demographic bonus to the demographic onus.* Asian Population Studies 1(2005): p. 207-226.

Ohnishi, N. (2006): *In a graying Japan, lower shelves and wider aisles.* New York Times, September 4, 2006.

Mainichi Shimbun (2003): *Susumu wakamono no nenkin fushin, nijûdai no nanawari minô*. Mainichi Shimbun, February 2, 2007.

6. Cultural and Social Changes

By Rolf Madrid, Yuka Tanaka, and Greg Taylor

Japan's economic development dates back to the Meiji Restoration, when the new government ended an isolationist policy and promoted the modernization and industrialization of Japan. Over the long history of modern Japan, society developed its own attitudes and cultural expectations of work, family, and life. Whether it was the cultural roots in Confucianism, Bushido, or just a home-grown *ganbaru* spirit, Japan flourished when its people worked hard and worked together.

The economic crisis in the 1990s challenged cultural expectations at the foundation of modern Japanese society. Working hard and working together were not producing the same success. Sacrificing oneself for the group was no longer paying its reward, and the government was unable to cure the economic recession. The long-held tradition of life-time employment was being violated, restructuring layoffs and forced early retirement left many Japanese without work late in their careers—a disastrous situation as companies still limited their hiring primarily to new college graduates. Furthermore, many new graduates failed to find full-time work, relying on part-time work to survive and missing the opportunity to be hired into a firm. At once, both the older and younger workforces saw the promises of and routes to a comfortable life compromised or shattered altogether.

Owing to major restructuring in governmental and corporate policy, the post-recovery Japanese economy is a very different playing field. But the effects of the changes and the recession were not limited to the business world; they left a permanent mark on the fabric of Japanese culture and society.

The End of Japanese Middle-Class Society

A major change that is widely discussed by the media and the public is the end of Japanese middle-class society. A need for corporate changes was realized during the recession that followed the collapse of the Japanese bubble economy. The ideas of life-time employment and the seniority system, which were thought to have driven Japan to become an economic superpower, began to fragment and break apart.

To survive the economic downturn, Japanese companies used Western-style solutions to solve their problems, such as outsourcing manufacturing to other countries, downsizing their staff, and replacing full-time staff with part-timers. In 1994, non-regular employees, part-time or short-term contract workers, made up 19% of the workforce and increased to 29% in 2004. This is in spite of the fact that non-regular employees earn an average of 40% per hour compared to their full-time counterparts. While this resulted in increased profitability for companies, the changes have increased the wage disparity in Japan, leaving many to struggle and slowly emerge as part of the lower class.

The use of Western-style solutions to solve a company's problems has forced workers to think from a Western point of view as well. Thus, it is no wonder that Western company culture has been spreading and has been practiced by Japanese workers in recent years. Workers no longer feel secure in a company and work there all their life because they know that, if a crisis similar to the bubble economy arises again, their heads could be on the line. Thus, this experience has changed their attitudes, not only towards work, but towards their lives in general as well.

Changing Attitudes towards Work and an Increasing Interest in Quality of Life

Japan has the second largest GDP in the word, but in terms of Gross National Happiness (GHP), a survey conducted by World Value Survey, Japan was ranked 29th out of 60 countries overall. This survey indicates that, even though Japanese households generally have sufficient income, it does not necessarily mean that they are satisfied with their lifestyle. Consequently, according to the 1995 National Survey of Social Stratification and Social Mobility, radical change was found among Japanese attitudes with regard to living in a post-modern society. The interests and priorities of Japanese people have shifted from "possession" to "existence" in general. Success was previously determined by the property and cash a person possessed. The Japanese believed that the more property and money a person had, the happier a person would be.

Nowadays, the situation is quite different. The focus on possessions to reach a high social status has changed, and people now focus more on lifestyle by reflecting on their own existence. In other words, Japanese have started to prioritize relationships rather than material wealth. This means feeling loved and trusted by other people, doing volunteer work, and playing an important role in society.

Research conducted by the Cabinet Office of the Government of Japan (2007) clearly illustrates the changes in people's views towards happiness. In 1970, 40.3% of Japanese considered happiness to be based on material possessions, while those who based it on "existence" were just 35.3%. Thus, it can be seen that, in the early 1970s, people determined happiness based on a person's material possessions rather than by their "existence." However, from the early 1980s, attitudes started to shift. By 1999, people who considered happiness to be based on their material possessions declined to 27.4%, while those who based happiness on their "existence" rose to 60.7%. Recently, more and more people base their happiness on their "existence," and the numbers indicate a trend in which people are increasingly viewing work as a route to self-fulfillment and discovery, and no longer strictly to pay the bills. Therefore, people's attitudes toward work have changed, which has in turn affected the working environment in Japan.

New Types of Labor

This change in attitude should be viewed against the background of pre-bubble and post-bubble economics. In the past, the typical image of the Japanese worker was the *salaryman*–the male salaried worker. These employees work for the companies in Japan and worked hard during the high growth period, and were considered to be the coal that kept the economy on fire. Their discipline, hard work, and dedication to their respective companies were unquestionable. They were used to spending long hours at work in return for life-time employment. It was common for *salarymen* to spend most of their time at work. They prioritized their careers over their families for the good of the company. Thus, to compensate for the lack of quality time spent with their children, fathers spoiled them with material belongings, hoping that the children would understand the situation.

Nevertheless, owing to improvements in Japan's economic situation in recent years after the bubble economy, young Japanese no longer feel compelled to live the life of a *salaryman*. Thus, there have been considerable changes in Japan's employment environment. In fact, new labor types are developing, which have been controversial among the Japanese public. One of the most frequently discussed groups is that of *freeters*.

Freeters

According to the data for 2007, the number of part-time workers between the ages of 18 and 34 reached 4.5 million. This includes men and women, students, and non-students. Japan's Ministry of Labor, Health and Work (2007) defines part-time workers as "workers whose weekly working hours are shorter than regular employees."

Recently, a group of part-time workers, known as *freeters*, has been increasing in number in Japan. The etymology of the term *freeter* comes from the English word "*free*" and the German word *Arbeiter*, meaning worker. It comprises people who hop between casual, low-paid jobs. According to the Labor Ministry, the number of *freeters* jumped from 1.51 million in 1997 to 2.17 million in 2003, with a drop to 2.01 million in 2005. The statistics include *freeters* who are aged between 15 and 34, school graduates, and unmarried women. Moreover, the Ministry of Labor, Health and Work defines *freeters* as those (1) who are currently employed and referred to as "part-time workers or *Arubeito* (temporary workers)" in their workplace, or (2) who are currently not working and neither doing housework nor attending school, but want to be employed as part-time workers.

Researchers and writers often separate *freeters* into different categories. Brender (2007) divides them into three categories:

dreamers, procrastinators, and those with no alternative to part-time work. Dreamers are those who strive to be musicians and other artistic occupations who work in part-time jobs in order to save money, with the hope that they will be able to achieve their aspirations. On the other hand, procrastinators are usually high school or college graduates who would like to take their time and feel no pressure or eagerness to be a full-time company employee. Finally, the last category comprises people who are not able to find full-time jobs for situational reasons, from a lack of training, down to pure bad luck. Thus, they lose interest in pursuing a full-time career and remain as *freeters* or drop out of society completely.

According to a report, the number of *freeters* aged 35, who typically work in convenience stores and on construction sites, will triple to 1.5 million by 2020. This forecast will cost 1.4 trillion yen annually in lost tax and pension contributions (Parry 2006). These numbers have truly alarmed the government because it will lead to the collapse of the social security system (NRI 2004).

This kind of lifestyle is upsetting for the Japanese frame of mind. The Japanese are shocked about the existence of *freeters* because the nation considers its highly trained, hard working labor force to be its most valuable source (Japan Economic Newswire 2005). Thus, it is not surprising that elderly people view *freeters* with disgust because they are not contributing to the retirement fund (Brender 2007). *Freeters* are still generally considered wayward youngsters who need to grow up (Kageyama 2005). However, the fact is that the increase in the number of *freeters* in recent years symbolizes the growing number of individuals who believe that an individually fulfilling life is more favorable than one filled with material wealth, a situation that characterized their parents and grandparents lives, a life based on work.

The Increase in *Tenshoku*

Besides *freeters*, another result of the change in attitude towards work and lifestyle is the increase in *tenshoku,* which literally means job change. Consequently, *tenshokusha* is "one who has changed job."

In 1989, the increase in *tenshokusha* was already noticeable. There were approximately 2.4 million people considered *tenshoku*sha that year, an increase of 110,000 people over the previous year. The majority were part-time workers aged between 15 and 24 who wanted better working conditions (32.4%), or had changed jobs due to household, educational, and health reasons (10.5%). However, a recent survey in 2006 reports a further increase in *tenshokusha*. The number of *tenshokusha* has risen to 3,460,000 among 25 to 29 year olds (21.3%), followed by those between 30 and 34 (17.9%), and those from 20 to 24 (12.7%). In addition, 76% of *tenshokusha* were full-time employees, part-time workers only 7.1%. This change was not only evident in the numbers, but shocked Japanese people in general (Nihon Keizai Shimbun 2007).

One of the main reasons why *tenshoku* has become such a big issue in Japan is because of the traditional Japanese mentality. Since the Showa period, people have believed that one's mission in life was to stay on track and to follow the norm. In respect of Japanese companies, this means passing examinations and overcoming ordeals, entering a well-known corporation, working through the company's seniority system for a lifetime, and being satisfied with a stable life (Jô 2006). Thus, the idea of *tenshoku* simply goes against the traditional way of thinking, which makes it a controversial issue in Japan, especially among the elderly and traditional Japanese.

In addition, the survey was also able to determine possible causes for *tenshoku.* This includes a feeling of anxiety about the company's future (30.9%) and dissatisfaction about the salary (23.2%). These two factors are strongly linked to the demise of the traditional Japanese management system. The wage system in Japanese companies is based on seniority. This means that, regardless of the amount of work one has done, young employees receive low salaries while senior employees receive high salaries. Moreover, Japanese management has also believed what matters more is the time spent by a worker at a company rather than what the individual actually contributes.

One of the key problems in failing to meet these conditions is the age imbalance among employees, which can be seen by looking at current demographic changes. Nowadays, the declining birth rate and the increasing lifespan of Japanese are prominent issues. As fewer young workers enter companies, the proportion of older workers increases, which strains corporate finances due to the high salaries paid to senior workers. As a result, the average monthly salary is decreasing. Compared to salaries in 2001, salaries in 2006 have decreased on average by 3,000 yen. Furthermore, employees aged 20 to 40 and those who are 50 and older have had their salaries reduced. Despite the change in the average salary, senior employees still prefer working for their respective companies due to the desire for a stable life and also for the retirement money they will receive. On the other hand, younger workers are more likely to change jobs if it means earning a higher monthly salary in another company. Moreover, employees' trust in a company depends upon forecasts of high and stable growth. If a company does not grow stably, employees lose confidence and trust in their respective companies and hesitate to remain in their present positions.

As some employees lose trust and confidence, they now find more options and freedom in their hands. They are now more conscious of choosing their careers independently. In fact, 17.8% of *tenshokusha* changed their jobs due to the feeling of being unappreciated by their employers for their skills and abilities; while 29.4% switched jobs because of dissatisfaction with the work they were assigned.

Thus, the notion of enriching a career independently has become accepted by Japanese companies and the number of experienced workers companies employ is increasing every year. Based on Works Institute's research (Works Research Institute 2006) with 7,469 private enterprises, the number of employees who were hired by mid-2006 was 1,626,000 people, which is a 32.4% increase on the previous year. Especially in the manufacturing industry, the rate for hiring employees in the middle of the year greatly exceeded the growth rate in the expected number of new graduates to be hired. The data clearly indicates the rising acceptance among companies towards hiring experienced workers from other companies.

While more people change jobs to enrich their own careers and to earn higher salaries, a larger number of employees are also changing jobs to gain more private time. Japanese workers are well-known for being overworked in a stressful environment. On average Japanese workers do some 2500 hours overtime annually, 1.5 times more than their European counterparts. As for paid holidays, Japanese workers take just half the actual holidays given them because it is not considered a "worker's right" as it is in Western countries, but a "company's blessing." (Jô 2006)

However, the situation is changing and people are now prioritizing their private lives over work. If Japanese workers are assigned to one of the following groups, "work-intensive," "hobby-intensive," "balanced-life," or "family-intensive," the first three groups have declined in size, while the "family-intensive group" increased by 4.1 % between 1997 and 2000 (Nitto and Shiozaki 2001, p.8). This is relates to the idea above that people now base "happiness" on their "existence" rather than on material possessions.

The difficulties in achieving a stable income due to recent economic developments and changes in society have resulted in more cases of *tenshoku* among Japanese workers. Moreover, a radical change in culture and mentality has occurred. Many workers have started to change jobs not only to have a stable life but also to fulfill their own personal aspirations. Thus, changing attitudes towards work explain why *tenshoku* has increased and become a controversial issue in Japan.

The End of the Japanese Dream

Accompanying the radical changes of the last decade, "radical lifestyles" have also emerged. These kinds of new lifestyles are increasing in number. Thus, these emerging radical lifestyles have been challenging social norms in a country generally regarded as conservative from a post-modern perspective.

NEETs and *Hikikomori*

One of these radical lifestyles is that lived by *NEETs*. It is an acronym from the U.K. that stands for "Not in Employment, Education, or Training." It is properly defined in Japan as jobless 15 to 34 year olds who are not housewives, students, or active jobseekers and workers. *NEETs* are generally either those who are free spirited, victims of Japan's economic problems in the 1990s, or those who choose to actively reject traditional Japanese values towards employment that are embodied most strongly by their parents' generation. In 2006, there were 640,000 *NEETs*, up from 490,000 in 2001. In 1993, 53% of *NEETs* were under 25, but now 61% are between 25 and 34 (Parry 2006).

Experts have discovered that several hundred thousand young people now fall into the *NEET* category. The Ministry of Health, Labor and Welfare described *NEET* youth as, "Non-working individuals between the ages of 15 and 34, unmarried school graduates who neither help with the housework not attend school." (Ministry of Health, Labor and Welfare 2007)

In addition, a further phenomenon that has developed recently is that of *hikikomori*, defined as those who are socially withdrawn. It involves hundreds of thousands of young people living at home who literally hide in their bedrooms. Because these people do not engage in any activities and remain in their rooms, they do not contribute to Japan's economy in any way. They even provide a potential threat to Japan's economic recovery if their numbers continue to increase. Like *NEETs*, they are considered to be "parasite singles," who are grown-up children well into their twenties and older, but who still live with their parents. One reason is the high property rates, especially in areas like Tokyo. They also do not want to take responsibility for their own lives.

There are several factors that have triggered these phenomena and their spread country-wide. First, people become *NEETs, freeters*, or *hikikomori* for personal reasons. There are experts who have noted psychological changes on the part of young people, but the specific causes have yet to be determined. Moreover, young people do not want to become *salarymen* and instead they try to find new career paths. Thus, they defy past standards of success by working in temporary jobs to finance their dreams. In other words, they dare to be different.

Second, there are family reasons. Young people who tend to become *NEETs*, *freeters*, or *hikikomori* belong to a generation that saw their parents, particularly their fathers, work very hard and dedicate themselves to the well-being of the companies they worked for. Young people now see how challenging it is to be a *salaryman* because they witnessed firsthand this kind of life.

Thus, few young people are willing to buy into the traditional Japanese employment package of becoming a *salaryman*.

In addition, there are also parents who do not want their kids to struggle in the same way as they did, and they do not push their children out of the "nest." Thus, it is common for a household in Japan to house and financially support children until marriage. Japanese society has been a wealthy society for decades and young people feel little pressure to become independent.

The emergence of these phenomena has also been due to economic and business factors. In a survey done by Nomura Research Institute (NRI 2004a), it found that respondents commonly cited economic reasons, such as recession, as why the number of *NEETs*, *freeters*, and *hikikomori* had increased. Businesses are also at fault due to changes in corporate hiring policies. The economic slump, particularly as the economic bubble burst, has encouraged firms to curtail full-time hiring and rely more on part-timers. Despite Japan's recent economic recovery, many companies still prefer to employ a certain number of part-timers due to their overall lower cost.

Finally, there are people who blame the government for exacerbating the problem. This stems from former Prime Minister Koizumi's reforms in which labor laws allowed companies greater flexibility in hiring temporary workers and part-timers. Thus, the demand for cheaper workers is increasing as companies try to remain competitive and cut back on hiring full-time employees with generous benefits.

Development of New Consumer Groups

Besides changes in work patterns, we can also observe new developments in the Japanese consumer market. The most widely discussed developments in the Japanese media are the development of new consumers groups. These consumer groups are the promising new targets for companies in Japan. These groups, which have a high purchasing power, are attracting attention in Japan today. Many companies would like to capture these promising target groups (Ishiwata 2006).

The New Rich

The erosion of Japan's "one-class" society has given way to a society of winners and losers. And the winners are winning big. The number of Japanese millionaires rose by 10% from 2001 to 2004 to 1.34 million individuals, and in 2002 the richest 20% of Japanese earned 50.4% of the nation's wealth, compared with 48.8% in 1999 and 44.3% in 1987.

The way of using capital is intensifying among the new rich. Some 23% of new rich tend to have 86% of their capital as savings. On the other hand, the remaining new rich tend to have a large proportion of capital in risky assets, such as stocks, bonds, and alternative products. Spending on alternative products is a strong characteristic of the new rich (Obinata and Miyamoto 2006).

They now flaunt their wealth, with a new taste for flashy consumption, particularly for foreign luxury items. Hirofumi Usui, president of a Tokyo company that provides advice on marketing to the rich, stated that in the past the majority of Japanese thought the rich were boring and tacky, and would have been embarrassed to drive a Ferrari. But the new rich have no qualms at all about driving a Ferrari, and the trend towards flashy consumption is accelerating (Usui 2006).

However, their wealth and their new courage in showing it off leads to strong reactions among the Japanese public. Prior to his arrest and conviction for securities fraud, internet entrepreneur Takafumi Horie was the iconic image of the new rich's flair for flashy consumption. Age 35 in 2007; he was known for his lavish 22,000 U.S. dollars per month apartment in posh Roppongi Hills and for cruising around Tokyo in his silver Ferrari. He famously stated that, "There is nothing money can't buy." And he is not alone. Cornes & Co., a major dealer of luxury cars in Tokyo, sold nearly twice as many Maseratis in 2005 than in the previous year, and, furthermore, nearly half of the buyers were under the age of 40.

The new rich's taste for the luxurious and exotic is driving the high-end consumer market. Mini city-within-a-city projects like Roppongi Hills and Tokyo Midtown are springing up all across Tokyo. These projects combine high-end office space, apartments, shopping, and entertainment in a self-contained playground for those who can afford it—an apartment in Roppongi Hills can cost up to 50,000 U.S. dollars per month.

The new rich gravitate towards luxury products, particularly those which allow them to flaunt their wealth, such as cars, designer clothing, watches, accessories, and jewelry. Even luxury versions of everyday products and services, such as crystal studded tissue boxes, are proving strong sellers (Hardach 2008).

Working Women

The number of women in the labor force was 27,320,000. As for types of employment, 16,800,000 were full-time employees, 4,140,000 were part-time employees, and 660,000 were day laborers. As regards breakdown of occupation, clerical work led at 7,050,000, followed by professional or technical work at 3,780,000, security or other service work at 3,320,000, manufacturing, production, machinery operation, or construction work at 2,960,000, and sales work at 2,690,000 (Japan Institute of Workers' Evolution 2003). Economist Nobuyuki Saji has noted that younger working women in their 20s and 30s are seeing their incomes rise as a result of an increase in merit-based pay. This restructuring will see income redistribution heavily in favor of younger workers who suffer low wages under the seniority-based system.

Eventually, the number of women in management positions will increase in coming years. It is forecasted that the number of women who will be earning 10 million yen a year will reach 160,000. These women will want to improve themselves and will be aggressive in making investments (Ishiwata 2006). Owing to these income changes, working women have become a focus of interest for Japanese corporations recently. Ishiwata (2006) also mentions three characteristics particular to working women's consumption patterns. First, they are very particular about quality and are willing to pay for products they consider "good." Second, because of their hectic schedule, they are considered loyal users or regular customers of good (quality) products. Basically, they know what they want and stick to it. Finally, with regard to their purchasing power, they are able to spend on fashion items, beauty treatment, and travel without financial challenge and without feeling family constraints. Commodities that have become popular among this consumer group include high quality bath salts, high quality seasonings, and lessons for self-improvement, such as golf or tango.

Moreover, working women are affecting more than just service industry bottom lines. The number of women signing up for mortgages is increasing by 10% a year and banks have responded with loan products tailored to the needs of the female buyer. Before 2000, banks were reluctant to lend to single women as they presumed they would get married, pregnant, quit their jobs, and have to renegotiate their loans. In practice, however, single women have a lower default rate than male workers, the former preferred target group.

Otaku

The word *otaku* in standard Japanese is a very formal way of saying "you," roughly equivalent to the English "thou." It was adopted by hard-core Japanese fans of *manga* and *anime* (comics and animation respectively) in the early 80s as a slang term for self-reference. The term has broadened in recent years to refer to fanatics of any number of hobbies, from car enthusiasts to collectors of *manga*-inspired dolls.

The stereotypical *otaku* is an unmarried male professional, usually working in a technology-related field; though this stereotype is hardly universal. *Otaku* range from young to old, male and female, and their hobbies are equally varied. The most stereotypical *otaku* hobbies and industries are those which have traditionally drawn fanatical followers: comics and animation, video games, and electronics of all types. The *otaku* market is not a single market segment and consists of many small niche markets which serve the particular tastes of the fanatics of that specific interest. There is one common theme for all the varied *otaku* groups—they spend liberally in support of their preferred hobby.

Nomura Research Institute (2004b) suggested that over 2.85 million Japanese could be categorized as *otaku* and that this market segment generated over 2.6 billion dollars annually. Furthermore, comic books, the largest of these *otaku* markets at over 350,000 people, are generating revenues of 83 billion yen per year. Five major classifications make up the bulk of the *otaku* market: comics (100 billion yen annually), animation (20 billion), idols (60 billion), games (78 billion), and PC assembly (32 billion).

There are several groups that fall under the category of *otaku*. For instance, comic (*manga*) *otaku* purchases include firstly the comics themselves, but also comic-themed products ranging from model figures of their favorite characters, trading cards, posters, clothing, accessories, down to trinkets such as bags, cell-phone tassels, pens, stationery, etc. Consequently, animation *otaku* have similar shopping habits and significant overlap with comic *otaku*, with animation DVDs replacing the comics, but other secondary purchases are similar. On the other hand, game *otaku* purchase games, but many prefer first-run, limited, or special editions of games, and they often purchase the same core game many times for additional content. Game *otaku* also overlap heavily with the previous two classifications, purchasing comics and animation based on their favorite games. Game *otaku*, who favor "network games," tend to also overlap into the PC assembly group, custom-building their PCs to play their favorite games on. The PC assembly market purchases cutting edge, boutique parts and builds PCs to meet their specific interests, be it the pursuit of a silent PC, or one which has colored fans and wiring inside, with custom case artwork outside. Finally, *aidoru otaku* are enthusiasts who are extreme fans of pop musicians, or "idols or *aidoru*," who visit concerts and purchase first-run or special edition CDs, books, magazines, DVDs, and any other material concerning their favorite idol singers (Kitabayashi 2004).

Baby Boomers

In 2007, 6.9 million baby boomers, or almost 9% of the nation's workforce, reached the standard retirement age of 60. Born between 1947 and 1949, baby boomers brought Japan out from post-war reconstruction to become the world's second largest consumer economy. Due to peak salaries during the lucrative bubble economy years, Japan's baby boomers have money to spend. Those over the age of 50 make up 39% of the population, but control more than 75% of the financial assets held by individuals. According to Bank of Japan statistics, these assets amount to more than an astonishing 1,400,000 billion yen.

Unlike previous generations, particularly those who lived through the war, the baby boomers are more likely to spend their savings and enjoy the hard earned fruits of their labor in their retirement. This desire to enjoy life can be seen through the characteristics of their consumption patterns. Japanese baby boomers would like to buy high quality products and are, in fact, willing to pay high prices for what they like. Nonetheless, price is still a serious matter for them for they value their hard earned money very much. They also favor long-selling products or goods that have been in the market for quite some time. Women spend more on communication-related activities to be in touch with their friends and family, while men spend on their hobbies and personal collections (Ishiwata 2006). In fact, in a recent survey done by MacroMill among 515 male Japanese baby boomers working for public or private employers, the top 5 answers to the question what they would like to do after retirement are as follows: domestic travel (72%), PC and internet (55%), overseas travel (49%), exercise for health (41%), and share or bond dealing (36%) (MacroMill 2007).

Thus, companies are lining up various products and services to cater to baby boomers' retirement lifestyles. For instance, the travel industry is expecting increased demand for tours and travel packages from retiring baby boomers. Toyota integrated its luxury Lexus brand in Japan in 2006 from foreign markets. Company president Katsuaki Watanabe specifically stated that baby boomers are one of their intended targets.

Several financial service companies have come up with the idea of retirement investment. Tome Sumida, an economist at Nomura Asset Management, believes the idea behind retirement investment springs from the fear of Japanese baby boomers that the Japanese are living longer and they might outlive their money. He also believes that in order to make savings last, annual returns of some 4 or 5% are needed. Thus, financial service companies have come up with standard models which are targeted at baby boomers. Such products invest in a variety of asset classes and use the gains to make regular payments to customers (Turner 2007).

Nevertheless, the consumption behavior of Japanese baby boomers cannot be generalized, but they will indeed be a driving force in breaking society free from mass production and mass consumption. The point is, many of these baby boomers will spend their retirement savings on themselves and that could dramatically change Japan's structure of consumption (The Nikkei Weekly 2006).

Developing New Work Patterns

The cultural and societal changes that have emerged from economic recovery pose a number of challenges for management. The old rules no longer apply and the new rules require change and adaptation to be successful.

In view of these emerging consumer groups, Japanese companies have been trying new work patterns that will cater accordingly to the different consumer groups. Companies are beginning to understand that, in order to succeed in their respective areas, they need to focus and customize their products and services properly to different consumer groups instead of following the work patterns based on Japan's corporate culture and tradition.

With the erosion of the life-time employment system, companies are less likely to keep their employees until retirement and, in turn, the employees are less reluctant to change jobs mid-career. The reduced tendency of the company to keep employees through good times and bad has reduced the loyalty that the employee pays to the company. Now, instead of companies just competing for recruits among new college graduates, they must also compete to keep their mid-career employees and the investment they have made in these people. To compete on this front, management must strive to keep the company an attractive place to work, not just for new graduates, but for all levels of experience.

On a more positive note, companies in Japan today not only have to adjust to workers but to consumers, too. In fact, with the changes in Japan's social environment, consumer demands are changing as well. This is in line with the different, influential consumer groups that have surfaced in recent years.

It is essential for companies to determine and cater well to these new consumer groups because these groups have the purchasing power to spend on the products and services that they desire. If companies are able to supply the products and services these consumer groups want, companies will be able to benefit accordingly.

If companies know how to cater to these surging consumer groups, company management will know how to configure employees with demand from consumers. For instance, an increase in the number of Japanese who would like to travel is expected, fuelled by the baby boomers who are about to retire, and from the working women who have a lot of disposable income (Ishiwata 2006). Thus, if companies, not only in Japan but also overseas, wish to profit much from these two consumer groups, they should employ staff who can speak Japanese and are used to the kind of service Japanese people expect.

In other words, companies which wish to acquire a profitable share among these proliferating consumer groups need to customize their products and services. The more customized these companies become, the more attractive and appealing they will be to their target consumer groups. Thus, it is indeed important for companies in Japan to research and study the possible consumption patterns of these groups in the future in order to detect upcoming trends.

Conclusion

The Japan of today is no longer the Japan of the past. Just looking at the current social environment, it can already be observed that the whole country is in a state of change, whether it is cultural or corporate. This has led to the emergence of new perspectives towards work and new consumer groups affecting the market.

In fact, the interaction between forces of social change is evident with regard to Japanese management. Corporate management formerly exercised great control over its employees while employees simply followed company culture, working late at night and staying with one company for a lifetime. The current conditions have changed this culture. Japanese workers now have more options than ever. Employees feel greater freedom in being able to change jobs. Potential workers now have an option to either work part-time or even not to work at all. These options were simply non-existent before.

Moreover, these changes have not only affected companies and workers; they have also affected the whole of Japanese society. Japanese perceptions of the meaning of life and how it should be lived are changing. People nowadays not only want to work—they also want to enjoy the fruits of their labor. Attitudes towards work have changed so much that quality of life now plays a more vital role than work life.

Therefore, these cultural and societal changes will surely affect Japan's future. Some of these changes, such as the *freeter*, *NEET*, and *hikikomori* problems, will have negative effects on the whole of Japanese society in the future if not taken seriously and if no measures are taken to address them. Possible future problems include the pension system, human resources, and taxation in Japan.

Nonetheless, from an optimistic point of view, having *freeters*, *NEETs*, and *hikikomori* is a sign of a developed society in an industrialized country. These kinds of people exist not only in Japan, but also in other industrialized countries. People who live in developing countries do not have the option of living a *freeter*, *NEET*, or *hikikomori* lifestyle because working is a matter of survival. If people in developing countries do not work, they would not be able to meet their basic needs.

As regards the emergence of new consumer groups, companies will benefit greatly if they are aware of these groups. Customizing and personalizing products would enable companies to acquire a good market share among these groups, making them more profitable. The niches that the said consumer groups represent can possibly rake in millions of yen for successful companies.

In the end, no one knows for sure whether these changes will positively benefit Japanese society in the coming years. What is certain is that values have shifted in Japan. What is imperative is that people are aware of these changes in order to be able to adjust accordingly.

Bibliography

Associated Press (2006): *Emergence of Rich and Poor Rattles Japan.* CBS News April 4, 2006. Downloaded from http://www.cbsnews.com on December 12, 2007.

Akita, M. (2006): *Japan Companies Concerned Over Employee Shortfall, Survey Shows.* Downloaded from www.bloomberg.com.

Brender, A. (2007): *Fretting over freeters.* Japan Today, October 18, 2007.

Cabinet Office of the Government of Japan (2007): *Kokumin seikatsu ni yoru seron chôsa.* Whitepaper 2007.

Cunanan, C. (2000): *It no longer pays to be middle class in Japan.* Asia Times Online, July 27, 2000.

The Economist (2007): *Changing how Japan works.* The Economist, September 29, 2007.

Faiola, A. (2007): *Conspicuous consumption shapes new Tokyo skyline.* Washington Post, March 11, 2006.

Foster, M. (2007): *When they're 64: Japan's baby boomers head for their gold watch.* The Guardian, November 7, 2006.

Hardach, S. (2008): *Japan's big spenders flaunt their new wealth.* International Herald Tribune, January 6, 2008.

Hattori, R. and Maeda, E. (2001): *Nihon koyô shisutemu ni tsuite.* Nihon ginkô chôsa geppô. January 2001.

Honkawa, Y. (2002): *Kôfukudo no kokusai hikaku.* Shakai jôhô deeta zuroku 2002.

Hyuga, T. and Hirano, K. (2007): *Around Asia's Markets: Nomura takes aim at Japan's boomers.* International Herald Tribune, September 7, 2005.

Ishiwata, Y. (2006): *Trends among Japanese Consumers and Promising Targets.* Presentation Center for Consumer Studies Dentsu Inc. Downloaded from www.hawaiitourismauthority.org on September 12, 2006.

Japan Economic Newswire (2006): *Some Japanese companies open doors to NEETs.* Japan Economic Newswire April 3, 2006.

Japan Institute of Workers` Evolution (2003): *The situation of working women.* Downloaded from www.jiwe.or.jp/english/situation/situation2003.html.

Jô, S. (2006): *Wakamono na naze sannen de yameru no ka? Nenkô jôretsu ha ubau nihon no mirai?* Tokyo: Kobunsha.

Kageyama, Y. (2005): *Job-hopping "freeters" growing in ranks in Japan—and authorities are worried.* The Associated Press, July 12, 2005.

Kakuchi, S. (2004): *Women flex economic muscle.* Asia Times Online, December 28, 2004.

Kitabayashi, K. (2004): *The otaku group from a business perspective: Revaluation of enthusiastic consumers.* Research Paper. Nomura Research Institute 2004.

Meek, C. B. (1999): *Understanding the Japanese employee.* Business Horizons 42(1).

Ministry of Health, Labour and Welfare (2007): *Hôdô happyô shiryô – Heisei 18 tenshokusha jittai chôsa kekka no gaikyô.* Research report on Tenshoku 2007.

Moffett, S. and Y. Hayashi (2006): *Japan's spending boom confers global benefits.* The Wall Street Journal, March 29, 2006.

Nakamoto, M. (2002): *Japan's economy sees silver lining in ageing population.* Financial Times, December 11, 2002.

Nakamura, A. (2007): *Being NEET not so neat for nation's youth.* The Japan Times, June 19, 2004.

Nihon Keizai Shimbun (2007): *Tenshokushasû, kako saikô no 346 man nin.* Nihon Keizai Shimbun, March 15, 2007.

The Nikkei Weekly (2006): *Marketers give tips on tapping boomer yen.* The Nikkei Weekly, November 6, 2006.

Nitto, H. and J. Shiozaki (2001): *Changing consumption patterns and new lifestyles in the 21st century.* Research Papers. Nomura Research Institute 2001.

NRI (Nomura Research Institute Press Release) (2004a): *Over 90% of people have a sense of crisis regarding the NEET Issue.* Downloaded from http://www.nri.co.jp on October 18, 2007.

NRI (Nomura Research Institute Press Release) (2004b): *The otaku group from a business perspective: revaluation of enthusiastic consumers.* Downloaded from http://www.nri.co.jp on October 18, 2007.

Obinata, T. and H. Miyamoto (2006): *Shinsedai fuyûsô no kenkyû.* Research Paper. Nomura Research Institute 2006.

Osawa, M. (2006): *Worklife Balance shakai e – Kojin ga shuyaku no hatarakikata.* Iwanami Shoten.

Parry, R. L. (2006): *A nation lives in fear of the Neets and Freeters.* The Times (London), November 2, 2006.

Pilling, D. (2005): *Japan's wageless recovery.* Znet, January 28, 2005.

Rowley, I. (2007): *A mortgage of her own.* Business Week, July 12, 2004.

The World Bank (2007): *Total GDP 2006.* The World Bank Statistics.

Taipei Times (2006): *Job-hoppers' want part-time life.* Taipei Times, June 2, 2006.

Turner, D. (2007): *Meeting the needs of demanding baby boomers.* Financial Times, January 8, 2007.

Usui, H. (2006): *Nyû richi no sekai.* Tokyo: Kobunsha.

Wiseman, P. and N. Nishiwaki (2006): *Income inequality shrinks Japan's middle class.* USA Today, July 23, 2006.

Works Research Institute (2006): *Waakusu chûto saiyô chôsa 2006.* Recruit K.K. February 2007.

Yamada, H. (2007): *Wooku fea.* Tôyô Keizai Shinpôsha.

Yang, J. (2007): *Asian pop generation.* SF Gate, July 7, 2005.

7. Human Resource Management

By Akihiro Kayama and Momoko Kusayanagi

Advantages of Life-time Employment and Seniority-based Wages

In Japanese human resource management, there are three distinct pillars which have supported Japanese management until the present. These three pillars are: life-time employment, seniority-based wages, and the trade unions. These three characteristics are thought to be the reasons behind Japan's economic miracle and success and the reasons why Japan has managed to become developed compared with other Asian countries.

Life-time employment, one of the distinctive characteristics of Japanese management, is seen as the most important characteristic of Japan's economic success (Billesbach and Rives 1985). This management technique, which seems to be unique to Japanese management, is found world-wide. However, unlike other countries in which life-time employment is predominant only in government and military organizations, Japanese management implemented this style in most organizations (Firkola 2006). Thus, life-time employment is an innate feature of Japanese management in Japan.

There are two main theories for explaining the spread of life-time employment in Japan. One is based upon cultural reasons going back to the roots of Japanese social structure and cultural beliefs (Firkola 2006). The second theory is derived from the Western influences in Japan after World War II (Hirakubo 1999).

In the dominant theory of life-time employment, it is thought to have evolved from Japanese culture. Life-time employment was established on the base that Japanese people mainly lived on farms as a collective group, cultivating land and growing rice (Firkola 2006; Kajimoto 1999). People would spend most of their lives in the village they were born in and it was the understanding that, once born into a family, the member would work for the family and help the village. Villagers were self-sufficient in providing their own resources to serve their best interests, which ultimately lead to serving the interests of the village itself to improve its efficiency. This laid the foundation for an individual's loyalty to the place where they belonged. After industrialization, this loyalty transformed from loyalty to the village to loyalty to the workforce. The notion of village life was that elders would teach the young and they would gradually receive more responsibility within the village as they grew older. This style of village life prevailed in the tradition of Japanese companies where young, new employees worked under their elders and received extensive training in order to accumulate tacit knowledge. In addition, Japanese companies incorporated the traditional Japanese village lifestyle into the wage system: elders were respected and received the best food or the most crops, and this system was transposed into the modern world as wages (Firkola 2006). This idea came from the strong connection between the moral, religious, and social norms of village people and Confucianism, Buddhism, and *bushido*. Thus, rice farming village ethics are said to be the main reason for Japan having life-time employment.

On the other hand, there is a further theory which states that life-time employment is a result of Western influence and post-war efforts by Japan. This theory was proposed by Hirakubo and was based on the idea that life-time employment did not evolve from pre-modern Japanese societal traits, but rather that it was a modern invention based on the efforts of the Japanese people after World War II to catch up with Western economies (Hirakubo 1999). Although both theories seem credible, pre-modern Japanese culture and lifestyle have played a dominant role in the creation of life-time employment in Japanese management and traditional values are more relevant than the influence of post-war ideas. This can not be ignored when explaining Japanese life-time employment.

Life-time employment is a management strategy that is used by Japanese companies to essentially hire their employees for their entire working career and they are usually hired up to retirement age between 55 and 60. Life-time employment is not an official or written contract, but a mutual agreement that guarantees that once a person enters the company they are assured a position there until they retire. However, when life-time employment was introduced, there were certain regulations and limitations. Life-time employment did not always apply to every person that entered the company. This unofficial contract and consent only applied between the company and male employees, who were mainly college and in some cases high school graduates. Women and part-time workers were not included in this category, and women were expected to get married and spend their lives as full-time mothers and housewives (Firkola 2006).

Associated with life-time employment is the concept of seniority-based wages. Structured upon the basis of life-time employment, during which long years of service and loyalty to the company are expected, the process of promotions and raises in wages is very slow. Under life-time employment, the longer the employee works and the older the employee is, the more responsibility and pay he receives (Japan Times 2003a). This can again be attributed to the cultural and social make-up of traditional Japanese life as the elders were wiser and had tacit knowledge based on experience, which was passed down. In this structure, life-time employment and the seniority-based wage system can work successfully. Thus, the seniority-based wage system is based on life-time employment under the premise that the longer an employee stays at a company, the more extensive knowledge through experience they will gain and pass down. Japanese management and learning techniques are based on on-the-job training (Firkola 2006). They cannot be learned from a book or through lectures as it is intangible knowledge. Thus, it is understandable to assume that older employees are given more power and responsibility, and thus better pay.

As employees stay for a long period of time through unwritten, mutual consensus, the employees become more attached to their companies. Thus, Japanese management style builds the relationship oriented around the company itself, rather than being based on an individual's abilities, and knowledge is shared and passed down to fellow employees. These particular aspects of Japanese knowledge management will be discussed in the chapter on knowledge management in greater detail.

The reason for having life-time employment and keeping employees in the same workplace for 40 years is that companies offer more promotions and wage raises to employees the longer they stay at the company. Japanese lifestyle from the pre-industrialized age, in which there was the concept of loyalty and a group-oriented society, has greatly influenced the establishment of the Japanese management style. The two concepts of life-time employment and seniority system come as a set. One concept is intertwined with the other. However, with the crumbling of both these concepts, as major corporations move away from these techniques, it can only be a matter of time before these concepts become a thing of the past. It is evident that an increasing number of people are quitting and switching jobs before retirement age and an increasing number of companies are recruiting middle-aged employees based on skill rather than only accepting new, young employees (Cortazzi 2006).

Since there is a mutual understanding on both sides that employees will stay at the company for a long time, companies too are motivated to train and educate employees intensively (Firkola 2006). The company will have no motivation or incentive to spend vast amounts of money and time on employees if they are only going to stay for a short period of time and "most managers agree that extensive training enhances the value of employees." (Billesbach and Rives 1985, p. 28) Through training, employees will acquire more knowledge and make bigger contributions to the company. As the level of employees increases, the level of the company will increase as well, which will lead to better pay and training, which will further increase the level of employees. There is a positive spiral which can be efficiently achieved through life-time employment and seniority-based wages (Kajimoto 1999). In addition, this style of management has long suited Japanese traditions and is embedded into Japanese culture and lifestyle (Wijers-Hasegawa 2006), and these management techniques also lead to a rise in productivity and efficiency within the company (Benson and Debroux 2004).

The company is willing to give its employees extensive training and education in exchange for their life-time loyalty. Although companies are limiting training to their own company, the company must have a way to motivate employees to stay with the company for a long time (Billesbach and Rives 1985). However, in recent years, with trends changing, in the post-crisis era more workers are changing jobs and companies are recruiting middle-aged workers who have experience and tacit knowledge (Hani 2003). Therefore, it is difficult for both companies and employees to take advantage of life-time employment and seniority-based wages.

In addition to life-time employment and seniority-based wages, trade unions are the third of the three pillars of Japanese management. Japanese unions are organized on an enterprise basis, and only full time employees are permitted to enter these unions (Benson and Debroux 2004). The main role of these unions is to ensure job security and good working conditions in the company. There are distinct differences between Western unions and Japanese unions. First, unions in the West are oriented not on an enterprise level, but on an industry basis. In the West, for an example, there would be a labor union for workers in the car manufacturing industry. In this type of union, there is a collective attitude among workers. This type of collectivity among blue collar workers in the automobile manufacturing industry, without the involvement of white collar workers in the same companies, establishes separate unions within the same industry (Billesbach and Rives 1985).

On the other hand, Japanese trade unions are established for the company, rather than at the industry level. In the example of the automobile industry, a union would exist for each individual company, whereas trade unions are established for all the companies in the West. Furthermore, in Japanese unions, there are no distinctions between blue and white collar workers as they are all part of the same company. Thus, a strong bond is built between fellow co-workers. The West takes a different approach, and blue collar and white collar workers unite together only with their fellow blue or white collar workers. Japanese management style is oriented around bonding in the company as a whole. Communication and relationship processes play a significant role in this system, whereas Western management focuses on departments and their immediate group, and workers in different departments within the same company are considered rivals.

The reason why these labor unions are special in Japan is because they create further unity within the company and help employees to have a sense of togetherness. If they are bound by the same union, it strengthens their collective identity. Furthermore, Japanese unions focus more on job security and working conditions than wages. Although wages are a big factor, employees do not have to worry about future payments as they are certain that wages will increase within the system of life-time employment and seniority-based wages. Moreover, it is important for employees to have a suitable environment in which to work as they will stay with that company for a long time. Creating a supportive, comfortable environment is vital to keep employees with the company, and these forms of unions lead to better communication within the company and enhance better employer-employee communication (Benson and Debroux 2004).

Challenges for Japanese Human Resource Management during the Economic Crisis

During the so-called "economic miracle" following World War II until the 1990s, Japanese management strived for success through the three pillars of life-time employment, seniority-based wages, and labor unions. However, this system posed problems and threats to Japanese management as Japan underwent economic and social changes.

First, there has been demographic change in Japan, and, since the end of the post-war period, the 1950s, there has been an increase in the aging of the population. The percentage of the population over 65 was 4.9% and, in the last 50 years, this segment of population has quadrupled and was 20.6% in 2006. Furthermore, for both males and females, the average life expectancy has risen by more than 20 years. This demographic change in age has caused major problems for Japanese management. During the high economic growth period, the age of the population was not a crucial issue as the economy was growing and companies were hiring a lot of people. However, as the economy slowed and the elderly population continued to increase, it became a problem for the human resources departments. The retirement age, once set at between 55 and 60, is now shifting to 65 (Shimizu 2004), and, as an increasing number of older employees stay at the company, there is less chance and a greater wait for younger and, in some cases, more able employees for promotion, and for wages to rise (Billesbach and Rives 1985).

In the 1990s, as the population aged and the economy slowed, the limitations and problems of life-time employment and seniority-based wages became more visible. During the bubble, these limitations could be ignored as the economy was doing well; however, along with the problem of aging, young workers were limited for choice of field and departments in which they desired to work (Firkola 2006). The Japanese economy underwent the so-called "miracle" in the post-war period until 1990 when the economic bubble burst. Japanese style management faced many challenges with the end of the bubble, and both employers and employees lost faith in Japanese human resource management. With this crisis, the three components of management—life-time employment, seniority-based wage, and trade unions—were questioned as to whether they were the right way to manage the Japanese company.

Life-time Employment

During the economic crisis from the 1990s, Japanese management faced difficulties and challenges, which led to a questioning and revision of the concept of life-time employment in management practices. Although life-time employment did not apply to all companies, and was only usual in large companies (Cortazzi 2006), some 20-25% of the whole Japanese market (Yoshida 2001), companies faced many difficulties. The crisis brought about a surplus of labor, with limited employment options. Furthermore, with the decline in the Japanese economy after the bubble, companies struggled to produce the desired profits. The norm of life-time employment no longer applied in the time of crisis and thereafter. During the bubble, there were jobs available for many workers; however, with the end of the bubble, companies could no longer support the great number of employees who were supposedly secure in life-time employment, and they undertook restructuring, laying off large numbers of workers (Kajimoto 1999). Although this did not necessarily indicate the abolishment of life-time employment, the unwritten mutual consent between workers and managers was in an ambiguous position. During the bubble, it was rare for companies to lay off workers, but "the restructuring boom clearly showed that many companies (were) willing to lay off workers." (Hanai 2000) This demonstrated that workers no longer had the job security that they once had enjoyed during the economic miracle. These were merely visible symptoms. Japanese management also took internal measures. To maintain the status of life-time employment, companies used transfers, early retirement (Mroczkowoski and Hanaoka 1999), in-house unemployed (Hanai 2000), and resignations. When conditions deteriorated for the company, they would ask their workers to resign, and companies would pressure those that did not want to resign with a reduction in their bonuses. This was so-called "voluntary" early retirement (Kajimoto, 1999; Yoshida 2001). In crucial times, companies would reduce working hours, make internal transfers, and limit employment of non-full time workers in an attempt to cut labor costs, but not lay off workers in order to maintain the myth of life-time employment (Mroczkowoski and Hanaoka 1999).

Western management believed that Japanese management was performing a miracle during the post-war period—from 1953-1995—simply because the unemployment rate in Japan was phenomenally low. The unemployment rate never exceeded 3%. It was seen as a phenomenon that Japanese management could keep the unemployment rate under 3% while life-time employment was still being offered. Even during the oil crisis from 1975-1978, the unemployment rate never exceeded 3%. However, there are interesting statistics which show that about half a million people in companies with more than 500 workers were laid off. The reason why the unemployment rate stayed so low was due to the emergence of small- and medium-sized firms that produced jobs for 1.7 million workers (Yoshida 2001). It has been mentioned before that only some 20-25% of companies extended life-time employment. This explains the survival of the Japanese economy through the oil crisis, in keeping low rates of unemployment, and in covering up for the failure of the life-time employment system.

Regarding the limitations on life-time employment, a survey was conducted in 2000 during the so-called "ice-age for job hunting," which showed that of the 591 companies surveyed only 9.5% continued to attach importance to life-time employment, while 38.3% did not. Thus, the majority of companies supported life-time employment only on a limited basis. As regards the decline in life-time employment, 65.2% of companies were cutting the number of full-time employees, and 59.2% of companies were actively hiring more part-time workers. The most important change in recent years is that 97.2% of the companies are increasingly shifting towards a more merit-based wage system as opposed to the traditional seniority-based wage system (Japan Times 2000a).

Seniority-based Wages

Owing to the problems associated with life-time employment, which is closely linked to seniority-based wages, the system is being revised. Major companies, such as Toyota, Canon, Matsushita and Honda (Japan Times 2003b; Japan Times 2003c), have moved away from this traditional seniority-based wage system to a more merit-based wage system in which employees are assessed according to their abilities rather than the number of years they have been employed. This is a movement away from the traditional wage system due to strong competition and pressure from the labor unions. Furthermore, it is helping to cope with the winds of globalization that swept through Japan after the bubble burst. The new wage system was introduced to compete not only domestically, but also to compete globally (Japan Times 2003a). As globalization spread through Japan, employees had the option of switching jobs (Hani 2003) as companies continued to invest in training new employees with their tacit and specialized knowledge. Companies were faced with employees being attracted to other competitors and they started incorporating merit-based wages (Billesbach and Rives 1985). Although the number of companies that have adopted merit-based wages is still small, there is an increasing trend for companies to switch from seniority-based wages to merit-based wages. On the other hand, younger workers who are entering or have just entered the company are concerned about their job security and feel that their salaries are assured under the seniority-based wage system and seek security rather than merit-based pay.

Companies such as Toyota and Matsushita, which have implemented merit-based wages, did so not necessarily for the benefit of employees, but rather they felt that wages could be cut, or higher wages for older workers could be avoided (Japan Times 2003b and 2003c). The main factor that contributed to this shift was in Japanese workers and managers' mindsets. In the past, during the economic miracle, workers had the idea that they were working for the company, which was of great significance in their lives. However, as the bubble burst and the crisis came, this mutual relationship collapsed and workers were no longer guaranteed life-time employment. As the Japanese population aged, workers were slow to be promoted, which eventually led to further distrust in Japanese management and the company, breaking away from the traditional attitudes (Kajimoto 1999).

Japanese Labor Unions

While life-time employment was established as the norm and the standard, workers placed value on their working environment and job stability. However, with the trend moving away from life-time employment, workers were not so keen on keeping their jobs and staying in the same company for their entire careers and started to enjoy the different choices available in choosing their careers (Benson and Debroux 2004). As mentioned before, life-time employment and seniority-based wages have not disappeared and are still predominant in today's Japanese management practices; however, workers are no longer restricted by these concepts. They feel less need to participate in Japanese labor unions as they have other options and opportunities in searching for other jobs that better suit their needs in better working environments and which still offer stability. Although this is not always achieved, and it is rare for them to be offered a better job position or pay, it is becoming easier to switch jobs, and this concept, once thought "taboo" in Japanese management, is now being accepted.

Although there is less participation in labor unions, it does not mean that employees have been given more power or a more powerful bargaining tool. However, the reality that employers must provide the employees with a suitable environment has certainly given employees some leverage. While the company was the predominant actor in deciding working conditions for workers, the company is now keen on "hearing the voice of the workers" and this can be seen through the emergence of merit-based wages. Although seniority is still a large factor in the company, and in all Japanese society, this is starting to change. Living in Japan and observing Japanese society first hand, it can be said that the orthodox system of seniority is changing and shifting towards a more flexible version, with younger generations having more options available when making their decisions. Japanese companies are accepting younger workers in more vital roles and are starting to pay merit-based wages and are considering the individual abilities of workers.

Labor unions are now given a different, yet vital role in assisting workers and managers. With the increasing number of part-time workers (Shimizu 2007), and with the significant increase in the female workforce, labor unions are placing more emphasis on supporting these groups of non full-time workers (Hanai 2000). Thus, Japanese trade unions are undergoing a rapid change in creating better working conditions and environments for those outside of full-time status, and so incorporating new strategies to adapt management styles to a wider population of workers.

Increase in Non Full-Time Workers

Following the collapse of Japan's economic bubble, one of the legal changes implemented by the Japanese government also influenced Japanese HR practices. Japanese companies began to focus on replacing full-time employees with part-time, contract, and temporary workers. The seniority-based life-time employment system made it difficult to cut the wages of older full-time workers. Therefore, employers shifted their focus on hiring more part-time workers, who can be paid much less, with few or no benefits. The main advantage is that they can be laid off more easily than full-time employees (Nikkei Weekly 2007a).

The figures show that there were 11.25 million non full-time workers in 2006, accounting for 20.5% of the nation's workforce, whereas in 1996 the figure was 8.7 million, or 16.6% of all workers (The Japan Times 2007a). This increase in part-time workers not only reflects a shift in companies replacing full-time employees with part-time workers in order to cut operating costs, but more importantly a shift away from life-time employment.

Although non full-time employees play a significant role in the labor force, their inferior working conditions, including wages, social welfare benefits, and job training opportunities, have become major problems. In 2001, the average hourly wage for regular workers was 2,778 yen compared to 1,026 yen for part-time workers (The Japan Times 2002a). This gap between part-time and full-time workers portrays the inequality suffered by part-time workers who are paid less than half the wage received by regular employees for doing the same work. Part-time workers are unable to receive the same benefits as full-time workers in areas such as housing allowances and congratulatory or condolence leave. However, some companies are revising and introducing training programs and opportunities for part-time workers in order that they can apply for full-time status.

The labor unions, originally formed to help full-time employees, have extended their membership to these non full-time employees to give them better working conditions and to narrow the gap between full-time and non full-time employees (Hanai 2000). Japanese labor unions are focusing on these part-time workers rather than on more stable full-time employees.

Pasona
Case Study

Pasona was established in 1976 as one of the first temporary staffing and full-time placement firms in Japan. Yasuyuki Nambu, the founder of the company, established the firm as a means to make Japan's labor market more flexible and to reduce inequality. When he was preparing to graduate from university in 1976, he was struck by the injustices of Japan's workplaces. There were gender inequalities in the hiring and payment of male and female workers, and women who left their jobs to start a family found returning to work almost impossible. In view of these conditions, Nambu had the idea of creating a non-profit organization (NPO) to place women in flexible, part-time jobs and, at his father's suggestion, he turned this job-placement scheme into a venture firm - Pasona.

Pasona's main goal is to provide solutions for challenges that businesses may encounter and to offer outsourcing, temporary staffing, and head hunting of the best available talent for a specific full-time job. It is a firm that now has annual revenues of approximately 2 billion U.S. dollars, and it outsources a quarter of a million people to a job everyday. Japan has numerous temporary-staffing agencies today, but Pasona was the first and is still one of the biggest.

Before Pasona was established, job placements were handled by a government agency. Part-time and temporary employees were treated like outcasts from Japan's corporate-welfare model, with the principles of life-time employment and seniority-based wages. However, these models depended on the length of service, rather than the quality of work and only privileged regular workers who obtained training and other benefits. Within the 30 years of Pasona's establishment, non-regular employees have gone from the periphery of the Japanese labor force to the core and the emergence of *freeters* has increased as well.

With this new *freeter* trend, Nambu focused on providing flexibility that is beneficial to both employees and employers. It also shows his concern about the inequality between regular and non-regular workers, and he feels that the best way to address such concerns is to extend some of the benefits offered to regular workers to *freeters* as well. With this idea, Pasona has increased the pay of temporary staff by reducing its own margins for full-time workers. It has promoted individual retirement savings accounts, even before they were implemented into Japanese law.

Nambu states, "We want to provide solutions to society's problems" (The Economist, 2007), and refers to his top managers as a "shadow cabinet" on the basis that they, rather than the government, are in a position to provide solutions to many of Japan's issues, such as declining birth rates and revitalizing rural areas, by establishing a more flexible labor market. He believes that the private sector, instead of the government, should lead this transformation. His innovative ideas were heavily criticized by government officials. They were worried that he was undermining traditional Japanese labor practices that served the country well by maintaining loyalty and equality. However, rather than undermining the social ties between employee and company; he is empowering workers by giving them more choice and flexibility.

Pasona has expanded its workforce services through subsidiaries which handle outsourcing projects, the recruitment of full-time staff, outplacement support to help redundant staff find new jobs, technical support, finding temporary jobs for the retired, and managing benefits schemes for other jobs. It has also expanded its business and services into other Asian countries and America, with around 4,000 staff, 75% of whom are regular employees (The Economist 2007).

Flextime

Flextime was first adopted by Japanese companies in 1970, but became more popular after standards were set under the labor law in April 1988. With the government encouraging companies to adopt flextime to "give people the opportunity to enjoy more diverse lifestyles and allow men to have a greater hand in child-rearing" (The Japan Times 2002b), companies now try to nurture family-friendly environments in firms, not just for working mothers, but for fathers, too. Flextime allows employees to select the hours they will work, with set core hours during which employees must be present in the workplace. Employees on a flexible schedule have the option to choose the hours they begin and end their work, giving more time for working parents to drop off or pick up their children at daycare centers or other facilities. Having the option to work a condensed week, working four ten-hour days, rather than five eight-hour days, allows employees to achieve more balance between work and private life.

This style of management is an attempt to attract workers to the company. If companies can attract workers with the work environment and evoke satisfaction, managers can expect loyalty from their employees. Flextime creates a choice for employees whereas, in traditional life-time employment, workers had no choice but to obey company demands and rules. Increasing the choices available for employees offers them freedom and control over their lives, which is becoming an important factor in Japanese lifestyles today.

Improving the Work-Life Balance

Besides the adoption of flextime in Japanese companies, the working environment in Japan is growing more diverse, with companies shifting their focus to improving the work-life balance for employees. "Traditionally, Japanese companies have demanded that employees prioritize their jobs over their lives. Now, however, companies cannot secure the necessary number of workers without drastically changing their policies to accommodate needs." (Nikkei Weekly 2007b) During the 1960s and 1970s, workers endured long working hours in the single-minded pursuit of economic growth (Kamiya 2007). However, more workers, both male and female, are increasingly valuing their personal lives outside the workplace.

With the advance of information technology, many companies have introduced innovative programs to provide more efficient and convenient working environments. Matsushita Electric Industrial has introduced a telecommuting system under which employees can work at home. Employees are able to work at their own pace and in an environment which increases the efficiency of work. They also have more time to spend with their families, especially those who have children. The company recognized the benefits and, in April 2007, expanded the program so that some 30,000 white collar workers could take advantage of it (Nikkei Weekly 2007b).

Similarly, NTT Communication Corp introduced a "free-working system" for customer-service representatives to help subscribers with internet connectivity problems. These representatives use home computers to connect to a special network that allows them to receive phone calls from customers, and they are allowed to take a break at any time by clicking a "leave desk" button and work whenever they want. This system has enabled NTT Communication to attract 850 workers, and, with the fear of labor shortages in the future, Japanese companies are trying to introduce programs that allow employees achieve a good work-life balance.

Family-Friendly Companies

As the birth rate declines, labor shortages pose a major challenge to Japanese companies. Therefore, companies are revising and improving working conditions for both female and male employees to help them balance their careers with their family lives. In 2006, the Ministry of Health, Labor and Welfare declared that, "helping people balance work and home life has become an issue of ever-greater importance amid the declining birth rate and drop in the working population." (Kamiya 2007) Japanese companies are now increasingly creating childcare programs that offer parents better support. These programs include lengthening maternity leave and leaves of absence, not only for mothers, but also for fathers, decreasing working hours, and introducing rehiring programs for female workers who have left the company in order to give birth.

Many Japanese banks have introduced better childcare support programs for working parents. Shinsei Bank started a "my-car" program in 2004, letting employees use its in-house day nursery and to come to the office by car and use its parking lots free of charge, which eliminates the inconvenience of taking children on crowded trains (Nikkei Weekly 2007c). Bank of Kyoto, a regional bank, lengthened maternity leave by three years to enable mothers to stay home to care for their children until they reach the age of four. Furthermore, employees with children up to the elementary school age of 6 are now exempt from overtime. This was raised from the previous age limit of

3 years old, and it also gives employees with young children a monthly allowance of more than 10,000 yen. Tokyo Star Bank made shorter working hour programs available to employees with children up to sixth grade level, that is, 12 years old, after a previous third grade limit of 9 years old. This new program allows workers to choose between working a five day, six hour shift, or a three day, eight hour shift.

There are two main reasons for having childcare support in companies. The most important factor is that there is a chronic labor shortage and, with an aging population and low birth rates, this problem will persist. By recapturing the female workforce, in some cases the male workforce, as fathers can also take leaves of absence, companies will be able to hire already trained and skilled workers. Furthermore, once the worker comes out of "retirement," they can be hired again as full-time employees and given the commensurate benefits. However, this is a rare instance as in most cases workers return as non full-time workers.

Second, such childcare support is a big incentive, not only for the partner that takes the leave of absence, but also for the other partner. Family-life and personal life are becoming a major component of Japanese lifestyles, thus, it is imperative that workers are given satisfactory environments in which to live and work.

While work was the most important factor for employees during the bubble economy period, workers are now placing emphasis not only the job or the job content, but on working conditions and the pursuit of personal life outside the company. Companies are thus trying to create a more desirable environment for workers to work in. Unlike the economic bubble period where employees "nurtured corporate loyalty under the life-time employment system" (Kajimoto 1999), Japanese lifestyles have become oriented towards satisfaction. Although the older workforce is familiar with this type of working life, the trend, especially after the collapse of the mutual agreement on life-time employment, is towards workers searching for jobs which provide better conditions as well as job security. Ultimately, the company must combine the two.

Conclusion

Japanese management seems to have undergone substantial changes, especially as regards the mindset of workers. Although changes have been made in Japanese management, not all problems have been solved and, in some cases, more problems have appeared.

Change is not always positive, and people are reluctant to change. Workers that have been working under the system of life-time employment and seniority-based wages struggle to adapt to these changes, especially the older workforce that has lived with the three pillars of Japanese management. They have worked under a system in which they have "often sacrificed their personal lives" and built up productivity and efficiency (Kajimoto 1999). Though changing the pillars of Japanese management is a desperate measure to revive the Japanese economy, older workers cannot adapt so readily to this change. Traditional Japanese lifestyle is reflected by the three pillars of Japanese management, and it is not an easy process to change the essence of Japanese life to adapt to globalization and Western pressures (Firkola 2006).

Uniqlo is an example of a company which has moved away from flexible working hours and has re-adopted a more traditional method of management. Like most other apparel retail stores in Japan, many of the workers consisted of part-time workers, and, even if they worked full-time hours, they did not receive benefits and were paid hourly wages. Uniqlo was not so proactive in acquiring new full-time workers for life-long careers, but took a step towards the traditional style, and, in 2007, it stated that it would upgrade 5,000 part-time workers to full-time status during the next two years. The company plans to upgrade workers to secure experienced shop clerks and to boost the firm's performance, as well as allowing workers to gain a regular status, earning 10% more per year and providing bonuses. Thus, there is a move to regularize the position of part-time workers as a means of reinvigorating the workforce. These new full-timers will receive benefits just like regular full-time employees. Uniqlo is still a rare case, but there are other companies in different industries, such as manufacturing and the automobile industry, which have adopted similar and more traditional methods of management.

Japanese human resource management is still thought to be the reason for the success of the Japanese economy. The three pillars that supported Japanese human resource management and the Japanese economy—life-time employment, seniority-based wages, and Japanese labor unions—have been adjusted over the years; however, we cannot assume that these management styles have disappeared. They are still predominant and play a vital role in Japanese management, despite the shifts and adaptations to the changes in the Japanese economy.

From a Western point of view, Japanese companies and management have changed in line with the growing challenge of globalization and attempts to adapt to this challenge. The Western point of view is that the three pillars of Japanese management that supported the Japanese economy during the post-war period and throughout the bubble economy are outdated and do not suit modern management techniques. As mentioned above, change is not always positive, and change has brought both positive and negative impacts to the Japanese economy and to management practices within the companies.

The positive impact is that a Western style of management has given Japanese management more scope and choices in management. However, this change has not been fully accepted in the minds of Japanese workers and managers, but has merely given them an alternative to how they operate. With this increase in options, both Japanese managers and employees can make better choices in choosing what suits their style and needs better.

The negative impact upon Japanese management is that this change does not suit the characteristics of the Japanese employee, and, thus, the characteristics of Japanese society. Employees that have been working under this system for many decades cannot suddenly cope with this style as the whole business structure of Japan has been based on the three pillars of management. Not only the workers, but the managers and the companies also have a hard time adjusting to globalization and to the methods that the West has introduced.

Life-time employment has been the key factor in Japanese management as it had its origins in Japanese societal structure. Many companies still choose life-time employment. It is still the standard in Japanese management, but now people have a choice, a choice to move to other companies and to seek alternative opportunities. People have gained the bargaining power of switching jobs and younger generations have dreams and ambitions that do not include being full-time employees. While the post-war era was characterized by hard work and dedication to the company, in the recent years, the emphasis has shifted to individuals pursing their own self interests.

The Future of Japanese HR Management

Japanese management is at a turning point and is currently undergoing change. However, as statistics and examples of companies show, it is not merely a switch from one set of management strategies, that is, the three pillars of life-time employment, seniority-based wages, and labor unions, to Western standards, with employees switching jobs freely and merit-based wages. The change is primarily intangible. It has emerged from the mindsets of workers and managers, rather than from a change in management strategy. The traditional three pillars of Japanese management are very much still alive. They have not disappeared as many may assume, but rather Japanese management has been given a choice between traditional and new management strategies. While some companies adapt to survive in times of economic depression, others change for competitive purposes. Some companies do not change their traditional ways as management believes that it is better suited to the company's strategies and goals. Like every form of management, every company is unique and therefore differs in its adaptations of concepts based on economic and societal changes.

Until the bubble burst, the Japanese economy had been successful mainly due to its unique and traditional methods of management. Western management was surprised at the Japanese success. Japanese management is oriented around the characteristics of Japanese society and, therefore, is understood as a style that best suits Japan. This was certainly the case during the bubble economy, but with globalization Japanese style management was required to make some adjustments. The myth of Japanese management has been greatly undermined. The three pillars, as Westerners often believed, did not exist in all companies. It was only common in large companies, usually with over a thousand employees, and life-time employment was only extended to some 25-30% of the entire workforce. Moreover, these pillars have not disappeared. Many Western managers assume that Japanese managers changed the system completely during and after the crisis in order to survive. The statistics do not vary much and the pillars do very much exist as they did during the bubble economy. The fundamentals have not changed, and, in some cases, companies have moved back to management that is based on the three pillars. It will not be as the same as before the crisis, but management is not static. Even through the bubble economy, there were shifts in line with the trends of the time and the demographic changes in the Japanese population.

We cannot formulate a single answer to all the different problems. It has become an age of choice, not determinism. Since the post-war period, and even further back to times of rice farming village life, Japanese workers have worked under a system that is embodied by the three pillars. Change is taking place, and management is choosing between traditional and new trends that have been introduced via globalization. Japanese management is evolving to adapt to globalization, but its traditional style is still the foundation and has not changed completely. Demographic changes are constantly affecting Japan and new trends and new groups of workers are emerging. Management has been pared down to three simple elements, but social, political, environmental, and economic factors, as well as all aspects of human nature and life, are interrelated and influence each other, which ultimately affects and shapes management styles.

BIBLIOGRAPHY

Benson, J. and Debroux P. (2004): *The changing nature of Japanese Human Resource Management, the impact of the recession and the Asian financial crisis.* International Studies of Management and Organization 34 (1), p. 32-51.

Billesbach, T. J. and Rives, J. M (1985): *Life-time employment: Future prospects for Japan and the U.S.* Advanced Management Journal 50 (4), p. 26.

Cortazzi, H. (2006): *Has Japan changed for better?.* The Japan Times, March 27, 2006.

The Economist (2007): *Changing how Japan works.* The Economist, September 27, 2007.

Firkola, P. (2006): *Japanese management practices past and present.* Economic Journal of Hokkaido University 35, p. 115-130.

Hirakubo, N. (1999): *The end of life-time employment.* Business Horizons 42, November-December 1999, p. 41-46.

Hanai, K. (2000): *Weak unions, weak economy.* The Japan Times, September 25, 2000.

Hani, Y. (2003): *We can work it out.* The Japan Times, July 13, 2003.

Japan Times (2000a): *Support down for life-time employment, survey shows.* The Japan Times, November 15, 2000.

Japan Times (2002a): *Narrow the wage gap.* The Japan Times, July 12, 2002.

Japan Times (2002b): *Flextime proving to be surprisingly inconvenient for big Japanese firms.* The Japan Times, October 2, 2002.

Japan Times (2003a): *Wage system headed for change.* The Japan Times, March 14, 2003.

Japan Times (2003b): *Matsushita to end seniority-based system for wages.* The Japan Times, November 27, 2003.

Japan Times (2003c): *Honda Motor abolishes wage based on seniority.* The Japan Times, January 26, 2003.

Japan Times (2007a): *A shrinking pool of jobs.* The Japan Times, April 4, 1999.

Kajimoto, T. (1999): *Century of change: job security feels tug of evolution.* The Japan Times, January 5, 1999.

Kamiya, S. (2007): *Office weighs less in the work-life balance.* The Japan Times, June 29, 2007.

Mroczkowoski, T. and Hanaoka, M. (1999): *The end of Japanese management: how soon?.* Human Resource Planning 21(3), p. 20-30.

Nikkei Weekly (2007a): *Firms recognizing importance of part-time workers.* The Nikkei Weekly, July 4, 2007.

Nikkei Weekly (2007b): *Workers cast away shackles of office.* The Nikkei Weekly, May 14, 2007.

Nikkei Weekly (2007c): *Labor shortage fear leads banks to more generous childcare support.* The Nikkei Weekly, July 6, 2007.

Shimizu, K. (2004): *What the government is trying to accomplish?.* The Japan Times, April 5, 2007.

Wijers-Hasegawa, Y. (2006): *New Keidanren chief urges Asia diplomatic thaw.* The Japan Times, May 25, 2006.

Yoshida, R. (2003): *Life-time employment myth fades amid jobless realities.* The Japan Times, March 9, 2001.

Further Sources

The Japan Times (2000): *A new breed of workers.* The Japan Times, July 7, 2000.

The Japan Times (2007): *Part-time all the time.* The Japan Times, October 27, 2007.

Kingston, J. (2006): *Salarymen: A dying breed of worker?.* The Japan Times, October 1, 2006.

Koitabashi, T. (2006): *Interview: Matsushita chief tells of company's family policies.* The Nikkei Weekly, August 14, 2006.

Nakamura, M. (2006): *Job, child care should be more compatible.* The Nikkei Weekly, September 25, 2006.

The Nikkei Weekly (2006): *Labor rules: IT Society blurs limits of work hours.* The Nikkei Weekly, August 16, 2006.

The Nikkei Weekly (2007d): *Government considers allowing companies to screen temp workers.* The Nikkei Weekly, January 11, 2007.

The Nikkei Weekly (2007e): *Unionized non-full-timers to get better pay, more recognition*. The Nikkei Weekly, October 4, 2007.

Toma, C. (2007): *Firms being more accommodating*. The Nikkei Weekly, April 2, 2007.

8. Production Management

By Natsuki Hayakama, Mari Okachi, and Pascal Kalbermatten

Production is a combination of the factors of labor, machines, and materials, with the derivative factors of planning and organizing, for the reason of performance construction. Industrial production employs the tools of division of labor, standardization, and automation to increase technical and economic efficiency.

Production management is defined as the management of manufacturing companies and involves coordinating the factors of production in addition to other derivative factors such as organizational performance planning. The definition is based on an integrative approach where production management includes the running of production processes, quality management, logistics, maintenance, industrial engineering, and production. Production management is the main concept and the core of so-called "Japanese management" and was a main factor in the success of the Japanese economy in the 1980s. Japanese production management is also referred to as lean management, a concept where the primary goals are increasing productivity while cutting costs through reducing cycle time, increasing flexibility, reducing stock levels, and shortening machine changeover times.

Basic Concepts of Japanese Production Management

Production management is considered the heart of Japanese management. Often seen as the most successful part of Japanese management, it gained worldwide fame with the introduction of the Toyota Production System, which is considered a strong factor in the company's success. There are several production concepts for which Toyota is particularly famous.

Just-In-Time (JIT) is an inventory strategy aiming to improve processes by reducing in-process inventory and its costs. Its main objectives are to assure quality and save time and costs. As the word "just" denotes, the manner in which this strategy is used in the production process is very precise and calculated: only specifically requested items in the correct amount "move through the production system as and when they are needed." (Beasley 2008) Through this method, Toyota successfully discovered a way to eliminate waste, such as stock and unnecessary labor, to reach the ultimate goal of saving time and costs. Also known as lean management in the West, JIT is one of the world's most innovative production systems. When the system was created, it opened up the world to a new production approach that decentralized mass production and offered a small lot production system that made limited production of diversified products possible.

Along with the JIT system, *kanban*, *jidôka*, and *kaizen* are some of the other production concepts that Toyota is well-known for. *Kanban* are tools which support JIT production. A *kanban* enables designated car parts to be delivered to a specified location, at a specified time, in the specified amounts. It is often referred to as the "subsystem" of the Toyota production system for its dominant role in facilitating the JIT system. The name *kanban* was adopted as the system uses cards, which literally translates to *kanban* in Japanese, in order to address the delivery information of each car part. By using *kanbans*, Toyota was able to eliminate stock and produce diversified products in the exact desired amounts.

Toyota also employs its original screening process, known as *jidôka*. The *jidôka* system blocks defective products from penetrating the production line. It is operated by means of thorough inspections conducted by workers and by a device that immediately halts the entire production system if defective products are detected. Toyota's *jidôka* system was another unique concept innovated by the company in that it integrated the human workforce into the screening process to increase efficiency in ways that could not be done with machines alone. For instance, by utilizing the human workforce, identified errors are processed by more flexible human minds that are capable of analyzing mistakes critically. Moreover, by employing humans, it also becomes possible to identify the flaws that may exist in machines. Since the system heavily relies on physical inspections by individual workers, there is often great pressure on workers, which has been a labor issue at Toyota. Nonetheless, *jidôka* has systemized an effective quality control, helping maintain Toyota's reputation for high quality cars.

In addition to *kanban* and *jidôka*, *kaizen* is another innovative concept practiced in the Toyota Production System. Unlike the previous two concepts, *kaizen* is a moral concept that is used by workers throughout the production process. *Kaizen* is a name for the five principles that constantly guide workers at Toyota to maintain cleanliness, orderliness, and a high discipline to achieve smoothness in the production process at all times. The five principles are: *seiri* (sort), *seiton* (setting in order), *seiso* (clean), *seiketsu* (systematize), and *shitsuke* (standardize). *Seiri* refers to discarding items which are unnecessary and only keeping the relevant ones for the production process. *Seiton* describes how all these leftover items are organized. *Seiso* means to clean all these items, as well as the workplace, and all other materials used in the manufacturing process. *Seiketsu* refers to making all the cleaning, control, and improvement processes a regular activity at the workplace, and *shitsuke* means to standardize and sustain the process to support long-term *kaizen* goals (Imai 1997).

Japanese production management became a leading worldwide influence in operations management in the early 1980s. Knowledge of its main elements became known beyond Japan. Manufacturers from many countries, including the U.S. and others across Europe, tried to apply Japanese production practices. Toyota became a role model for its production processes all over the world, and the Toyota Production System (TPS) is supposed to be the most successful of its kind. Toyota's corporate culture has transformed it from a small manufacturer into a market-gobbling giant famous for its practices of quality circles and, as opposed to traditional practices in other manufacturers, giving workers control over production lines. By trying to implement various Japanese practices such as these, many manufacturers from Western countries achieved improved performance ratios.

Implementation and Adjustment

Although the Japanese production management system has been implemented widely throughout the world, sometimes it is hard for the company to apply the system in full. Some companies in the United States have indicated that these methods have led to only limited success. Japanese production practices might not be particularly suited to the company's manufacturing activities, or management might not completely agree with the basic principles behind these practices. In these cases, companies adapting Japanese production management systems adjusted Japanese practices to their specific needs, which is appropriately termed "local adoption." Using this method, Japanese practices are less intrusively diffused and it allows company employees to easily grow accustomed to the changes. Local adoption not only means implementing foreign practices into the local workplace, but can also lead to new practices—JIT purchasing has been adapted by a U.S. firm based on the principles of JIT production. Adopting JIT practices, the company eliminated unnecessary and redundant processes and simplified its cost management and performance evaluations.

Success and Failure

Despite numerous success stories, there is plenty of anecdotal evidence showing failure—in some cases implementation of new production methods has even led to bankruptcy. Japanese practices, as implemented by manufacturers, do not always interlock with the existing work environment and practices and might be rejected by some of the workers and management. Western business practices can be at odds with Japanese practices. One of the characteristics and features of Japanese production management is that corporate growth is not achieved through takeovers and acquisitions, as in the West, and this disconnect between management cultures can cause difficulties when implementing foreign principles. Difficulty in transferring management practices has also proved to be a challenge in exporting TPS to Toyota factories overseas. Toyota's North American manufacturing subsidiary is one example. A general manager at one of Toyota's plants has been quoted as saying that, "While new American hires often had difficulty at first with some tenets of the Toyota Way, they quickly caught on." The same general manager was also initially hesitant towards Toyota's practices and had difficulty in understanding their logic. The "Toyota Way" makes workplace problems more visible for management, and the same hesitant general manager saw how Toyota business practices were positively affecting management. These changes led the way for smoother implementation of JIT production practices despite regional differences between the country of origin of these principles and the factory where they were adopted. Although it might be difficult to adjust to a new idea, or methods, at first, there are many models where a company has been successful at adjusting.

Japanese Production Management after the Recession

The economic crisis and the globalization process have left their mark on Japanese production management as well as in the environment of Japanese production. In a world of rapid globalization, consumers are increasingly becoming more demanding. As a result, the need for businesses to constantly incorporate innovative ideas to meet these demands has risen. Many large American and European companies have long been aware that radical and inventive ideas are the key to stay atop in the modern global market. Firms from developing nations, including China and India, have also emerged to compete in the same realm and have increased their competitiveness through implementing innovative market approaches. Despite past successes and their high technological and manufacturing prowess, Japanese companies face various challenges that will make it difficult for them to remain globally competitive.

Traditional Structures and Management Styles of Japanese Manufacturers

The main problem in adapting to international standards is said to be the Japanese company structure and the traditional ways of Japanese management. Prior to the economic crisis, the Japanese corporate system was praised by many foreign companies. However, after the crisis, and as the continuous expansion of globalization has taken place, the traditional corporate system has come under criticism from abroad.

Many Western companies and analysts have pointed out that Japanese firms need to shift from a collective culture to a more individualistic culture. While collective culture has been in part Japan's strength, helping enhance company teamwork and making the detailed manufacturing process possible, from the Western perspective, some view this mentality as outdated. Moreover, it seems that the collective culture of Japanese companies does not always allow them to compete effectively with global competitors. Traditional Japanese corporate culture now looks as if it lacks any real edge in the eyes of Westerners, whose individualistic culture seems to better cultivate the innovative taste in products.

In addition, the traditional structures and management styles of Japanese manufacturers consist of various predicaments whose difficulties often seem to overshadow the actual doing of business, the introduction and production of marketable products. For instance, the previously mentioned collective culture of Japanese manufacturers can be problematic in that, for any action to take place, the consensus of every member in the team is needed. Thus, any new idea that is introduced to the company must go through a long routine procedure, which is extremely time-consuming. Furthermore, it must be noted that there are often a great number of people involved in viewing the new product proposals, many of whom could be conservative members of the company who are likely to oppose radical ideas. Consequently, not only is it time-consuming for new products to be accepted, but the chances of acceptance for novel, radical, and innovative ideas are very low.

Another example of traditional corporate culture that is slowing the acceptance of innovative ideas in manufacturing companies is the bottom-up culture. The bottom-up culture is a culture where the staff in the lower management levels and various divisions in a company set-up their own ways of adopting new ideas, instead of following the orders given from top authorities. This can be an effective system in that the people who will more frequently use or deal with those ideas are in control of their implementation. However, this could also give rise to various other problems, such as the aforementioned time-management issue.

Hiroyuki Chûma (2007), a professor at Hitotsubashi University, conducted research at more than 20 different semiconductor-related companies in Japan, as well as in foreign countries, and discovered some of the reasons Japanese factories were unable to adopt MES (Manufacturing Execution System) software as quickly as Western companies. According to Chûma, the bottom-up system hindered MES software from being swiftly integrated into the companies. In a bottom-up system, he stated, workers from various levels and divisions of a company must cooperate to find out ways to adopt a new system, which is often a highly time-consuming procedure. Therefore, Western companies that typically operate in a top-down system, a system where the authority decides and controls how the new ideas will be instilled in the company, were able to implement MES quickly, while it took much longer for Japanese manufacturing companies. Thus, for these reasons, traditional Japanese structures and management styles have drawn negative feedback from many Western observers.

Increasing Competition

Another major issue Japanese manufacturing management is facing is the rising competitiveness of the new economic power China. Well-known for its cheap labor costs, China has for many years been recognized as an economic threat by many countries. However, recently, confidence in the Chinese economy has grown as an increasing number of Chinese companies have begun to incorporate new technologies and make drastic advancements and achieve high growth. Although this is a common challenge to all major industrial economies today, it poses a greater threat to Japan, whose strength lies in incrementally perfecting products manufactured by mature industries. As Chinese firms become more specialized in manufacturing and develop rapidly, it is likely that more companies (both Japanese and foreign) will see China as an alternative to Japan as a site for advanced manufacturing. China, however, is not the only rival in Asian manufacturing. In recent years, ASEAN countries and NIEs have also shown potential. The Philippines, Malaysia, and Indonesia, to name a few, have slowly begun to show economic growth, as more developed economies are beginning to make direct investments and shift production plants to these countries.

China, due to its production costs, has therefore experienced a massive influx of foreign production plants, including those of Japanese companies. Although Japan is still currently recognized as the second largest economy after the U.S., the emergence of the Chinese economy is nonetheless a major threat to Japanese production industries. Moreover, as a result of the shifting of production overseas, Japan has started to suffer an industrial hollowing-out. In 2003, there were 12.22 million manufacturing workers. This is a 3.47 million decline from 15.69 million people in 1992, the year in which the number of manufacturing workers peaked (Itô 2007).

Shortage of Domestic Technicians

As a result of long years of economic slump after the bubble crash, many workers, including veteran technicians and engineers were laid off. Moreover, with the recent retirement of the senior generation, who had supported the Japanese economy after the war, the shortage of experienced technicians has become a major issue in Japanese production management. Labor shortages are a major concern for many production industries and particularly in the software sector. According to The Kobe Shimbun (2007), the software production industry is facing a shortage of some 100,000 workers. Software is a core product of almost any electronic product, such as flat-screen TVs, cellular phones, and even automobiles. Furthermore, as products have become more technically sophisticated, the need for technicians has equally become a growing concern for Japanese production management. In addition, some companies have begun recruiting technicians from Korea, indicating the acute shortage of technicians in Japan nowadays.

Trends in Japanese Production Management

Owing to Japan's economic crisis in the 1990s and rising competition and globalization, Japanese companies and the government have been forced to react. Besides shifting production facilities to low-cost countries and moving closer to end-customer markets, Japanese companies have taken various measures to improve the competitiveness of production in Japan. The government enforced reforms to increase the competitiveness of Japan as a production location and to boost the creation of new jobs in the country. The measures are subsequently presented in two parts. The first part describes the trends in production management in and between companies. The second part is about trends in the environment, such as government initiatives, which influence production management and production in Japan.

The heart of Japanese production management is the so-called "Toyota Way." Today, many large companies, particularly in the automobile sector, use this management concept, but in recent years new trends have emerged. Japanese managers have incorporated some Western practices, and, in some cases Western managers have been transferred to Japanese companies. The Toyota production system and lean production are also not yet widely used in many small- and medium-size enterprises and outside the car and electronics industry, but the number of Japanese companies which are implementing these processes is increasing.

Influences of Western Management and Managers

Troubles at Japanese companies in recent years have allowed foreign managers the opportunity to come in and break with tradition. Carlos Ghosn, CEO of Nissan, believed that foreign managers could only implement changes if they maintained respect for their employees. Other examples of foreign ownerships are DaimlerChrysler's (now revoked) stake in Mitsubishi Motors, Ford Motors in Mazda, and General Motors in Isuzu and Suzuki. Nissan's restructuring plan included strong cost cutting targets for suppliers, factory closures, and halving the number of suppliers, which even caused consolidation in supplier industries. Further, the number and complexity of components were reduced to an equivalent of the Western platform management strategy. Lastly, global alliances were established and production was further globalized. Also in the electronics industry, traditions were broken and Japanese companies sold factories to foreign contract manufacturers. For example, in 2000, Sony sold two of its Japanese factories to the U.S. contract manufacturer Solectron and Hitachi. Moreover, Toshiba and General Electric merged their nuclear fuel operations. Such changes indicate a shift towards a "multi product" strategy, which eliminates redundancy and attempts to raise efficiency through compatibility.

Total Productivity Management

Many Japanese firms have implemented Total Productivity Management (TPM) to achieve their corporate-wide targets. TPM works with a top down approach and reduces the goals to tangible objectives and numerical targets for specific corporate activities. For example, if a company-wide goal requires a 10% cut in production costs for a certain product, appropriate adjustments would have to be made throughout the company. This concept is at odds with the traditional Japanese method of decision-making. Traditionally, decision-making was a comprehensive process which included everybody from the top management down to the blue collar worker. This led to more democratic and incremental rather than radical change inside companies.

Steps within TPM comprise corporate goal setting, top down enrollment, implementation, and assessment, and such measures are applied to the whole value chain, leading to changes throughout the entire company. The main difference to bottom-up approaches, such as TQM (Total Quality Management), is the cost reduction emphasis and increased awareness among employees about how they contribute to the whole. TPM has led to a new phenomenon in Japan, with an increased recognition of trade-offs between product quality and costs.

Toshiba, for instance, applies TPM throughout the company. In a plant, where plain paper photocopiers are produced, the lead time for delivering frame side panels and molding was to be cut by 25%. The target action plans were worked out to improve the speed and efficiency of the work, the use of machine tools, setup times, as well as productivity and quality. After the plans were executed, the goals were achieved.

Cell Production and Jidôka

Cell production is a new human-centered production system that replaces the traditional line system, which has been employed in many companies. There are various other terms for cell production, such as multi task spiral line or one man production line system. In the cell system a single worker or small teams (up to five members) perform multiple production jobs in short segment lines. The cells are arranged in a U-shape and components enter close to the point where they leave as finished products. A wide range of tools and equipment is placed around the worker so he or is able to perform various tasks as well as customize the products. It allows the production unit to react very flexibly to changes on demand. The cell production system allows factories to produce small-lot products efficiently. The optimized cell design and the highly skilled workers lead to productivity increases. There are three basic types of the cell production system in existence. One is the divided production system (*bunkatsu hôshiki*), where four or five people work in one cell and each of them performs specialized tasks. The second type is the one-man production system (*hitori hôshiki*), where one person performs all required tasks in one cell, including inspection. The chase production system (*junkai hôshiki*) is the third type. It consists of two or three workers who perform all operations in turn and nearly at the same speed. The use of cell production is increasing and it is often combined with the *jidôka* concept. It optimizes role sharing between workers and machines and leads to robot support in the cell production. Thus, quality can be increased as well as the efficiency of the workers. *Jidôka* also makes it more difficult for Chinese companies to imitate the Japanese production system. Robot companies even offer robots which can completely replace workers in a cell production system. The cell production system has been praised as less capital intensive, more flexible, better for the motivation of the workforce, efficiency improving, and more supportive in sharing knowledge between workers.

Radical Innovation

It has become increasingly necessary for Japanese companies to be more globally competitive as Japan continues to integrate more fully into the global economy. As a result, some Japanese corporations have started to leave behind the me-too (*yokonarabi*) strategy and have established, through radical instead of incremental innovation, strong unique selling propositions. In response to this pressure, some Japanese companies have turned to radical innovation from incremental improvements, and, furthermore, there is increased focus on using core competencies as a unique selling point to consumers. Toyota exemplifies this strategy shift in the hybrid car market. The company developed radical innovations in car engine technology for the large-scale market and met growing concerns about global warming and scarce energy resources. Sony also shows some movement towards focusing on differentiated selling points and is known for its miniaturization of laptops in its VAIO line. Nintendo developed new differentiated gaming systems that focused on innovative features over pure technological advances such as competitors like Sony. Nintendo DS software has thus far included language training and voice narrated cookbooks, while the Wii has physical training software. The value for both products has been created through software that takes advantage of unique technology in the two respective systems, making it difficult for competitors to imitate Nintendo's exact success. The DS's unique library of software and the Wii's motion sensing controls attract consumers, ranging from young women to elderly adults – the new market groups that Sony has been less able to attract with its technologically powerful PSP and PlayStation 3 systems.

Toyota
Case Study

Toyota is the world's second largest automaker after General Motors. Toyota Motor Corporation was founded in 1937 by Kiichiro Toyoda. The company was first owned by Kiichiro Toyoda's father, Sakichi Toyoda, who then spun off Toyota Industries to his son to create automobiles. Although it is the second largest automaker, Toyota is ranked first in net worth, revenue, and profit. Toyota is also the only car manufacturer to appear in the top 10 of the BrandZ ranking, which is a brand equity database. This database holds data from over 650,000 consumers and professionals, across 31 countries, comparing over 23,000 brands.

Right now, Toyota owns and operates Toyota, Lexus, Scion, Daihatsu, Fuji Heavy Industries, Isuzu Motors, and engine, motorcycle, and marine craft manufacturer Yamaha Motors. In these operating companies, Toyota has a majority shareholding in Daihatsu, but does not own the company, and the same applies to Fuji Heavy Industries in which it has a minority shareholding.

As many people already know, Toyota is the largest company to push hybrid vehicles and the first to commercially mass-produce and sell such vehicles. Toyota used a lot of resources for the development of its radical innovation—a hybrid engine for a mass market car. The company did a great amount of research and learned that people were becoming more and more conscious about the environment, and they wanted to do something new and better than having just the best equipment and technology. They also wanted to gain a reputation for being environmentally friendly. By e-mailing the potential customers, they also got feedback and ideas. Contacting people interested in the product proved successful.

Furthermore, Toyota was able to roughly estimate how many people would be interested among the potential customers that they already had. This then gave the company an idea of how much to produce, and, from the feedback, what a typical customer would like.

A hybrid car or hybrid electric vehicle is a vehicle which combines a conventional propulsion system with an on-board rechargeable energy storage system to achieve better fuel economy than a conventional vehicle, without being hampered by range from charging like a battery electric vehicle, which uses batteries charged by an external source. It took more than 25 years after development work began, and, afterwards, millions of dollars were spent worldwide after designing many prototypes. Toyota launched the hybrid car Prius in 2000.

Toyota Prius is one of the first mass marketed gas-electric hybrid cars. Toyota decided to produce hybrid cars in the United States because most of the population owns a car, and uses it every day. Recently, globalization has been in the media and is a big issue. Thus, Toyota in North America wanted to do something good for the environment and capitalize on the good reputation they have with cars and trucks. To achieve that goal, they also asked their suppliers to be environmentally friendly as well.

By introducing its hybrid car in the United States in year 2000, Toyota has increased its sales and revenues. The Prius has become the top selling hybrid car in the United States. Toyota is not selling Prius as its sole hybrid car; it has already introduced other models such as the Lexus 450h hybrid sedan and the Camry hybrid in 2007. They have further hybrid cars lined up for the future.

On June 7, 2007, Toyota Motor Corporation announced that global cumulative sales of Toyota hybrid vehicles had topped the 1 million mark, with approximately 1,047,000 units sold worldwide as of May 31, 2007. The success was such that they even had customers waiting for the cars to be produced. Additionally, not wanting customers to wait for the car, they doubled production to meet the rapid spike in demand in the United States.

There are many other hybrid cars out there which customers can purchase, but Toyota Prius stands out from all other hybrids and still benefits from the first mover advantage. Toyota competitors have had little success in approaching the sales levels of Prius, but it is not for lack of trying.

Active Information Gathering

Today, many successful Japanese companies extensively conduct R&D and have patents all over the world. New products are developed strategically based on the results of an explicit search for new opportunities. Toyota, for instance, first determined an attractive market for luxury cars and developed and acquired the necessary technology and knowledge for the market entry—this led to the establishment of Lexus. Now, owing to new information and communication technologies, communicating and gathering information directly from the consumer are much cheaper for companies than they have been in the past, allowing easier access to market information.

Global Supply Chain Management

In the past, there was a lack of IT, especially information management systems, in Japanese companies, which led to a productivity and speed gap between Japan and Western competitors. The Ministry of Economy, Trade and Industry (METI) (2004) suggested a more efficient use of information technology, such as Supply Chain Management (SCM), Computer Aided Design and Engineering (CAD/CAE), and

Customer Relationship Management (CRM), to stimulate Japanese manufacturing and technology industries. SCM is the management of a supply chain of goods as a process, from the supplier of raw materials or components, through to the manufacturer, the distributor, and the wholesale buyer, down to the end consumer. Supply chain management involves the actual products moving through the chain, but also the management of all the information (data) about the product. CRM is a business strategy built around the concept of being customer-centric. The main goal is to optimize revenue through improved customer satisfaction. CRM collects and analyzes customer information supported by information systems.

It will be important for companies, who have their business driven by global demand, to remain closely integrated with SCM. Japanese companies procure materials globally, have production sites and suppliers outside Japan, and export their goods to multiple international markets. Companies have to combine their international and regional strategies in an optimal manner to respond to challenging global market conditions; therefore, a global supply chain that encompasses all information is a crucial success factor. Furthermore, it enables the company to focus on core competences and allows smooth and close collaboration across company borders (virtual corporation). Presently, it is a new era of large quantity, but also small scale production and short product life-cycles. This makes it crucial for the manufacturer to lower the inventory level by using a production system that matches production with demand as closely as possible and shortens the time from product development to market-delivery.

On the hardware side, there have been major changes recently in Japan, as well as throughout the world, with the boom in inter-modal container systems. This makes transportation of goods more efficient and cheaper. On the software side, state of the art information systems have led to agile management—

today, Toyota car plants are linked to the sales offices and can react in real-time to changes in demand, such as increases in sales of a certain model or color. Furthermore, the increased use of information systems, mainly in larger companies, allows for improved financial control and helps support decision-making. Hitachi, for example, reorganized procurement, personnel, and accounting functions through business process re-engineering, which not only helped improve efficiency, but also led to the establishment of new firms that provide specialized services to Hitachi group companies, helping transform Hitachi in part into a service company.

Regarding the use of information technology, the majority of large Japanese companies have recognized the necessity of state of the art information systems for global supply chain management and already improved their infrastructure.

Improvement of the New Product Development Process

The product development process has to become faster in every way due to shorter product lifecycles and increased competition. Some Japanese companies, such as Mazda and Toyota, build cross-functional teams. To develop a new car, Mazda creates a "Parts Management Team," which includes the leaders of all departments and sections and which carries out a variety of tasks from design to production preparations. To cope with the problem of diverging tasks between different departments, there is a digital innovation system, which allows computer-aided three dimensional designs and gives employees in all departments' access to all available data. When a problem is too difficult to be solved in the team, meetings are called, and employees can ask for support from all other departments through the system. The Mazda Roadster (Miata in U.S. markets) was the first model developed using the management teams approach and won the Japan "Car of the Year" award for 2005-2006 in its category. This development approach supported cross collaboration within Mazda and successfully used knowledge throughout the entire company to speed up product development to produce a successful car.

Another tool to speed up time to market, which is used, for example, by Toyota, is platform management. The company has a number of platforms, which include basically everything in the car. The development of new models is based on existing platforms, therefore, the development time is much shorter and the company can react more flexibly to new market trends. In 2007, Toyota needed around one year to completely develop a new model based on an existing platform.

Technological progress also forced companies to build alliances with partners in other industries to develop innovative products. For example, microelectronic (sensor), information, and communication technologies are becoming increasingly important in the automobile industry. Therefore car producers collaborate with electronics companies to develop car communication and navigation systems and to coordinate the research activities of various partners.

Innovation in large Japanese companies has become more international. International teams work on innovation projects, and there is international collaboration between companies, for example, between Renault and Nissan. Some corporations established R&D facilities abroad, next to globally famous universities, or in large foreign markets like the United States.

Increasing Production in Low Cost Countries

The effects of globalization have caused a shift of production facilities from Japan to low cost countries and closer to the end-consumer markets. Labor costs in China are up to thirty times lower than in Japan. Therefore, many Japanese companies, large producers as well as smaller suppliers, have shifted parts of their production to low cost countries. Companies also procure from local suppliers in addition to suppliers within Japan. In 2002, two-thirds of Japanese production overseas was carried out in Korea, Taiwan, Hong Kong, Singapore, Malaysia, Thailand, Indonesia, China, and the Philippines. The Chinese share has continuously increased. For example, Japanese foreign direct investment in China in the first half-year of 1990 was 3,072 million U.S. dollars, and, in the first half-year of 2000, it was 5,588 million U.S. dollars. Interestingly, in the same period, foreign direct investment from European and United States companies in Japan grew about 400%, which shows the opening of the Japanese economy and the increasing level of globalization. Some companies are now only performing corporate functions such as management, R&D, and design in Japan. For example, Mabuchi Motor Corporation has shifted about 90% of its micro motor production to China and no longer produces anything in Japan. Japanese SMEs mainly invest in neighboring Asian countries, while only large corporations are able to go to the Americas and Europe. Especially for those companies producing in Asian countries, most output is exported to Asian and other overseas markets rather than back to Japan. Today, a modern Japanese production network, such as Hitachi or Sony's, consists of subsidiaries, affiliates, and joint ventures with subcontractors, suppliers, service providers, as well as partners in strategic alliances. The value chain is broken down into a variety of functions, which are located wherever they can be carried out most effectively. Production is increasingly centralized and production lines will be located entirely overseas, although in recent years there is a small trend towards having production split between overseas and Japanese factories. Overseas production also differs from the past in that key parts were sent from Japan overseas to specific markets, whereas now overseas factories specialize in certain products for the international market. Often the R&D and marketing activities for products produced in a certain factory are done on-site.

Japanese suppliers have also followed large corporations overseas, and, in 2002, almost 88% of suppliers of electronics components planned to expand their overseas production networks over the next three years, with fewer SMEs planning to invest in upgrading their domestic operations. This is leading to the disappearance of a vibrant and flexible domestic base of supplier industries, a major traditional strength for Japanese corporations. Nevertheless, Japanese firms still try to retain an unequal division of labor that keeps the development and production of leading-edge and high value-added products and production stages in Japan. A reason for this is the pressure on Japanese global players to combine the expansion of production in Asia with upgrading their domestic production and innovation systems. Laying-off workers in Japan would be very costly, and the reputation of a good employer must be maintained in order to attract high-potential employees in Japan. They also try to minimize possible leakages of technological knowledge. Experts estimate that a part of these functions, which need a higher degree of skill, knowledge, and technology, will also be outsourced in the future. On the other hand, the leading role of Japanese industry in the robot industry could help companies stay competitive, even with large production facilities for mass products inside Japan.

Horizontal Networks

Unlike in the past, when Japanese companies only collaborated with partners inside the *keiretsu*, an increasing number of horizontal networks are being created in Japan, including with companies from abroad. Horizontal networks are alliances with companies which are active in the same stage of the value chain. The number of horizontal alliances of Japanese companies, or of between Japanese and foreign companies, is increasing. For example, there is an alliance between Hitachi Kenki and Furukawa Kikai to develop earth-moving equipment, another between Hitachi and NEC to develop large memory semiconductors, as well as one between Honda and General Motors that sells each other's engines. This phenomenon is called "coopetition," because it includes cooperation in certain areas and competition in others. The determining factors for these alliances are to speed up the development phase and economies of scale in the production phase. There is a move away from market share expansion to profitability as a measure of success. Alliances with foreign companies, such as the alliance of Sanyo with the Chinese company Haier, are encouraged by the Ministry of Economy, Trade and Industry (METI), but still result in strong protests from many sides. Nevertheless, the trend will lead to vertical specialization and the outsourcing of non-core activities.

Rediscovery of "Made in Japan"

Many Japanese companies still base their strategic centers in Japan. R&D and technology intensive parts of the company are still in Japan. Today, there is much investment in production lines in Japan, and forecasts point out growth in manufacturing investment by Japanese companies of 8.7% in 2008, and, since 2002, there has been a trend towards increasing investment in equipment in Japan. Although a lot of production was and is still displaced to low cost countries, there is a trend to rediscover "Made in Japan." The reason for this is the strong protection of intellectual property in Japan, improved quality control, as well as the preference of Japanese customers for domestic products. For example, Japanese customers have strong preferences for medical products which are made in Japan. Customers are ready to pay a price premium for products that are produced in Japan. However, this strategy is controversial.

The Japanese Ministry of Economy, Trade and Industry (METI 2006) traditionally plays a strong role in the Japanese economy. It has very strong ties to the major *keiretsu* and acts as a kind of manager of "Japan Inc.". During the economic crisis, intense analysis was done and action plans were developed to bring Japan back on track. It was discovered that there was a serious lack of entrepreneurship, low activities in promising business sectors, as well as weak collaboration between universities and R&D departments of companies. This led to a lack of high tech industries in Japan. Owing to the strong competition of low cost countries and the outsourcing of many production activities in these countries, Japan needed more innovation and had to find opportunities in the field of production of high tech products.

Reform in the Japanese Innovation System

In the 1990s, there was a decline in the rate of entry of new enterprises. As Silicon Valley demonstrates, these high-tech start-ups are crucial for the advance of new technology markets. In 1999, a new law for facilitating the creation of new businesses was enacted. In 2001, the Japanese government drew up a "Science and Technology Basic Plan," which gave top priority to life sciences, IT, environmental sciences, and nanotechnology. The reform also included measures for closer industry-university collaboration, such as the deregulation of research funding, special tax treatments, as well as the support of spin-offs. Tax advantages were later established and the minimum amount of capital to found a stock company was reduced to 1 million yen and special stock markets were opened. Start-ups were allowed to use stock options in their compensation schemes. There is also an e-government initiative which aims to simplify both the communication industry and public administration functions to create a more efficient and customer friendlier administration.

The goal of the reforms is to facilitate better technology transfer and to enable joint research projects. Universities should generate more resources through professional licensing management. There was also an initiative in intellectual property policy that included stronger laws as well as the promotion of the creation, protection, and exploitation of intellectual property. Lastly, a special court was established to deal with patent litigation, and universities were forced to improve their education about patent law and management. Many small ventures in the semiconductor or the mobile data communication market were established and have found their niche beside large Japanese corporations and have had a positive influence on the Japanese business community.

New Economic Growth Strategy

In 2006, METI presented a new economic growth strategy that included a virtuous circle of growth in Japan and Asia as well as one for demand and innovation. The target of the first circle is to contribute to the development of neighboring countries in Asia and to create an environment for growing together. Further, a business environment, which offers a free flow of people, goods, and capital, should be created and more foreign direct investments should be attracted.

The expectation is that successful Japanese companies abroad and neighboring economies in Asia will have a positive influence on the Japanese economy. The second circle aims at maintaining a lead in research and innovation and in improving research in areas like environmental protection. METI's target is closer collaboration between academia, public institutions, and industry in research to bring technologies faster to markets, to improve cross sector research, and to focus on strategic research fields. Skills of workers are to be improved through practical education at technical high schools and junior colleges.

Through a new "promotion strategy," in areas such as fuel cells, robots, and digital consumer electronics, the Japanese government plans to bolster the Japanese economy and create cutting edge products in the fields of automobiles, medical equipment, biotechnology, energy, and environmental aircraft. There are measures to facilitate a business environment for the commercialization of the new technologies and to support companies by building brands and strengthening international marketing power. Through the promotion of a new vision of IT management, the government wants to improve productivity all over the country. Furthermore, a cluster policy will establish six large clusters in different areas of Japan. The new economic growth strategy has targeted the creation of 40,000 new businesses by 2011.

The Example of Green Tech

An example of the strong policy initiatives is the promotion of the environmental industry. The new fields offer growth potential for Japanese industries. There are subsidies and incentives from the government to push businesses, such as economic assistance, pro-environment regulations, and public spending for environmental projects. In addition, the government is being proactive about the six percent emission reduction plan under the Kyoto Protocol and has introduced many policies and programs to achieve the target. Industry participants are very proficient in recycling technology, pollution control equipment, and membrane filtration.

METI specified in its first cluster plan 300% growth in the field of renewable energies. Many large companies, such as Toshiba, Sanyo, and Hitachi, are already active and successful in the field of photovoltaic technology, with Japanese companies leading in these fields. Japan is today the second largest photovoltaic market in the world, and 50% of the world's photovoltaic cells are produced in Japan.

Conclusion

During recent years, Japan had positive GDP growth rates and it looks as if the economy will recover from the crisis of the 90s. Many companies changed their R&D, production, and procurement networks, introduced new production concepts such as cell production, introduced total productivity management, and increased the use of IT. As the adaptation of Japanese management in Western countries shows, it is not possible to completely adapt business concepts from foreign cultures. Nevertheless, benefits can be gained from these foreign concepts and, through adjustments; they can provide valuable contributions to success. The government has also taken measures to strengthen innovation through closer collaboration between companies and universities as well as boosting the number of new businesses in cutting-edge industries. There are examples such as Nissan, which turned around its fortunes by blending Western and Japanese management, and companies such as Nintendo, which have achieved strong positions in new markets through radical innovations. Another successful example is Toyota, which is a global market leader in both the automobile industry as a whole and in the environmental car market category. Japan is also showing strength in newer industries with its dominance in photovoltaic technologies. Studies estimate that around 40,000 businesses were created due to the first strategic recovery plan between the years 2001 and 2005.

Despite these successes, there are gaps between the traditionally successful Japanese consumer electronics and car makers and other industries, implying that there is still potential and a need for improvement. This will be difficult to achieve, though, as the breaks with Japanese traditions, such as life-long employment or the target of attracting more high-skilled workers from abroad, are not universally accepted in

Japanese society. Another challenge is to transfer production management knowledge, which in Japan is to a great extent tacit knowledge, from the high number of retiring workers to the young generation.

Manufacturing was in the past the flagship of the Japanese economy. This changed, as in every other highly developed economy, and the service sector is becoming increasingly important in Japan. Nevertheless, there is still a lot of production done in Japan and Japanese companies are world leaders in the application of certain production concepts—in their factories in Japan as well as all over the world. The Japanese economy and the government have recognized the need for reforms and new concepts to stay competitive and to assure jobs in Japan. The shift of labor intensive standard activities, which do not require a lot of knowledge, to low cost countries will continue in the future. Nevertheless, flexible and innovative production concepts as well as the adoption of robots can increase the competitiveness of Japanese production. Another opportunity is the creation of new companies and jobs in upcoming industries and the development of innovative products which offer attractive perspectives for the future. Furthermore, there are also external factors such as the exchange rate of the yen, the demographic changes, or issues in international politics which can influence production management. Japan has to focus on its strengths, but has, at the same time, to further develop the economy from a production to a globalized service and knowledge society in order to remain competitive and to be able to maintain and increase welfare.

The Japanese economy has a long list of capabilities, a high number of large and strong companies, a sense of necessity for reforms, and innovation friendly government policies. These are positive factors for successful Japanese production companies, but Japan has to innovate continuously, improve the concepts, and adapt to new environmental conditions to be able to sustain competitive advantages as a production location.

Bibliography

Adam, D. (1998). *Produktions-Management.* Wiesbaden: Gabler Verlag, 1998.

Automotive News (2000): *Toyota commercializes e-mail.* Automotive News, October 12, 2000.

Beasley, J. E. (2008): *Just-in-time.* Downloaded from http://people.brunel.ac.uk/~mastjjb/jeb/or/jit.html on January 28, 2008.

Caryl, C. (2007): *Why Apple isn't Japanese.* Newsweek, December 1, 2007, p. 22-24.

CIA Factbook (2007): *The World Factbook - Japan.* Downloaded from www.cia.gov on December 6, 2007.

Chappell, L. (2007): *Would Toyota System work in U.S? NUMMI was a test run: part 2 of 2.* Automotive News, October 29, 2007.

Chen, M. (2004): *Asian Management Systems.* London: Thomson.

Chûma, H. (2007): *Handôtai seisan shisutemu no kyôsôryoku jakka yôin o saguru: meta shûriawase chikara no shiten kara.*

Research Paper, Research Institute of Economy Trade and Industry (RIETI). Research Digest 2007, No. 3, p. 1.

Ernst, D. (2004): *Searching for a new role in East Asian regionalization.* Working paper 68, East-West Center, Economics Study Area, 2004.

Fruin, W. M. and Nakamura, M. (1997): *Top-down production management: a recent trend in the Japanese productivity-enhancement movement.* Managerial and Decision Economics 18, p. 131-139.

Geist, L. C. (2004): *Web pinpoints Toyota prospects; e-mail reaches tech-savvy potential buyers of the Prius Hybrid.* Automotive Marketer, November 20, 2000.

Ghosn, C. (2002): *Saving the business without losing the company.* Harvard Business Review, January 2002.

Gualier, G., Lemoine, F. and Ünal D. (2004): *China's integration in Asian production networks and its implications.* MAS Staff Paper No. 42, Monetary Authority of Singapore.

Haghirian, P. (2007): *Markteintritt in Japan.* Vienna: Lexis Nexis.

Hasegawa, H. and Hook G. D. (1998): *Japanese Business Management.* London: Routledge.

Hattori, K. (2003): *Trend research shows how R&D is developing.* Roland Berger Executive Review 2003, p. 16-25.

Hayashi, S. (2004): *Japanese manufacturers shift toward a global operation model.* The Japanese Economy 32(1), p. 132-152.

Hideaki, E. (2005): *Mazda achieves record-high profits, wins "Car of the Year" award.* Nikkei Business, November 28, 2005.

Imai M. (1997): *Gemba Kaizen.* Mc-Graw Hill.

Isa, K. and T. Tsuru (2002): *Cell production and workplace innovation in Japan: Toward a new model for Japanese manufacturing?.* Industrial Relations 41, p. 548-579.

Itô, M. (2007): *Hollowing-out of the Japanese manufacturing industry and regional employment development.* Downloaded from www.jil.go.jp on December 10, 2007.

Japan Statistical Yearbook (2007): Statistical Research and Training Institute. Tokyo: Ministry of Internal Affairs and Communication, 2007.

The Japan Research Institute (2004): *A forecast of the Bank of Japan's short-term economic survey.* Research Report. Tokyo: The Japan Research Institute.

Kashiwagi, A. (2007): *Why Apple Isn't Japanese.* Newsweek, December 10, 2007, p. 37.

The Kobe Shimbun (2007): *Gijutsusha fusoku ga shinkoku keitai denwa nado no kumikomu sofuto.* December 27, 2007.

Kono, T. and St. Clegg (2001): *Trends in Japanese management.* New York: Palgrave.

Maynard, M. (2007): *Say "Hybrid" and many people will hear "Prius."* New York Times, July 4, 2007.

Ministry of Economy, Trade and Industry (2006): *New Economic Growth Strategy.* Tokyo, June 2006.

Ministry of Economy, Trade and Industry (2004): *White Paper on International Economy and Trade 2004 - Towards a new value creation economy.* Tokyo 2004.

Ministry of Economy, Trade and Industry (2006): *White Paper on International Economy and Trade 2006.* Tokyo 2006.

Roland Berger Strategy Consultants (2003): *Making Money in Japan: Eine Studie zur Gewinnsituation deutscher Unternehmen in Japan.* Tokyo: Deutsche Industrie und Handelskammer Japan, 2003.

Solarbuzz (2005): *Fast Solar Energy Facts: Japan.* Downloaded from http://www.solarbuzz.com on December 11, 2007.

Toyota Corporation (2008): *Toyota jidôsha kigyô jôhô.* Downloaded from www.toyota.co.jp on January 28, 2008.

Whittaker, D. H. (2002): *Crisis and innovation in Japan: A new future through techno-entrepreneurship?* MIT working paper. Cambridge: University of Cambridge.

Wideman, M. R (2006): *The Role of the Computer. Max's Project Management Wisdom.* Downloaded from www.maxwideman.com on December 6, 2007.

Wiseman, P. (2002): *China's low-cost labor lures Japanese firms.* USA Today, November 20, 2002.

Young, M. S. (1992): *A Framework for successful adoption and performance of Japanese manufacturing practices in the United States.* Academy of Management Review 17(4), p. 677-700.

9. Marketing

By Jun Nishida and Anna Sanga

Of all the business disciplines, marketing is by far the most culturally sensitive. Therefore, it is essential to understand Japanese culture in order to understand marketing in Japan. Japanese marketing has gone through various stages of development to reach what it is today. Early Japanese marketing concepts first came from the United States and were moulded to fit Japanese values and beliefs. Hence, American marketing style was "Japanized" in order to create a unique marketing philosophy. Certain American marketing constructs, ideas, and practices were modified in order to adjust to Japanese culture and values. Japanese companies have traditionally placed special emphasis on production, based on the belief that the company's main mission is to create good products. Also, Japanese companies have always placed special emphasis on keeping strong ties with their customers and have, thus, developed a very sophisticated marketing approach, which is communications and human relations oriented. In addition, they have a tendency to be more intuitive and subjective in their marketing approach.

Japanese Customer Relationship Management

Customer service, product quality, and after-sales service are the three pillars of Japanese marketing. Therefore, Japanese companies willingly go the extra mile in order to research what the customer wants and work hard to try to satisfy customer demands. The Japanese company, being very relationships and communication oriented, has maintained strong cooperation between the production, distribution, and sales divisions. The sales division is responsible for marketing the products. However, it does not force products upon customers, but, in fact, concentrates on building a long-term relationship based on trust in order to sell products. While building this long-term relationship, the sales division is able to absorb the demands of the market and give feedback to production. Therefore, aiming for customer satisfaction is vital in the Japanese management process. Dealers are regularly measured by means of customer satisfaction surveys as regards sales and service. This is useful in improving the development of systems and people. Another aspect which is distinctively Japanese is the fact that no matter how illogical a request is to the supplier; they will never say "No." The supplier will make an effort, or at least show that they are making effort, to meet demands. This is a key factor in keeping customer loyalty high, especially in a time when customers can easily access information about various choices, and can, therefore, switch between different brands.

Japanese marketing focuses primarily on customer satisfaction and on building a strong, lasting relationship with customers. Probably, this is also the reason why there are so many customer service centres, ready to react to complaints. These voices help improve products. Kao Corporation, one of Japan's most successful companies, exemplifies this Japanese business philosophy in their mission statement: "Each product must be useful to society; it must use innovative technology; it must offer consumers value; we must be confident we really understand the market and consumers; and finally each new product must be compatible with the market." Kao demonstrates how Japanese companies strictly follow the Japanese philosophy of creating products which will satisfy their consumers. They believe that if a quality, lower-priced product is produced based on consumer information people will buy it.

However, this is only one of the aspects of the Japanese philosophy which leads to marketing success. Japanese companies are not only very close to their customers, but they also try to grow and develop with them. This is the key to acquiring, maintaining, and growing the customer base. Japanese marketing also concentrates on emerging demographic categories, such as baby boomers and single female workers, as a marketing technique. Companies also work to respond quickly to satisfy the demands from each of these segments. Their strength in creating products that suit the demands of each demographic group is the key to building strong customer relationships. The fact that Japan is an island of a comparatively small area makes it also geographically easier for companies to remain in close touch with consumers.

Shinhatsubai and the Focus on New Product Development

As Japanese household incomes rise, more people are able to change to new products quickly. Not only is it socially "unappealing" to buy used products or an old model, the product is often functionally out of date. By the 1980s, basically, every household in Japan had every kind of product they needed. Thus, there was no need to buy any new products. Fearing a slackening of growth in sales of products, companies worked to create new, remodelled goods in order to motivate consumers to exchange the old products for newer and better ones. This created the clamour for newness in the 1980s, which led to the launch of new designs, new models, and new products throughout the year. This gave consumers even more choices than before. Using their marketing strength of building strong ties through their customer relationship management, Japanese companies could provide products that reflected customer demands. This was the key to continually selling "new products" to consumers. Japanese customers also tend to prefer new products and those with more sophisticated features.

To keep consumers buying products, there must be a continual renewal of products, often seen in the release of *shinhatsubai*, a new or newer version of existing products. Companies have always created new products (*shinshôhin* in Japanese) because they believe that the moment a new product is released its freshness declines, so the company must develop new products, and improve on previous ones. New products are also quickly imitated. Therefore relatively innovative companies have to keep releasing new models and product improvements as competitors follow at their heels. The Japanese are very talented in taking a pre-existing product and brushing up the design, modifying the price, and so forth, in order to improve on it. These new products vary from a renewal of an existing product to an expansion of an existing line of products. This continual release of new products distinguishes Japanese marketing. A *shinshôhin* by itself carries a newness and style of branding, which makes consumers feel they are ahead of the trend. As stated above, it is important to recognize customer demands when marketing in Japan. But Japanese companies do not solely respond passively to customer desires, they also drive changes that are advantageous to their products. Therefore, not only the creation of *shinshôhin* is important in satisfying customer demands, it also represents a marketing technique to guide and lead market preferences with new products.

Best Service and Quality in the World

Success among Japanese firms is also based on their service and quality orientation. In Asia, Japan is often held up as an icon of service. Politeness, courtesy, and attention to detail are some strengths of Japanese culture. This is, therefore, a Japanese hallmark in the field of service. Indeed, Japanese consumers are considered to be the toughest in the world to satisfy and the most critical about the quality and safety of products they purchase. Companies, therefore, are carefully attuned to customer voices. With the economic crisis, consumers have become more value conscious than ever before. Using the information available on the internet, customers can compare similar products and locate the best choice. Japanese consumers have a fetish for service and quality that trumps their fellow American consumers. High standards govern service expectations. Therefore, companies follow guidelines strictly in order to provide customers with a consistent level of service. The Japanese view service as a labour-intensive function that demonstrates how much the customer is valued. Some companies even have mottos that read "the customer is god," and will go the distance to satisfy their customers at all times, no matter how unreasonable a complaint or demand may seem. The drive for quality of service comes from the Japanese concept of *giri*. Japanese employees have a deep sense of duty to fulfil their obligations to their supervisors and their customers. Japanese consumers also have a reputation for being very picky and difficult to satisfy, and they tend to be very demanding about obtaining a high quality product at a reasonable price. Japanese consumers also pay great attention to a product's appearance and packaging, as well as to its functions. Consumers also have a reputation for rigid definitions of quality, and expect more in the way of service. Value-added is important not only as regards the product, but also the service that accompanies it. Therefore, we see that Japanese customers demand a high quality of service. The Japanese are extremely finicky about the appearance of a product and often reject a product if there is a scratch on the package. Food products must be fresh and must look fresh. Thus, retailers take extra care not to damage their merchandise.

Retailers have been aided significantly by wholesalers who give priority to customer services. Before the 1990s, wholesalers in Japan delivered even the smallest quantities to retailers upon request, accepted unsold goods without complaints, and granted special discounts to long-term clients, and offered them credit for up to five months. However, there has been a decline in this trend as the number of cash and carry wholesalers has increased.

Strong Company Brand Orientation

Building loyalty to the company is the key in standing out from competitors. This is what the Japanese value. Unlike in Western business culture, Japanese pursue such questions as, "Am I a leader in business? How do I compare with my competitors?," rather than, "Am I making any money?" or "How much?" Thus, companies work to create a company brand in order to stand out from competitors. Japanese consumers tend to be loyal to stores and consider the store's reputation a guarantee of product performance. Valuing the product goes beyond the physical product to include the store in which it was purchased. For example, a cookie in a paper bag from a prestigious department store has more than twice the value of one bought in a regular supermarket. There is also a considerable amount of status-oriented consumption. Well-known, global brand names are highly valued. There is also an emphasis on newness in products and brands. Companies, therefore, have a brand-driven customer relationship program in order to maintain a good brand image of the company. The image of the brand has a great impact upon the company's business opportunities. No matter how prestigious a brand is world-wide, if it is not a known brand in Japan, it will not gain an equal reputation and equal credit. Therefore, it is extremely important to establish the right brand image in order to conduct business in Japan. However, even if a company has a good brand image, it doesn't necessarily mean that the product will sell, since the brand image must fit what the customer demands. Today, there is a gradual shift towards functionality rather than status and brand. Yet signs of the latter behaviour are still present among Japanese consumers. Companies have lessened their focus on company brands, and have shifted their focus to product brands. However, at the same time, consumers still associate functional quality with company brand names.

New Consumer Group and their Effects on Japanese Marketing

Japanese consumer behaviour underwent considerable shifts after the economic crisis. Developments in new consumer groups and values have greatly influenced marketing behaviour. Not so much has there been a radical change in marketing strategy nor industry structure in Japanese marketing in the post-crisis era, but rather transformation of the users has prompted changes in Japanese marketing. Japan's emergence from the shadow of the economic bubble saw the development of a renewed sensitivity towards price, and the emergence of different consumer groups which have influenced the types and ways of marketing.

Indeed, demographic shifts have played a significant role in the emergence of new consumer groups. The most notable of these are young working women, single men in their 20s to

30s, and elderly retirees and aging baby boomers, otherwise known as the "silver" market.

Nowadays, the group of single working women is a key consumer group. In the 1990s, women comprised more than 40 percent of the labor force and the percentage of unmarried women (presumably most of them working) almost doubled in the 15 years from 1980, when it was just 24%, to 49% by 1995. Since most of these women earn healthy sums of money from working and often still live with their parents at home, they have a considerable disposable income, which is often spent on indulgences and luxuries such as travel, fashion, brand products, beauty, and health clubs. Also, this group is characterized by a new attitude towards gender roles, with more men and women placing less emphasis on the domestic duties of women as their primary function. This increase in the financial independence of Japanese women, combined with the changing perceptions of gender roles over time, has led to the development of a distinct group of young working women whose levels of consumption are very high. Therefore, in recent years they have become a growing target for new product developments and marketing strategies.

Another newly established consumer group consists of aged retirees who have accumulated large sums through saving (seen traditionally as good) and through receiving their *taishokukin*, the monetary benefits handed out to retiring workers. The people comprising the silver group have much money and time to spend. Generally being well educated, and with money in hand, this group tends to be an active consumer of services, especially travel. To capitalize on this group's ability and willingness to spend on health, fashion, vacation packages, magazines, and other goods, products are tailor-made just for this segment. The emergence of new groups has had an impact on the nature of recent marketing activities. For example, Sharp released its steam oven Healsio, which reduces the amount of fat and salt contained in food, whilst retaining the vitamin C. It became popular among mothers with small children and with the elderly, who are willing to pay for good health.

Characteristics of Japanese Consumer Behavior

Japanese consumers are less loyal to established Japanese companies. In the past, and to a lesser extent in the present, large corporations used their corporate names as umbrellas to promote and market various types of products. This is most clearly seen in television commercials where the company logo is often featured at the end. In many cases, it is the corporate brand that is emphasized, and not the product brand, as seen in Sony's television commercials featuring the tagline, "It's a Sony." Often in the past, products had few or no defining, differentiating factors from similar products on the market other than the corporate brands. However, in an age where individuality and experimentation are highly valued by consumers, brand building seems one of the viable options to differentiate one's own products from those of competitors and is one of the marketing strategies more commonly developed by companies today.

These new consumers are also characterized by their price sensitivity and value consciousness. Traditionally, Japanese associated high price with quality. Cheapness of a particular product did not matter as much as its function, aesthetics, brand image, or newness. However, since the economic bubble burst, consumers have become more conscious of value, because being less financially stable, they tend to emphasize functionality over brands or status.

Also, owing much to this increased sense of price sensitivity is the new desire of Japanese consumers to comparison shop. This involves using available channels to find any information on the product, whether it be researching the prices of the same product at different stores, or traveling overseas and buying products at cheaper prices. Kakaku.com is one website where this increase in price sensitivity can be seen. This site offers prices on various products, such as digital cameras, apartments, and funeral plans, allowing users to compare prices and exchange comments on products.

With international travel booming, the opportunities for Japanese consumers to compare prices on a global scale has become easier, thus encouraging value consciousness and price sensitivity. The emergence of various discount stores and other less pricey channels of distribution is a sign of this. Discount stores such as Don Quixote and American bulk retailer chain CostCo have become increasingly popular with price conscious Japanese consumers. Previously, the Japanese bureaucracy viewed consumers as needing to be protected from price competition, and did not encourage aggressive pricing. However, with the burst of the economic bubble and the rising financial instability of many households, combined with the vast opportunities for price comparison, price competition had to be implemented. Japanese consumers have to some extent learned that high price and good quality are not synonymous—competition and exposure to overseas markets have taught Japanese consumers that lower prices do not always mean lower quality.

However, high demand for quality still exists amongst Japanese consumers, and they remain demanding as ever, with an insistence on flawless, perfect products. Japanese consumers are not satisfied only with functional products, but also seek a high level of quality. This means that they not only value the function of a product, but also its appearance, packaging, delivery time, and after sales service. Japanese consumers demand high quality standards and will not purchase a product, even if it appears to be a little scratched. Even though more and more Japanese consumers are price conscious today and prefer to buy inexpensive products, they are still willing to spend large amounts on high quality products.

Another aspect valued by Japanese consumers is the idea of a product being new. Japanese consumers are highly sensitive to trends, called "*bûmu.*" For example, there has been a recent increase in the popularity of mangoes, with everything from "limited edition" mango liquor to mango ice cream hitting the supermarket shelves. These trends have had a profound impact on the product development of companies, necessitating the need to develop strong ties with consumers in order to obtain virtually instant feedback and devise products that are in demand.

Although many writers and analysts argue that producer power wins over consumer power in Japan, it is true that the changes that have occurred among Japanese consumers are prompting changes in production, distribution, product development, and especially in marketing, marking a change from a producer-driven to a consumer-driven market.

New Values of Japanese Consumers

Generally, the character of Japanese consumers has changed markedly since the bubble burst. Owing to the emergence of various social groups whose values and attitudes differ greatly, a diversification of consumer needs has occurred. Japanese consumers are becoming more heterogeneous, and companies now have to develop new strategies that recognize the continually developing segmentation of the Japanese market. Also, as Japanese consumers are becoming more price sensitive, various channels of distribution have opened up and have affected the Japanese market.

A value shift has occurred from a traditional, relationship-based interaction between customer and store/brand to one where consumers care less about the size or place of a company within an industry. When purchasing products, traditional consumers placed emphasis on their relationship with a particular brand or salesperson from whom they purchased goods on a regular basis. Nowadays, however, consumers are more willing to compare prices from different sources. They are no longer very loyal to stores and do not see the store's reputation as a guarantee of the product. It may be said that the emphasis has gradually shifted from personal relationships and a loyalty towards a brand to a stronger affinity with product value.

Japanese Marketing is Back

Following the burst of the economic bubble, the Japanese economy is now back on track. Owing to the changes among Japanese consumers, companies have had to adapt marketing approaches and strategies in order to cater to the needs of these consumers. Such adaptations include marketing products to specific segments and social groups, developing new marketing strategies, and fusing the Japanese approach to marketing and advertising with more Western methods.

Challenges for Traditional Distribution Channels

The increase in price sensitivity has influenced distribution methods. The traditional Japanese *keiretsu* have been under pressure from the growing price sensitivity of Japanese consumers. Many companies have shifted their production to less costly Asian countries as a direct response to increased price competition and the demand for cheaper products. The development of low price distribution channels, such as discount stores and convenience stores, has also put pressure on the traditional distribution system. In the past, the traditional Japanese distribution system was known for being complex and numerous intermediate suppliers brought products to independent retailers.

Recently this system has changed, as the pursuit of low prices has led companies to eliminate middlemen from their distribution networks. Since 1994, well-established department store Mitsukoshi bought directly from suppliers abroad, bypassing entirely old supplier networks. Another example is the low-price apparel retailer Uniqlo, which has worked together with Mitsubishi Corporation in order to develop an original equipment manufacturing (OEM) system in which they follow the product from its manufacture through to the storefront. Thus, they have managed to cut out middlemen completely, lowering production costs and providing consumers with low-price apparel.

From Company to Product Brands

The decrease in brand loyalty and the changing attitudes of Japanese consumers towards corporate brands have prompted companies to develop products tailored to consumer desires and to develop product brands rather than corporate brands. Consumers no longer follow companies blindly, and solely relying on traditional relationship-based marketing and on the corporate brand image is becoming more difficult and ineffective. Whereas the traditional, pre-bubble era customer bought products from well-established, "trustworthy" big brands or from specific salespersons, the new customer compares products and prices from various sources before purchasing a product. With Japanese consumers becoming more highly informed and able to gather information on products, companies cannot merely release products and expect them to sell well. As a result, they have developed their product brands in order to gain popularity. For instance, a recent television commercial for the Hitachi Wooo features the product name "Wooo" several times, both visually by featuring the Wooo logo as well as in the voice-over, with only a small version of the corporate Hitachi logo in the bottom corner of the frame and at the very end of the commercial.

Shiseido Case Study

Shiseido is a case in point where marketing techniques have changed dramatically toward a brand orientation. In the past, they had many lines of cosmetics and toiletries, but recently the company has moved to a small number of lines, while at the same time strengthening *burando ryoku* (brand power).

In June, 2005, Shinzo Maeda took over as the new president of Shiseido in order to turn the company around. With its new leader, Shiseido began to design a new strategy to build a so called mega brand. Until then, the marketing style constantly changed to fit consumer demands for diversity. In the 1970s, the main marketing technique was mass marketing, and everyone basically wanted the same good products. But, as time elapsed, in the 1980s the ideology of individuality spread. Consumers began to demand greater variety to fit individual demands. Thus, the marketing style shifted to target segment marketing. Ten different people demanded 10 different types of product. Now the market has changed once again and 1 person demands 10 different styles. After the 1990s, the marketing technique evolved to one-on-one relationship marketing, forcing the company to create a large number of different lines.

With the increase in variety of marketing channels, such as the rise in number of drugstores and convenience stores, for each channel, the company was forced to create products that suited buyers. The number of brands, series, and lines increased 7 times from 1970 to 2003. In 2005, Shiseido had a large number of lines on the cosmetics market, such as Proudia, Pieds Nus, Uno, Geraid, Integrate, White Label,

Elixir, and many more. However, this large number of corporate brand weakened the backbone of Shiseido brand power.

With so many lines, inevitably the promotion budget for each line decreases. In order to avoid competition between different lines of cosmetics, the company executed its advertising campaign twice a year. In spring, it promoted Proudia, and in the fall Pieds Nus. This weakened the appeal of each brand to consumers. The company also continued to introduce new products whenever the sales of an existing product declined. Once a new product was introduced, the company focused on promoting it. This split the sales drive into numerous lines, weakening the promotion of major lines. Display space in stores shrank inevitably, automatically leading to a fall in sales. When sales dropped, the company introduced yet another line of products, feeding the vicious cycle. Mr. Maeda, trying to explain the proliferation of lines, was quoted thus in the Financial Times: "In the past, we had a passing-of-the-baton system."

In order to break out of this cycle, the company decided to eliminate underperforming lines and began working on the profitability of key domains to improve market efficiency. Thus, the company introduced new mega product lines: Maquillage, a women's cosmetics line in August 2005; Aqua Label, a series of skin toners in February 2006; the shampoo and conditioner Tsubaki in March 2006, famous for its recognizable red bottle; and re-launched the men's hair products line Uno in August 2005. The company renovated and promoted its mega product lines in order to acquire top market shares in the respective categories. Mr. Maeda commented in the Nikkei Weekly that Shiseido has worked to "grow the Shiseido label into a mega brand" and also to "boost brand power." Now, the company can concentrate on promotion to a wider, larger extent and spend greater portions of its budget on each brand. Shiseido also intensified advertising for the shampoo and conditioner line Tsubaki by investing 5 billion yen in advertising, using popular actresses such as Yukie Nakama and Yuko Takeuchi to highlight the beauty of Japanese women.

The strategy turned out to be a great success for each mega-line, all of which achieved top sales in their respective categories. Successful results can be best observed by way of example of the shampoo and conditioner line Tsubaki. The shampoo and conditioner market had long been dominated by three labels: Kao Corporation with Asience, Unilever Japan with Lux, and Procter and Gamble Co. with Pantene. In the month it was launched, sales of Tsubaki reached 4 billion yen. This was a tremendous improvement in sales for Shiseido. Before this product, Shiseido ranked fourth as regards market share for shampoos and conditioners, yet its share jumped to number one after Tsubaki was launched.

Shiseido, thus, was able to rejuvenate its position in the field of cosmetics. However, rival brands are not inactive. They have come up with their own countermeasures against the "new front-runner" and have released new products or strengthened advertising campaigns. In March, 2006, Unilever re-released an existing product under a new name. Procter and Gamble strengthened promotion for Pantene, highlighting its effectiveness in repairing damaged hair. Kao also increased its number of TV commercials by 10%.

In order to maintain the position of Shiseido's brands as top shareholders, the company needs to strengthen repeaters and sales in each channel. Shiseido must continue to promote its brand recognition and strengthen its share in department stores, specialty stores, discount stores, and drugstores. The company is, admits Mr. Maeda, still weak, especially in certain retail channels, including drugstores, and, therefore, needs to secure the shelves in these areas. With the increasing importance of retail channels such as drugstores, it is even more crucial for Shiseido to improve its sales. Shiseido must accelerate its reforms and innovate in order to survive in the scramble for top market share in the highly competitive field of cosmetics.

Adapting to the New Japanese Consumer

With Japanese consumers becoming less homogeneous, companies have also had to adapt to demographic changes and learn to market products to specific niches, segments, and social groups. For example, electronics maker Matsushita developed a small-scale, easy to operate version of its camcorder, which was targeted at housewives who had the time and opportunity to make recordings of their children. Confectionery maker Nestle ran an extensive advertisement and public relations plan for its Kit Kat chocolate, targeting the product at *jukensei*, middle and high school students studying rigorously in order to pass high school and university entrance exams. They used a pun on the word Kit Kat, by associating it with the phrase *kitto katsu*, a Japanese phrase for "sure winner," gaining street credibility as a lucky charm among teens. Nestle used the symbol of the cherry blossom, traditionally associated with youth, graduation, and exam time, printing images of cherry blossoms on the Kit Kat package and collaborating with Japan Railways to place advertisements featuring the cherry blossoms in trains which many students use to get to schools where these exams are held. Nestle also collaborated with hotels in the Tokyo area, where many Japanese students from all over the country stayed to spend the night before exams to cram. Hotel staff gave students free samples of Kit Kat bars as a lucky charm.

The motorbike manufacturer Kawasaki has developed innovative measures to capitalize on new distribution channels. It utilized the vast membership and popularity of the video mega-chain Cultural Convenience Club (CCC) and produced a "safe rider" video that was distributed to CCC outlets, where Kawasaki then proceeded to track the borrowers of the videos in order to present more promotional materials. The growth and development of new channels of distribution and new consumer groups has led to changes and innovations in marketing strategies.

New Marketing Channels

New types of marketing are also emerging, prompted by changes in consumer behaviour and advances in technology. Cyber marketing has become more important in the post-bubble era, with social network marketing becoming especially popular. Networks such as Mixi, launched in February 2004, with similar features to the American MySpace, allow users to write blogs and connect with friends. With 5 million users in 2006, Mixi has become a useful site on which advertisements can be featured to reach a mass audience. One of the unique features of Mixi, the 900,000 communities, ranging from school alumni through to favorite cartoon characters, renders it available to advertisers in order to narrow their marketing strategies to certain groups.

Another rapidly growing field is that of mobile marketing. With 85 million subscribers to mobile phone services, among whom 74 million have a phone able to browse the mobile internet, it is a growing medium. Japanese urban dwellers usually experience long commuting hours and spend little time at home, which makes it easier for the mobile internet and mobile marketing to flourish. Mixi is available through the mobile internet, along with Google and Yahoo! Users can upload photos and videos along with their blog entries. Significant innovations are being made in this area. For example, Mobile provider KDDI's EZWeb offers the search engine Google, which displays mobile sites and related ring-tone sites and music stores in addition to the regular listings found on an equivalent PC web search. This both reflects and attempts to satisfy the tendency of present-day Japanese consumers to shop around for options. Mobile messaging and campaign sites have also become popular recently. Movie, music, game and software mega-retailer Tsutaya has capitalized effectively on the development of the mobile internet channel. Tsutaya was also one of the very first companies in Japan to utilize a system that electronically tracks customer tastes, inventories, and demographics, allowing them to adapt to consumer demands.

Foreign Competitors Create New Challenges

The entry of foreign companies and products into the Japanese market is also becoming more commonplace, partly due to the change in Japanese consumers' sensitivity to price and decreased brand loyalty towards long established Japanese brands. However, foreign entrants have had to adapt their products and marketing strategies to the Japanese market in order to achieve success. An example of this is the French Beaujolais Nouveau wine of which Japanese drinkers consume nearly a quarter of the vintage—11.5 million bottles. This year, the established company Sapporo Beer and young luxury apparel retailer Tomorrowland designed the labels for Beaujolais Nouveau, hoping to attract a younger, wider market. A Beaujolais Nouveau spa also opened in Hakone, a popular hot springs resort, where visitors can bathe in the wine while they drink it. In this way, more widespread methods of marketing and advertising are used by companies. Foreign entrants are increasingly successful when tagged with established Japanese companies that have a strong corporate brand image and know-how of Japanese markets.

Japanese Marketing Goes to Asia

Japanese companies have used their strengths in customer relations and marketing in order to expand their operations overseas. The Japanese strength in building, maintaining, and growing with their customers while developing strong ties with them, as well as the ability to adapt quickly to changing consumer demands, have contributed to the growing levels of business they receive overseas. For example, Shiseido has developed the women's brand Aupres and the men's brand JS specifically for the Chinese market. Still considered a rarity in China, it reflects a Japanese strength in building a strong relationship with customers. Also, Japanese jewelry brand "The Kiss" has long shown an interest in the Asian market, recently opening stores in Taipei, Hong Kong, Seoul, and Singapore. All sales staff at these stores are Japanese, reflecting a strong emphasis on quality service. As a couples' jewelry store, specializing in pair rings and other forms of silver accessories, The Kiss has been successful in Asian markets among young couples.

Future Challenges for Japanese Marketing

Traditional advertising practices have not changed drastically in recent years. It remains difficult for foreign companies to break into Japan. Besides high costs, which are several times that of the U.S., there is also an oligopoly in the advertising industry, basically ruled by Dentsu, Hakuhodo, and ADK, which account for 48.1% of sales. The top three companies show continuous growth, while small- and medium-sized advertising agencies struggle to grow. They also dominate TV commercials and advertising in other media. In particular, Dentsu enjoys a share of 93% of TV commercials. The type of advertising used has also remained relatively constant, with SP advertising or TV as the top media. These types are followed by newspaper, magazine, radio, and internet advertising. Although there has been some flux due to the economic crisis, the relative ratio between each medium is largely unchanged. The traditional emphasis on TV as the primary source of marketing and advertising can be seen as a challenge as regards marketing in Japan. Some advertising and public relations projects, such as that organized by Dentsu for Toyota's "Bb," a small car with an in-built music player, represent a diversification in advertising channels, in which not only television commercials, but also advertisements on public transport, street posters and events were used. In the future, Japanese marketing will face the challenge of how well agencies and client companies can utilise a variety of media to target specific audiences, as TV commercials alone are unlikely to reach certain audiences, which can be more easily reached through media such as the internet and magazines.

Conclusion

The challenge faced by both existing Japanese companies and foreign newcomers is how to adapt specifically to the Japanese market, on the understanding that Japan will never in a complete sense become "Westernized." With consumer behavior and attitudes changing, and new channels of distribution and new media developing rapidly, companies can no longer rely merely on their corporate brand image or on conventional modes of marketing and advertising. Instead, they must fuse the old with new when marketing products. For example, traditional emphasis on corporate logos and brands can be combined with individual brand positioning, emphasizing the product brand as well as the corporate brand. More widespread PR strategies can be used, as seen in the case of Kit Kat bars, to market products to specific segments and social groups. A more holistic approach to marketing and advertising can be used, spanning different types of media. Japanese corporations can also use their strengths in relationship marketing, strong customer focus, and service provision to market different products effectively.

Changes in the Japanese market do not mean the creation of a Westernized Japanese market, but rather the emergence of a distinctly Japanese consumer market. It is, therefore, increasingly important for companies to develop marketing strategies that cater specifically to the Japanese market and to understand the changes that have occurred in consumer behavior and in new media development following the burst of the economic bubble.

Bibliography

Andruss, P. L. (2000): *Japanese market expanding ad reach.* Marketing News, October 23, 2000.

Campbell, W. (2007): *Can Japan sales save Beaujolais Nouveau?.* The Japan Times, November 11, 2005.

Clammer, J. (1997): *Contemporary urban Japan—A sociology of consumption*. Blackwell Publishers, Malden.

Czinkota, M. R. and Woronoff J. (1993): *Unlocking Japan's markets.* Rutland: Charles E. Tuttle Company.

Fields, G., Katahira, H., Wind, J. with Gunther, R.E. (2000): *Leveraging Japan—Marketing to the New Asia.* San Francisco: Jossey-Bass Publishers.

Fields, G. (1989): *Gucci on the Ginza—Japan's new consumer generation.* Tokyo: Kondansha International.

Herbig, P. (1995): *Marketing Japanese style.* Westport: Quorum Books.

Johansson, J. K. and Hirano M. (1999): *Japanese marketing in the post-bubble era.* In: Aggarwal, R. (Eds.): Restructuring

Japanese Business for Growth. Boston: Kluwer Academic Publishers, p. 243-257.

Kaikati, J. G. (1993): *Don't crack the Japanese distribution system—Just circumvent it.* Columbia Journal of World Business, Vol. 28, p. 34-45.

Kim (2007): *Keio keizai ronbun.* Tokyo: Keio University.

Katayama, L. (2006): *Social networking sites catch on in Japan.* Downloaded from http://www.japantoday.com on December 12, 2007.

Madden, N. and Sanders, L. (2004): *Nestle broadens efforts to bond with consumers.* Advertising Age 75 (32), p. 4-32.

Malkin, B. (2007): *Japan opens Beaujolais Nouveau spa.* The Telegraph. Downloaded from http://www.telegraph.co.uk on December 13, 2007.

Matsuo, Y. (2007): *Sapporo biiru no beaujolai noveau, raberu desain o Tommorrowland ga tantô.* Downloaded from http://blog.nikkeibp.co.jp/nd/news/2007/07/140809.shtml (Nikkei Design) on December 13, 2007.

Mooney, S. (2000): *5110 days in Tokyo and everything's hunky-dory.* Westport: Quorum Books.

Kobayashi, Y. (2006): *Broadening the concept of advertising; Japanese advertising (kôkoku) on holistics approach.* Aoyama Journal of Business 41(3), p. 3-18.

Kobayashi, Y. (2007). *Probing into the realities of advertising trade in Japan.* Aoyama Journal of Business 42 (1), p. 21-44.

10. Knowledge Management

By Alison Onishi

Traditional assets of a Western organization generally referred to land, capital, and people. Applying those same assets to a country, by the turn of the twentieth century, many Western countries had reaped the benefits of increasing national wealth through industrialization, with basically a focus on growing capital investment. People were not generally thought of as the key components to economic growth. For Japan, however, much of its economic success post World War II was said to be due to its focus on growing and developing human resources. The reason for this was simple: Japan had almost no land or capital. The archipelago nation is over seventy percent mountainous and has few natural resources, such as oil, or precious stones, or metal, unlike Latin American countries, such as Argentina or Brazil. In addition, after its crushing defeat in World War II, it faced an economic fiasco with inland transportation pushed to the brink of ruin, over thirty percent of the Japanese had lost their homes, food shortages resulted in starvation for many, many industries were on the verge of collapse as they were reduced to one fourth of their prewar potential, and the yen had depreciated to barely one hundredth of its prewar value, which meant that Japan not only lacked natural resources, it also lacked capital. The country actually had no choice but to focus on people. However, this worked to its advantage. While much of the American Occupation succeeding the war was related to reforming Confucian, feudal Japan (Hall 1968), one of the important foundations for setting the stage for the economic miracle was the ability to effectively manage knowledge within the company.

For many Japanese companies, knowledge management, particularly how to best share, transmit, and keep knowledge in the company, has been a natural component of doing business that was most likely not only influenced by Japanese culture, but also served to influence post-war corporate culture to create a unique competitive advantage for the *kaisha*, the Japanese firm. The main difference between a Japanese company of the time and a Western one was that the Japanese one was less concerned with dividends, shareholders, and share prices and placed a higher emphasis on business growth and achieving it through its focus on people versus capital and reinvestment in that resource. The idea of viewing people as a long-term investment was a major part of what enabled many Japanese companies to grow and prosper. Because the workers were seen as long-term investments, they became storehouses for information and knowledge that were often highly specific, that is, specific to the company that they worked for rather than a specific skill set, such as accounting or welding.

Japanese knowledge management practices enabled many companies to not only manage existing knowledge, but it also allowed the companies to facilitate the creation of new knowledge as discussed by field specialist Ikujiro Nonaka. In addition, some of the interesting aspects of knowledge within a Japanese company are that it is freely shared with other members of the company, a situation that is highly unlikely in a Western company, and there is a focus on the tacit (experiential and routine) aspect of knowledge more than the explicit. However, while it may be easy to chalk the differences in knowledge management practices, or, in some Western companies, the lack thereof, to cultural differences, the willingness to share and pass on knowledge by senior members to junior members in the company is no accident. Japanese companies, through many institutions such as lifetime employment, job rotation, the *sempai-kôhai* system, and the preference for the group as opposed to the individual, created a unique incentive scheme to motivate its workers to share and keep knowledge within the firm as the people who held the largest stake in the company. This chapter aims to not only discuss the past successes of knowledge management, but also to discuss the present situation and the future, concluding with a case study that addresses one of the challenges Japanese knowledge management faces and will face in the years to come.

Japanese Knowledge Management

One of the competitive advantages of post-war Japan has been the firm's ability to effectively induce the knowledge-creation process, a dynamic, not static process, by which an organization creates, maintains, and exploits knowledge in a spiral of seemingly contradictory concepts, such as chaos and order, micro and macro, and tacit and explicit (Nonaka and Teece 2001). One of the field's leading experts on the topic of Japanese knowledge management, Hitotsubashi professor, Ikujiro Nonaka, defines knowledge on the basis of the idea that knowledge itself is created through a dynamic process of interactions between individuals and organizations. However, he notes that knowledge and information are two separate entities, and in order to be considered knowledge, information must be put into context (von Hayek 1945), and the transformation from information to knowledge happens through the interpretation of an individual or individuals in a group.

Nonaka also argues the importance of *ba* (meaning "place," not only in the physical sense, but also in terms of time and space) in the knowledge creating process. *Ba* refers to the "shared context that knowledge is shared, created, and utilized in and ultimately resulting in it being the place where information is transformed into knowledge." (Nonaka and Teece 2001, p. 22) It is the shared context and platform of knowledge creation where people interact with one another, setting just enough conditions and boundaries for the integration of applied knowledge into a certain time or space. By sharing time and space, necessary for knowledge conversion to occur in the socialization and externalization process of Nonaka's SECI process, *ba* creates a common language between two otherwise different individuals.

Tacit versus Explicit Knowledge

Knowledge can be further broken down into one of two categories: explicit and tacit knowledge. Explicit knowledge is the more systematic and more formalized of the two, easily shared, processed, transferred, and stored in things such as databases, specifications, and manuals, whereas tacit knowledge is highly personal and subjective, such as insights, intuitions, and hunches, thus making it relatively more difficult to communicate and share with others than explicit knowledge. Tacit knowledge, with its tendency to be time- and space-specific, can, therefore, only be acquired through shared experience, such as through spending time together or living in the same environment. While traditional Western management has focused on the management of explicit knowledge, Nonaka expresses that both are necessary for the creation of knowledge as they are complements of each other and proposes that knowledge creation is based on three elements: *ba*, the SECI process, and knowledge assets.

Knowledge Creation by the Group

The SECI process is the process of knowledge conversion from tacit to explicit knowledge by way of socialization (conversion of tacit knowledge to tacit knowledge), externalization (tacit to explicit), combination (explicit to explicit), and internalization (explicit to tacit), thus creating a spiral, not a circle, that grows and further prompts the creation of even more knowledge. As Nonaka's SECI dynamic spiral of never-ending organizational knowledge creation grows larger, it has the potential to expand from the individual level to the point of "transcending sectional, departmental, divisional, and even organizational boundaries," and, thus, is constantly improving and "upgrading" itself (Nonaka and Teece 2001, p. 20). Summarized, the SECI process would start with the employees empathizing with their colleagues and customers, diminishing barriers and setting the stage for the sharing of knowledge (socialization). Then, once the individual commits himself to the group, and, thus, becomes one with the group by aligning his intentions and ideas with that of the group (externalization), and the new knowledge created through externalization is available to the group through digital or analog signals (combination), the individual can then access the knowledge of the group and even the entire organization (internalization) (Nonaka et al. 2000).

This process, however, is not only limited to knowledge creation within the firm or among its subsidiaries. It also can apply to related parties such as customers or suppliers of the firm. An innovative new manufacturing process could trigger other changes in the processes of customers and suppliers, which could thereby trigger even more innovations for the firm, but more importantly, simply by interacting with customers and suppliers, a company can gain much insight in regards what to pursue organizationally by drawing on the tacit knowledge of the consumer or supplier to add to their own tacit knowledge base (Nonaka and Teece 2001, p. 21). Japanese companies, for example, devote a significant amount of resources every year to researching consumer desires and gathering consumer feedback, generally though surveys and questionnaires.

Knowledge Assets

After *ba*, the final components in the knowledge creation process are the firm's knowledge assets, which are essentially the "firm-specific resources that are indispensable to creating value for the firm" and are the "inputs, outputs, and moderating factors of the knowledge-creating process." Divided into four categories – experiential, conceptual, systemic, and routine—what sets these assets apart from other company assets in terms of value is that their full value is only realized when they have been built and are used internally. They also are dynamic and constantly evolving, making it difficult to assess their true value, and they are not so easily purchased or sold (Teece 2001 in Nonaka and Teece 2001, p. 28).

The explicit knowledge based on the four categories is conceptual and systematic. Conceptual knowledge assets are articulated through images, symbols, and language; key examples being product concepts and brand equity. Systematic refers to the fact that it is systemized, packaged, and readily transferable as in the case of documents, specifications, databases, and manuals. On the other hand, the tacit knowledge based categories are experiential and routine; experiential referring to the fact that it is shared though common experiences and routine referring to the fact that it is routinized and embedded in actions and practices. Examples of experiential knowledge assets are skills, know-how, trust, security, energy, and passion, while routine is daily operational know-how and organizational routines and culture (Nonaka and Teece 2001, p. 29). These aspects of tacit knowledge based assets are some of the factors that enable the company to motivate its workers to share knowledge with other employees of the firm, rather than hoarding it.

Knowledge Management Practices in the *Kaisha*

Western companies have traditionally been characterized by their focus on explicit knowledge, top-down models of management, and, thus, their merit-based incentive system. For a Western company, it is no surprise that employees have a tendency to hoard information and display a certain unwillingness to share knowledge with their fellow employees, often believing that sharing knowledge would decrease a person's unique competitive advantage. From the perspective of the employee, sharing knowledge might result in the loss of one's job or the worker in the next cubicle getting the promotion and pay-raise. However, for those working in Japanese companies, particularly after the war and even today in the 21st century, the emphasis on sharing and exchanging tacit knowledge on a group level is natural in many companies. Japanese style management, with its elaborate incentive system that rewards the sharing and acquisition of knowledge both explicit and tacit and unique "education" system for uniting the interests of its workers, has many other systems and institutions in place to facilitate the knowledge creation process within the firm.

Trust within the Group

The Japanese organization can also be described as a clan. The clan is an organization whose members have come to a mutual understanding and are bound to each other over a very long period of time. This clan will also achieve equity serially, rather than on the spot, as in the case of a market, where equity is achieved when payment is rendered for the goods or service.

Serial equity as described by Ouchi (1984) is basically when a member makes sacrifices for several years before his true contribution is known. However, he will not leave the group, rather all the members know that his contributions will be appropriately recognized, he will be justly compensated, and equity will be achieved in the end. Japanese firms have used the concept of a clan within the organization and when used in conjunction with "corporate memory" to remember those who have contributed something of value in the past and those who have not, it ensures that the contributors are rewarded and the shirkers are punished at the end of the day, thus motivating workers to give their utmost despite it not being reflected in their pay (p. 28).

Trust is based on shared experience and is derived from interdependence. More importantly, it is the "emotional gatekeeper that determines whether any individual or team member will generate or share knowledge." Essentially, without trust, tacit and explicit knowledge cannot be aligned (Ballon and Honda 2000), which means that Nonaka's outward spiraling SECI process of knowledge creation will not be possible. With the clan and trust at the base of Japanese corporate culture in order to facilitate the sharing of knowledge, a completely different view of management has arisen.

Long-Term Stakeholding: Security

Return on investment for the shareholder becomes of less importance when there is a long-term relationship at stake. Japanese management basically sets the stage for its operations on the basis that it is looking for a return on the relationship or valuation of people over profits. Whether it is external, between the firm and its consumers or suppliers, or internal between its workers, the people with the largest stake in the company are not the people who own the shares of a company, like in Western management, rather they are the employees and managers. They associate themselves not with a specific occupation or skill, but their affiliation, in this case, the company. Japanese employees do not work for the company; they are the company. Knowledge sharing within the firm is possible only because trust is being nurtured among members who have a vested interest in the long term, which ultimately means that unlike the relationship between an employee of a Western company and his employer, this relationship is not a contractual one in which an unhappy employee will quit his job and the employer can fire the employee for poor performance or when he ceases to have use for the employee. The role of the Japanese firm is not to maximize profits, but to "safeguard the company in terms of its employees and the jobs they perform." (Ballon and Honda 2000) When one's job is not constantly in jeopardy, it is much easier to facilitate the knowledge sharing process among workers.

Personally Transmitted Training for Generalist Skill Sets

Japanese firms, with their relatively decentralized internal information structures, focus on autonomous problem solving on the part of individual work units within the firm and the horizontal communication between functional units based on knowledge sharing made possible by the dedication of the firm to developing the workers' integrative skills, which makes the firm effective in optimizing the work process quickly in order to adapt to a constantly changing market and technological environment. With job descriptions being far more fluid and ambiguous and the implementation of a job rotation system that requires workers to rotate jobs throughout a given period of time so that they can be trained at each function, there is a lower degree of specialization involved, which ultimately results in the facilitation of knowledge sharing among workers, allowing all the workers to become familiar with the entire work process. Also, in the event of complex tasks, rather than reading a manual and trying to do it themselves, it forces the less experienced to seek the guidance of the most experienced, in essence, the *sempai-kôhai* system. One of the original strengths of Japanese style management comprises operational decision-making. Japanese management has proved time and time again to be more practical when making operational decisions, such as ones regarding consumer satisfaction and consumer demand, effectively incorporating the concept of *kaizen*, or incremental improvement of goods or service, as most of the decision-making power is decentralized to the lower levels of the firm. Having generalists with a deep understanding of many aspects of the product for example, it is very easy to correct product defects or develop products according to consumer demands (Aoki 1988). By teaching workers much of what would be needed to advance their career on the job, people stay in the company to learn and develop their generalized, yet highly specific skill set—generalized in that there is not much depth to the functions that each person performs, but specific only in terms that it was specific to one and only one company: the one they work for. In addition, conditioning, developing, and breeding generalists, rather than specialists, partially ensures that at least workers will not leave the company, take their skills, and sell them to the highest bidder in the labor market. Japanese workers are not necessarily increasing the depth of their jobs, but rather they are generalists and laborers of scope, doing many different jobs throughout their career as a result of the job rotation system, never really specializing, but networking and sharing information among each other. Therefore, as the employee moves up, he increases the scope of his generalized knowledge regarding the company as well as his human network, or *jinmyaku*, resulting in a multi-functional worker capable of working anywhere in the company doing just about anything (Aoki 1988). This was the key to the success of the system popularized by the highly efficient automobile manufacturing company Toyota, the *kanban* system, epitomizing the strength and advantages of the implementation of post-war Japanese management.

An Incentive to Share Knowledge

Western management rewards individual achievement, not the sharing of knowledge and information. The incentive system of the Japanese firm is structured so that people realize that associating with a group, instead of thinking about oneself, is the key to success within the firm. Therefore, with group association, there is strong pressure within the group to communicate and cooperate to avoid burdening others and that the only way for a person to do well and succeed is if the team or group he is a part of does well. Therefore, by implementing a system to convince and encourage workers to cooperate and share information, and by rewarding the acquisition of tacit knowledge, or, rather, there being a strong disincentive not to cooperate, the firm is able to maintain a competitive environment while decentralizing much of the internal information, reacting quickly to changes in the market or problems on the shop floor using autonomous problem solving and group consensus mentality—an incentive structure known as hierarchy of rank (Aoki 1988).

In addition, those in white-collar positions should be able to also mediate the conflicting interests of subordinates through the use of their personal networking system that results from the job rotation system, bringing understanding and relatively swift and painless resolutions to conflicts, with minimal time and energy spent on the issue at hand, thus bringing him to his hypothesis that the value of the employee is assessed based on his "contextual skills" over a long period of time (Aoki 1988). A successful career and its recognition by society are tied to the success of the company and to an employee's contribution to this success (Ballon and Honda 2000).

While it might seem outrageous to spend seven or eight years of precious company resources in trying to figure out whether an employee has potential or not, this "individual incentive scheme," which evaluates and thereby rewards employees in the long term for acquiring tacit knowledge, developing contextual skills, and cooperatively utilizing them, is a unique way for management to differentiate between its employees in pay and status over the long run, thereby indirectly promoting competition, while encouraging employees to share information and knowledge for the good of the company. The seven to eight years are not necessarily in vain, especially if the company views its workers as a lifelong investment, but rather these years are used to mold the workers to fit into the organization, determining in the process whether or not the person is good at networking and is able to acquire a generalized skill set in the context of the firm. If he is what the company is looking for in a worker, then he is promoted into the fast track to become a high-flying individual working at the main branch doing something important.

In addition, the firm traditionally encouraged its employees to develop their careers for the long term, lifelong if possible, through an association with the firm by making the monetary aspect of compensation directly connected with a rise in one's position, which considerably improved with seniority, and upon the development of contextual skills. Also, "severance pay" upon retirement may be quite substantial and not directly connected to an increase in productivity. Therefore, employees with tremendous potential and ability to acquire tacit knowledge have a great deal of incentive-based wealth at stake should they quit mid-career. This rise in compensation with seniority combined with the large lump sum severance pay received upon mandatory retirement make up the final parts of the incentive system that encourages life-time employment within the Japanese firm (Aoki 1988).

Through an efficient and effective incentive system, which not only emphasizes the sharing of information and values, but which also makes it beneficial and natural for people to acquire, store, and share their knowledge by rewarding the same, a unique learning system is created involving concepts such as learning by doing, learning by using, and learning by interaction. Learning by doing, most closely related to on the job training, reduces costs and energy consumption and is the foundation for *kaizen* within the company. Learning by using is done through the feedback of accumulated experience between different entities. It has made significant contributions to the improvement in quality of capital goods because of the long-term relationship between the producer and consumer.

Current Challenges for Knowledge Management in Japan

During its economic resurrection after the war, when Japan was still trying to build up national wealth, from the thinking that employees were the most valuable resource as they held much of the knowledge within the firm, it made sense to have an incentive system that rewarded the sharing and acquisition of tacit knowledge and the development of a contextual skill set and vast network resulting from constant job rotation. For Japan, not working together and trying too hard to be an individual would have indeed resulted in everyone's loss.

With the pressure of the clan and corporate memory working in full swing, the firm was able to motivate its employees to compete, while still working together to share information, by rewarding those best able to conform to the organization with more opportunities and responsibilities, rather than simply more pay. In addition, the goal of striving to keep people employed was not an economic impossibility due to the fact that the economy was growing at an extremely high rate. Also, when the production goal is to simply add value to the manufactured products and *kaizen* was sufficient for corporate growth because the economy was booming, consensus and decision sharing within the firm worked rather well. Today, low economic growth and the increasing pressures of globalization are challenging traditional ways of managing knowledge. Post-bubble economy Japan faces not only economic problems such as a stagnant growth rate that fluctuates intermittently between inflation and deflation, but it also faces a myriad of social issues as a mature economy, such as an aging society, a declining birth rate, and an increase in social phenomena such as *freeters* and *NEETs*.

Retirement of the Baby Boomers

Currently, the most pressing issue is the problem of the retirement of the baby boomers. With many of the baby boomers retiring within the next five years, many companies are now strapped with retirement bonuses and more importantly the problems of who will replace these people, how will the company retrieve all that information and knowledge stored within a large portion of their workforce, and whether or not they can even afford to support a system such as this during times of low economic growth

At the pinnacle of the corporate ladder, the baby boomers are the most expensive workers on the payroll, their current contributions being of only marginal value to the company, their sacrifices already having been made and recognized by the company during Japan's period of high economic growth. Baby boomers, the first of whom were born between 1947 and 1949 and who represent more than 8% of Japan's workforce, were lauded as "foot-soldiers of Japan, Inc., building up Japan to become an economic powerhouse." (Hogg 2007) Therefore, as the key drivers of the economic miracle and who, although it was never made official by law, worked and lived under the life-time employment system, the baby boomers are essentially storehouses for experience, information, know-how, knowledge, both explicit and tacit, and they hold vast networks and connections both inside and outside of Japanese firms, and were the employees best able to flourish under the system as evidenced by their reward with the highest positions today.

As storehouses for knowledge and information specific to a particular company, rather than an industry, occupation, or skill set, the retirement of the baby boomers means that, because of their sheer numbers, their retirement will be a tremendous loss for companies. It is this very problem of retrieving and ensuring the transfer of highly firm-specific knowledge in a timely manner that Mazda found itself facing.

Mazda Case Study

Ten years ago, Japanese automobile manufacturer Mazda foresaw a management problem, a human resource one to be specific, and was able to make proactive provisions that would ease much of the stress that many companies face today in 2007. According to the company website profile, Mazda was founded in 1920 with the original core competency of producing commercial trucks, but, by the 1960s, had branched out into automobiles and had a specialization in rotary engines. While two-thirds of its revenue is generated out of sales from abroad, it still operates out of its original factory, headquartered in Hiroshima, prided on being one of the largest single-site plants in the world, with an annual production capacity of over 400,000 units (Mazda Fact Sheet 2007). Mazda's problem, however, was not a problem with motivating and retaining workers, a human resources problem that many Western companies have faced in the past and continue to struggle with today, instead, it was a problem that is more deeply rooted within something beyond the scope of the firm's control: population growth, or rather, the lack thereof.

Mazda's Hiroshima factory employs 5,000 salaried workers; however, of these 5,000 workers, 27% are over the age of 55 years old. Yet, the Japanese automaker cited that it had no way of ensuring that the skills and knowledge of these workers would be passed on to the younger generation before they retired (Tsukahara and Ueba 2007). Workers, such as 56-year old master lathe operator Junichi Ueno, demonstrated their wisdom and knowledge resulting from years of experience within the company. Through a simple visual test, the operator showed that just by observing the color and shape of a spark, he knew exactly what metal he was working with. It is this very type of tacit knowledge, knowledge that is gained through experience and often goes unrecognized, or is undervalued in the eyes of those who work in Western companies, that Mazda was attempting to retrieve. In the case of Mazda, because they did not have the luxury of being a manufacturer of great magnitude like Toyota, with over a quarter of its labor force retiring in the near future, they knew they needed to find an immediate solution to begin preparing for the transition.

What Mazda implemented in 1996 was a training program designed to have the older generation teach the younger generation in the form of a 24-course program. Since time was of the essence, it appeared that the traditional *sempai-kôhai* system of transmitting knowledge over an extended period of time would no longer be sufficient for the company, which had an extremely high number of highly skilled employees approaching retirement age. Therefore, of those 27% that would begin retiring in 2007, the company selected 33 extremely seasoned employees to train and hone skills such as the heat treatment of metal parts, the production of sand molds, and engine assembly. These instructors would take on two trainees for a period of two years a time. Mazda, in order to give factory workers an incentive to participate in the program, rewarded those who completed the course with not only a pay raise comparable to the work-group heads, who are at the highest rank for factory engineers, they also received privileges, status, and recognition.

This effort to suddenly pass on knowledge and skills may be seen as selfish on the part of the company. However, Mazda did recognize the importance and necessity of not just workers, but skilled technicians. Being in the automobile industry, today, much of the manufacturing process has been automated through the use of robots. However, the plant's staff manager made an astute comment that it is not the robots, but the "skilled technicians who instigate technical innovation,"—a powerful statement that demonstrates that companies are not only made up of core competencies that exist in the manufacturing process. The manufacturing efficiencies are what bring in the revenue today. What the training program ultimately achieves is the development of not only high-level problem solvers, but also inventors who think of the next opportunity for increasing value, which will keep the company going by generating the revenue of tomorrow (Tsukahara and Ueba 2007).

Increase in Part-Time Workers

With the number of *freeters*, who are basically professional part-time laborers, floating from part-time job to part-time job, and *NEETs* on the rise, compounded with the increasing number of workers who are deciding to change their occupation mid-career, Japanese companies face a problem as their knowledge base is now looking less and less trustworthy and because workers are less motivated to be the ideal kind of worker that brought Japan much of its success and growth after the war. While there are other chapters of the book dedicated to these social phenomena and their supposed effects on society and management practices for Japanese corporations, in terms of knowledge management within the firm, there are several major problems that will arise as a result of these changes in labor patterns.

Mid-Career *Tenshoku*

The first of these problems is related to the increasing number of workers who are changing occupations mid-career. For workers, once they leave the company, their skills and networks will be of little use to another company and there is hesitation on the part of other traditional companies that utilize traditional Japanese management to hire such persons. The suspicion is that if the person left in the first place there must be something wrong with him. He must be unable to fit into the company or the company culture, since Japanese corporations typically do not lay off people or fire them for a lack of ability.

From the management perspective of the company from which the worker has left mid-career, this is already an unfavorable situation, as there has been a heavy investment in the person. If the worker leaves the company, there is no return on the investment, as the expectation of the typical Japanese firm is that the worker will produce value for the company over the course of his lifetime, his contextual skills and human network being of particular use to the company. There is also nothing for the company to do but to replace this individual right away, as they cannot very well hire someone from outside. They must simply promote internally to cover this person, which may not be the easiest thing to accomplish, as it is difficult to measure one individual's tacit knowledge and network base against that of another individual. For a Japanese corporation that is already losing its baby boomers at the pinnacle of the pyramid, losing people in the middle is a further worry; however, there is yet another problem for the company at the base of the pyramid.

Shrinking New Labor Force

Japan suffers from a low birth rate, not even clearing the bar for replacement in society at 1.3 for the average woman during the course of her lifetime. Fewer children for the nation already signifies a problem for educational institutions, which means the pool for selecting potential employees is shrinking and companies will be in less of a position to be selective since they are losing people at the top, as well as in the middle, and replacing the workforce will be of the utmost priority over the next few years.

An End to Seniority-based Pay?

The original problem that Japanese companies faced had to do with the fact that the baby boomers at the top were expensive, especially since the economy was no longer growing at 10 percent as it had during the seventies and into the eighties. After examining their finances, companies were initially worried that they were going to be unable to maintain the seniority-based incentive system because it was too expensive. However, they could not simply lay off people because of a business downturn, as this would jeopardize their reputation as a company and they would lose face with the Japanese public and have severe issues with recruiting in the future, which is why traditionally during business downturns, they often shipped people out to their subsidiaries or suppliers in the form of *shukkô*. Japanese management could not lay off even 100 employees like a Western organization would during times of financial difficulty, as their entire incentive system would collapse and the safeguards that motivated people to share knowledge would disappear. People shared knowledge within the company and were, thus, able to produce value for the company as described by Nonaka in his knowledge-creating process, partly because of the security the firm provided for them.

Although some companies are switching to a partially merit-based pay system as a cheaper alternative to the seniority-based system, the actual conundrum that the Japanese companies are facing is how to best motivate their workers, which ultimately determines how willing employees are to share knowledge, a key component of Japanese management practices. Are Japanese workers still motivated by security, or are they more motivated by short-term financial gain, like most workers in Western organizations? The sharing of knowledge only exists when there is an appropriate system that rewards the acquisition and transfer of it in place and, as many Western organizations can ascertain, there can be no willing exchange of information and knowledge when there is a merit-based pay system. Corporations could hire part-time workers, but, as far as trust within the company goes, it would prove to be difficult to trust them with anything since they are part-timers, and they could leave at any time, taking with them any knowledge or skills, thus making it a poor investment on the part of the company.

Since high turnover in the future is an inevitable challenge, more Westernized explicit knowledge storage methods can be implemented, such as the creation of extensive manuals to store knowledge. However inadequate this storage system may be, it is still a first step towards consolidating the knowledge that had been previously stored within employees. However, the result will be that the need to transmit knowledge personally and on a group level will lose its meaning, thus bringing companies to the issue of how to best manage tacit knowledge in the 21st century, the sharing and exchange of which was at the heart of Japanese success.

BIBLIOGRAPHY

Aoki, M. (1988): *Information, incentives, and bargaining in the Japanese economy.* Cambridge: Cambridge University Press.

Ballon, R. J. and Honda, K. (2000): *Stakeholding: The Japanese bottom line.* Tokyo: The Japan Times.

Hall, J. W. (1968): *Japan: From prehistory to modern times.* Frankfurt: Tuttle Publishing.

Hayek F. (*1945*): *The use of knowledge in the society*. American Economic Review 35, p. 519-530.

Hogg, C. (2007): *Baby boom sets Japan 2007 problem.* Downloaded from www.news.bbc.co.uk on November 9, 2007.

Mazda Homepage (2007): *Mazda Company Profile.* Downloaded from http://www.mazda.com/profile/outline on November 9, 2007.

Ministry of Internal Affairs and Communication (2007): *Statistical Handbook of Japan: Chapter 2 Population.* Downloaded from http://www.stat.co.jp on November 9, 2007.

Nonaka, I. and Nishiguchi, T. (2001): *Knowledge emergence: Social, technical, and evolutionary dimensions of knowledge creation.* New York: Oxford University Press.

Nonaka, I., Reinmoeller, P. and Senoo, D. (1998): *Management focus: The "ART" of knowledge: System to capitalize on market knowledge.* European Management Journal, 16 (6), p. 673-684.

Nonaka, I. and Teece, D. J. (2001): *Managing industrial knowledge: Creation, transfer, and Utilization.* London: Sage Publications.

Ouchi, W.G. (1984): *The M-Form Society: How American teamwork can recapture the competitive edge.* Reading: Addison-Wesley.

Takeuchi, H. and Nonaka, I. (2004): *Hitotsubashi on knowledge management.* Singapore: John Wiley & Sons (Asia).

Tsukahara, M. and Ueba, H. (2007): *Baby boomer special: Passing down skills key to success.* Downloaded from http://www.yomiuri.co.jp. on November 9, 2007.

11. Distribution

By Matthew Cabuloy and Megumi Aoki

Characteristics of the Japanese Distribution System

The Japanese distribution system is viewed as one of the most complex and expensive systems in the world. This complex system is comprised of multiple layers of wholesalers, who have developed close personal relationships with other wholesalers, manufacturers, importers, and retailers (Kennedy 1993).

Unlike in Western-style business practices, Japanese business practices prioritize the personal relationship between business partners over the logistics and ramifications of the business endeavor itself. In Japan, it is perfectly acceptable to do business among friends, and to mix business with pleasure. "Personal, emotional ties are regarded not only as more important than abstract legal rules but also as a short-term economic advantage." (Batzer and Laumer 1989, p. 100) This concept stems from the strong emphasis in traditional Japanese culture on personal relationships, especially regarding the responsibility of fulfilling obligations and reciprocating loyalty.

The foundation of the Japanese distribution system reaches back into feudal times, during the Edo Period. Then, Japan was divided into approximately 500 self-contained regions. Because of the geographically separated nature of Japan, manufacturers developed complex distribution systems on a local level. These systems were highly organized, involving many intermediaries. Wholesalers played a crucial role in the survival of small manufacturers, providing financial support, and helping to store, distribute, and even market products to other regions. Since these systems depended on many individuals in order to be successful, the products being distributed were often overpriced. These characteristics continued even after the feudal system was abandoned and they became the base of the traditional distribution system until the 1980s. There were three intermediary channels between producers and retailers:

1. primary wholesalers;

2. secondary wholesalers based on region;

3. tertiary wholesalers.

The role of tertiary wholesalers was to provide storage and financing to small retailers as well as buying back unsold commodities.

Between 1945 and 1959, Japan needed employment because many soldiers were returning from the war, and the government encouraged the formation of small and medium-sized enterprises and the establishment of retail shops. During the 1960s and 1970s, Japan had a booming economy as a result of the growth of manufacturing and the expansion of exports. The relationship between manufacturers and retailers became more intensively linked. Many of these retail outlets were basic "mom and pop" stores that relied on larger Japanese manufacturers, industrial groups, or trading companies for support when it came to securing credit or storing large inventories because of extremely limited space and high storage costs. "The strength of the multiple layer system is in the ability of the Japanese wholesalers, in their capacity as middlemen, to provide appropriate and timely market information as well financial support to smaller manufacturers and retailers with limited resources." (Kennedy 1993)

Relationship Orientation

Japanese retailers have not exhibited a willingness to forgo intimate, longstanding relationships with other Japanese companies, even if a foreign exporter can provide materials at a superior quality or lower price. This is an attribute which is not seen in foreign distribution systems, and would be considered incredibly inefficient in Western terms. From a Western point of view, the relationships between Japanese companies are unnecessarily close, and, as many people are involved, the product is more expensive for the consumer.

However, these strong ties between Japanese companies do in fact have several key advantages. For example, Japanese distributors and retailers can easily suggest product modifications and improvements. Since the designers and engineers of suppliers have good relationships with the designers and engineers of final assembly companies, communication is open, and there is less time wasted and more product innovation. Open communication results in reduced uncertainty and more can be achieved efficiently and in a shorter period of time. Moreover, all Japanese companies benefit as a whole since the system is conducive to information sharing regarding product trends, innovations, competition, and overall market opportunities. The system in itself serves as a forum to discuss progression and improvements, and it provides valuable insights for everyone involved. Finally, the deep sense of loyalty exhibited by Japanese retailers and distributors leads to an extremely cooperative business atmosphere. There is less friction between parties, and everyone works collectively for the mutual benefit of the group as a whole. This can be contrasted with Western business practices, where sheer profitability usually overrides business loyalty. In such a business environment, tension and uncertainty can often lead to cut-throat competition (Kennedy 1993).

Emphasis on Customer Service

It can be argued that Japanese wholesalers and retailers have the highest level of customer service in the world. This is a direct result of the extremely demanding nature of the Japanese consumer. In such a competitive market, exceptional customer service is not only a priority, but a necessity. This intense dedication to customer service can be seen in many business practices common to Japan. For example, Japanese stores tend to be open later than in other countries, provide a wide range of goods to satisfy consumer demands, and store employees are overwhelmingly polite and possess adequate knowledge to answer the customer's questions before and after the sale. Furthermore, since prices are almost always set by the manufacturer, retailers cannot compete against one another by offering lower prices. Instead, competition happens in the area of customer service and convenience.

Such a customer service-oriented environment affects the distribution system as well. In many cases, Japanese shops will deliver products directly to the customer's home, promptly and free of charge (Batzer and Laumer 1989). Retailers strive to deliver products to customers the fastest, giving them a competitive advantage. This principle can also be applied to wholesaling, which will be described in the following section.

Unique Attributes of Japanese Wholesalers

Wholesalers have more impact on the market structure of Japan than in any other country, and wholesalers themselves exist in a complex, multi-layered system. A manufacturer can rarely sell a product directly to retailer, but usually relies on a network of wholesalers that each have a specific role in the distribution process. A product can pass from a manufacturer through as many as five wholesalers before it reaches the retailer. As a result, the price of the product is highly inflated once it reaches the retailer.

As in feudal times, the wholesaler plays a role that differs from wholesalers in Western countries. For Japanese wholesalers, customer service is often the utmost priority. For example, the wholesaler actively trains retailers to sell the respective product, how to display the product most effectively, advertising strategies, and passes on knowledge about the product.

Although retailers assume the risk of selling the product, in many cases they can sell the product back to the wholesaler without much difficulty. However, we must keep in mind that this custom also results in further inflation of the product price to accommodate the extra risk born by the wholesaler. The retailer can often return unsold goods to the wholesaler, even after a year has passed. In the clothing industry, 8 to 10% of standard goods, such as tights and underwear, are returned to the wholesaler or producer, and the amount of returned goods ranges from about 15 to 25% for more specific types of clothing, such as seasonal goods and gifts. Since returning unsold goods to a foreign wholesaler would be more troublesome as well as expensive, this is another reason why retailers would prefer to work with a domestic wholesaler rather than a foreign one. Interestingly, although the majority of returned goods are bought by the seller under normal purchase contracts, they are accepted back by the wholesaler under customary law. In fact, the process is similar to consignment, and the purchase from the wholesaler is not considered to be complete until the products are actually sold to the customer. In other words, the retailer is simply providing a selling space for the wholesaler's goods. Some larger retailers, such as department stores, even charge wholesalers or producers rent while providing their sales staff to sell the products. Moreover, in the Japanese system, wholesalers will usually deliver even the smallest shipments at a retailer's request. Japanese wholesalers also tend to supply smaller quantities of goods to retailers to reduce the risk of unsold products and costs of storing a larger inventory. They also contribute bookkeeping and other customer services. Wholesalers also offer retailers product discounts if they agree to work exclusively with one wholesaler (Batzer and Laumer 1989).

The wholesaler also plays a unique role for foreign companies that are able to successfully enter the Japanese market. In such cases, the wholesaler usually handles the marketing duties for the foreign company and its Japanese business partner, cultivating a Japanese market for the product. Thus, it is crucial that the foreign company and Japanese business partner cooperate to maintain a good relationship and sufficient communication with the wholesalers. The wholesaler has no obligation to work any harder for the foreign company than it needs to, so it is essential that the foreign company and its business partner convey confidence in the product and dedication to the market in order to motivate the wholesalers (Kennedy 1993).

Determination of Proper Distribution Channels

A Japanese company chooses its distribution channels based on two primary factors: first, the demands of the consumer; and, second, the production technology used in manufacturing the product. As a result, the type of product the company sells and the nature of the industry significantly influence the choice of distribution channels for that product. These factors can motivate a company to engage in forward integration, from manufacturing to retailing, as well as backward integration, from retailing to manufacturing. For example, in the apparel industry, many successful Japanese firms have integrated both manufacturing and retail activities. Since the lifespan of products in the apparel industry is short, this type of aggressive integration would allow a firm to successfully meet the needs of a demanding consumer market. The firm has more flexibility in producing products that they know that customers will purchase and when they want. The ability to satisfy rapidly changing consumer demands is crucial to a company's survival in a competitive industry where faster production equals greater profits. Although consumer demands and production technology directly affect the selection of appropriate distribution channels, some companies opt for alternative distribution methods (Miwa and Ramseyer 2001).

Another example of the influence of the type of product on the way it is distributed is the case of Japan's large food industry. There are more than 1.6 million retailers in Japan, and nearly half are food stores. According to a 1981 survey among housewives in Tokyo, New York, London, Paris, and Bonn, Japanese women went food shopping the most. Furthermore, Japanese consumers prefer fresh food, such as fresh meat, and fish, over canned or frozen foods. The strong emphasis on the freshness of the foods has a huge impact on the manner in which food is distributed in Japan. For example, usually small but frequent shipments of food are delivered from wholesalers to retailers, partially a result of the limited amount of storage and refrigerator space not only in stores, but also in consumer's homes. Also, since Japanese consumers only buy food in small amounts, many feel enriched by the familiar interaction with neighbors and store employees at the local grocery store. This, in turn, affects the business practices of the food retailers, especially small- and medium-sized shops, which make it a priority to establish personal relationships with their customers (Batzer and Laumer 1989).

The automotive industry in Japan is yet another example of how the nature of a product affects the distribution system. The automobile distribution system's primary function is simply to link manufacturing technology to consumer demands. For example, most American consumers would go about purchasing an automobile by doing some independent research about car models which would fit their specific needs. They would then visit a car dealership, find a car that matches their ideal choice, test-drive it, and, if the price is right or somewhat in the ballpark, finally purchase it. However, a Japanese consumer would take a very different approach. Approximately 60% of the time, the Japanese consumer orders the specific make and model of a car from a salesman who visits the consumer's household. The salesman simply sends the order in to the manufacturer, which then sends the order to the factories. The finished automobile is delivered to the consumer in about one or two weeks. This method is very different to its counterpart in the United States, where automobiles are pre-made based on what the company expects the customer will want (Miwa and Ramseyer 2001).

One of the reasons for this difference can be attributed to the lack of space in Japan compared to the United States. While American automobile dealers exhibit their models in showrooms in the United States, Japanese dealers cannot afford that luxury since space is scarce and rents are expensive. As a result, Japanese car dealers are better suited sending salesmen from house to house armed only with a catalogue. This method has proved to be successful since most Japanese car salesmen are extremely well trained and knowledgeable about the different models (Nariu and Torii 2000).

Importance of a Japanese Business Partner

As mentioned above, most foreign companies which enter the Japanese market do so with the aid of a Japanese partner. It is extremely important that a qualified business partner is carefully selected, since the Japanese business partner plays several critical roles in the establishment of the foreign company in the Japanese market.

For example, a Japanese business partner is the most important resource for a foreign company which has no experience in the Japanese market, especially in conducting the research and development of the target market. The Japanese business partner can provide priceless information regarding the target group of consumers for the respective product. Without the help of the Japanese business partner, the foreign company would have no way to obtain this knowledge. Furthermore, a foreign company can utilize a Japanese partner to identify and investigate existing distribution channels for similar products already being sold in the Japanese market. With adequate knowledge of consumer demographics and existing distribution channels, a capable Japanese business partner can provide an invaluable insight into the selection of appropriate distribution channels (Kennedy 1993).

Moreover, the Japanese business partner plays a central role in the development of a close relationship between the foreign company and the wholesaler. Since relationships are regarded as a priority in Japanese business practices, a foreign company and its Japanese business partner must invest even more effort than a local Japanese company to prove to its wholesalers and retailers that it is committed to the relationship. This can include making business trips and even socializing at drinking parties. Batzer and Laumer refer to a Japanese business partnership as "a kind of marriage, that is to say, a long term alliance." (Batzer and Laumer 1989, p. 100)

Sôgô shôsha

Another unique feature of the Japanese distribution system are the general trading companies, which are called *sôgô shôsha*. They play an important role in importing and exporting. *Sôgô shôsha* create unique business models, which do not exist in foreign countries. Examples are C. Itô, Mitsubishi, Mitsui, Sumitomo, Marubeni, Toyota Tsusho Corporation, and Sojitz, formerly Nissho-Iwai. They have several hundred subsidiaries and affiliates within Japan and overseas. However, the *sôgô shôsha* are not always the most profitable affiliates to work with, especially in the case of foreign importers (Kennedy 1993).

Sôgô shôsha engage in trading and act as supply and sales intermediaries. They deal with 10,000 to 20,000 products, such as metals, energy, chemical products, machinery, textiles, foodstuffs, etc. What makes *sôgô shôsha* different is that they trade all over the world. Because of this, *sôgô shôsha* also play an important role in industrial development. Their roles in industrial development are industrial investment, intermediation in technology transfer, financial intermediation, and intermediation in the goods market. Especially, they are identified with the role of financial intermediation. In the Tokugawa period, for instance, the House of Mitsui dealt with financing as well as the trading business. Then, after the Meiji Restoration, the finance arm came to be separated and the company then focused on trading. However, the financial power of the *sôgô shôsha* is still one of their biggest strengths (Yoshihara 1986).

Challenges for Japanese Distribution after the Economic Crisis

The economic crisis caused many changes during the 1990s. Although prices were not fixed as in a cartel, there was an unspoken agreement regarding the appropriate price for nondurable goods. This implicit agreement provided stability and reduced competition between companies. Companies abided by this unspoken agreement to show potential business partners and wholesalers that they were trustworthy enough to engage in business endeavors with. However, this practice combined with the unwillingness of Japanese retailers to discount certain products due to the complex process required to discount items, encouraged higher prices. Japanese consumers had no choice but to pay higher prices in comparison with prices paid by consumers in other countries. Other changes included the emergence of in-store brands, developed by retailers to become less dependent on producers and wholesalers.

After the 1990s, the number of small retailers decreased. Larger wholesalers gained more dominance and smaller wholesalers began to lose business. Instead of working exclusively with Japanese companies, wholesalers ventured out into business relationships with foreign suppliers, and importing became an important part of the wholesale system.

Furthermore, new foreign companies have tried to bypass Japanese wholesalers and work directly with the retailers. Importing goods from foreign wholesalers can often be much more profitable for Japanese retailers, costing them approximately 30 to 45% of the product's final in-store price. Japanese wholesalers themselves are also becoming more Western in practice. For instance, increasingly cash and carry wholesalers refuse to accept unsold goods from retailers, and they are not inclined to cultivate personal relationships with other businesses as in traditional practices.

New Supply Chain Models

During the late 1990s, new supply chain models emerged. Companies such as Zoff, Uniqlo, and Daiso transformed the Japanese business model by dealing with all aspects of a product, from research and development, down to marketing and sales. More companies began to exercise backward integration, for example, Uniqlo began to produce and retail its own products. Another innovation was the birth of the discount and 100 yen shops. The importing of goods in large quantities and the absence of wholesalers allowed for a dramatic decrease in prices, greatly influencing the Japanese market structure (Chen 2004).

Recently, 1,000 yen shops, which began with the "Miracle 1000" store established by a Japanese trading company by the name of 4H-Club, have emerged and are starting to grow in popularity. These shops sell brand-name imported goods for a fraction of the normal price and new stores have been opening in the Tokyo region. Because of 4H-Club's strong ties with wholesalers, it was able to secure a range of products that could be sold at a discounted price, at as much as one-tenth of the original price, while meeting consumer demands, a precedent in the Japanese market (Maruko 2000).

Uniqlo
Case Study

The emergence of Unique Clothing Warehouse, commonly known as Uniqlo, had a huge impact on the Japanese distribution system in the 1990s. Uniqlo came up with a completely new distribution system as part of its management strategy. Uniqlo is a clothing store managed by a company called First Retailing. They sell casual clothing at a reasonable price and their fleece jackets became a big hit with all kinds of customers, from kids down to their grandparents. The combination of color, quality, and reasonable price made the goods a hit.

However, why was Uniqlo so successful at selling high quality, fashionable, and reasonably priced clothing? The reason was simple. According to the president of First Retailing, Tadashi Yanai, Uniqlo created an original distribution system which does not have any intermediaries between manufacturers and retailers. Everything including the planning of products, manufacturing, logistics, and sales is done by one company. Uniqlo does not have any manufacturing facilities and 98% of its products are produced in China, following the specifications provided by Uniqlo. In the factories in China, a selected number of products are produced in a high volume. At least one type of clothing is produced in the millions. Manufacturers can know exact costs and do not have the risk of having to take back goods. These conditions have enabled Uniqlo to achieve a fusion of high quality and low price. This distribution system is very similar to the one in which manufacturers are selling products only at shops under their direct management.

In the past three years, Uniqlo has successfully sold millions of fleece jackets, and one in three Japanese has at least one fleece jacket from Uniqlo. But in December 2001, sales fell 24.6% compared to 2000 according to Takayuki Suzuki, an analyst at Merrill Lynch Japan. One of main reasons for this decline in sales was the failure in opening up new stores in the UK. Following the grand opening of a shop in London, a local managing director resigned because of different opinions about management.

To overcome this difficult period, Uniqlo decided to improve its product and sales force. First, the product should be standard, but highly fashionable. Thus, Uniqlo strengthened the "Uniqlo Design Laboratory," which concentrates on product development. Next, Uniqlo had to strengthen its sales force. Each employee was given a clear goal, and was trained. Uniqlo has an original training system, which is called the "Super Star Shop Master System," to train the best shop master. In the retailing business, inventory is a key factor which has a direct influence on sales. A shop master is required to directly contact customers, find out their needs, estimate demand, and control inventories based on the information collected. Therefore, a good shop master is crucial for Uniqlo's success.

After 2003, Uniqlo gradually recovered and started to reach its goal, step by step. By implementing new advertising strategies and through interest creation, Uniqlo became competitive against foreign casual clothing shops such as GAP and ZARA. Also, Uniqlo uses the internet as part of its distribution system. In 2007, the sales through online shopping reached the highest level yet: some 12.5 billion yen, representing 3% of total sales.

In just a decade, Uniqlo expanded its business rapidly, though it had to struggle with declining sales. By basing operations around employees who have leadership qualities and who are eager for improvement, Uniqlo will reach a higher level and it will be possible to respond to problems swiftly and with the cooperation of all the employees. As Yanai says, "I mean that companies that are enjoying high growth truly are eager for future high growth. We at Fast Retailing are eager to create a totally new industry through our own efforts, and in that sense our approach to business and our basic outlook is totally different from old-line clothing firms. Right from the start we have had the global marketplace and future markets in mind."

This quote underlines the future potential of Uniqlo. Building on the previous success of Fast Retailing, which created a new distribution system with no intermediaries between manufacturers and retailers, it will probably expand business worldwide and may change the style of Japanese distribution once again. Also, other retailers might be motivated by the innovative attitude of Fast Retailing to grow and expand (Asahi Shimbun 1999, AERA 2000; Asahi Weekly 2001).

Revision of the Large Scale Retail Law

Since the introduction of the Large Scale Retail Law (LSL) in 1973, it has had many effects on the Japanese retail industry. The LSL is based on the idea of the Department Store Laws from 1937 to 1973. The Department Store Law was designed to protect small retailers. Since World War II, the Japanese government has sought to ensure that all Japanese citizens can earn a living (Batzer and Laumer 1989, p. 52) and was trying to protect small- and medium sized retailers from the influence of big stores such as department stores and supermarkets. The LSL states that any big stores of more than 3,000 m^2 in big cities, and more than 1,500 m^2 in other cities, need permission from a government committee. This law was tightened in 1979 because many small retailers closed during the oil shock.

In 2000, the LSL was completely abandoned and three new laws were introduced. These changes made it easier to build supermarkets. One of the laws is the SuperStore Environment Law, which aims to protect the environment around the supermarket. The second law is the Revised City Planning Law to revive the areas which used to have small shops around the station in the countryside. The third law is the Activating City Center Law, which is designed to restrict the location of supermarkets in the center of the city. This type of government intervention is very important for Japanese small- and medium-sized retailers and it has helped traditional shopping arcades survive.

After the economic crisis, mom and pop shops felt threatened by the introduction and expansion of larger, more resourceful shops. In fact, the Japanese government enacted initiatives to protect and maintain the existence of these smaller shops as well. For example, the government limited the amount of real estate available for department stores.

Discount Shops

"The number of discount retailers in Japan is continuing to grow, and discount shops have been very successful in market share development, especially in the markets such as electrical appliances, men's apparel, and wine." (Goldmann 2000, p. 48) The growth and success of discount shops in Japan could also imply changing values and behavior among Japanese consumers. "Discount retailing is associated with shopping and buying patterns that are totally at odds with the ones assumed to characterize Japanese consumers." (Goldmann 2000, p. 47) The increasing number of discount shops in Japan is not only an implication of change in consumer rationale, but also a change in manufacturer and wholesaler mentality.

However, since the environment surrounding discount shops in Japan is not identical to the environment surrounding discount shops when they first appeared in the West, the same outcome cannot be assumed. For example, Japanese discounters are only using basic methods of discounting, which were evident in the early stages of discounting in the West. This has proven to be a limiting factor for the progression of discount shops in Japan, as many Japanese consumers are unwilling to sacrifice accessibility and customer service for a lower price. Japanese discounters have not yet taken advantage of more advanced techniques that are common practice in modern discount retailing in the West (Goldmann 2000, p. 48). Discount shops are seen as a means to purchase generic products at low prices. Discount consumers in Japan are, therefore, also consumers of high-priced brand products.

Convenience Stores

The convenience store originated in the United States to accommodate the changes in customers' needs. When the first convenience store arrived at Japan in 1970, there were already

11,620 shops in the Unites States. The aim in Japan was not only to satisfy customers' needs, but also to circumvent the Large Store Law and expand the supermarket business. In 2007, there were more than 42,000 convenience stores in Japan. The major Japanese convenience stores include Seven-Eleven, Lawson, Family Mart, Sunkus, Mini Stop, and am-pm. These stores have focused on "convenience," such as longer shop hours, proximity to consumers' houses, and a variety of goods to differentiate them from retailers like supermarkets or department stores. Because of their accessibility and commitment to providing excellent customer service, convenience stores are among the most successful businesses in Japan (Nihon Keizai Shimbun 2001).

In the retail business, marketing and merchandize are very important. Merchandizing is the cycle of buying, inventory, and sales. At a convenience store, point of sales is used in order that managers can know when, what, at what price, and how many products have been sold. This system is useful to adapt to customers' various needs.

In 1991, Lawson opened "Natural Lawson" in the metropolitan area already saturated with convenience stores. Natural Lawson targeted health conscious people, especially women. Through segmentation, Natural Lawson sought the loyalty of customers. The variety of products at Natural Lawson is very different from a normal Lawson store. For example, the vegetables in the rice balls are largely free of agricultural chemicals. There are also organic products such as sandwiches, snacks, and eggs.

As a new innovation in convenience stores, financial services were introduced at Seven-Eleven stores in the same year as Natural Lawson was launched. Seven-Eleven placed ATM machines in newly opened stores. Beyond selling products, convenience stores started providing new, convenient services to customers. In 2007, electric money, such as Suica, Pasmo, or Edy, was introduced as a means of payment as an alternative to cash. This eliminates the need to carry cash, and payment is easy. Following suit, Seven-Eleven started its own electric money service "*Nanako*," at 11,000 stores in Japan.

Modernization

Recent changes in the Japanese distribution system indicate a move toward greater efficiency. For example, there has been a decrease in the number of smaller retailers and wholesalers. This is partly a result of the reformation of Japan's Large Scale Retail Store Law, which was originally designed to protect smaller "mom and pop" type operations by preventing the establishment of larger retail stores, including foreign retailers.

The modifications to the law during the 1990s have made it easier for larger retail stores, such as supermarkets, department stores, and chain stores, to open new stores and establish themselves in the Japanese market. New retailing enterprises, such as discount shops, convenience stores, and e-retailers, have appeared as Japanese lifestyles change and shifts in consumer values and behavior necessitate new and innovative product solutions.

BIBLIOGRAPHY

AERA (2000): *Uniqlo, jôshô no shukumei hashiri tsuzukeru uzu to natte*. AERA, December 11, 2000.

Asahi Shimbun (1999): *Yanai Fast retailing shachô*. Asahi Shimbun, June 26, 1999.

Asahi Weekly (2001): *Uniqlo shinwa hôkai uriage ôhaba daun kôsan no kaigai demise*. Asahi Weekly, November 30, 2001.

Asano, Junji (2000): *Retail Finance ryûtsû o kaeru innovation*. Tokyo: Shinano Shuppan.

Batzer, E. and H. Laumer (1989): *Marketing strategies and distribution channels for foreign companies in Japan*. Boulder: Westview Press.

Chen, M. (2004): *Asian management systems*. Thompson.

Kennedy, E. (1993): *The Japanese distribution system*. Business America, May 17, 1993.

Kinoshita, Y. (2002): *Konbiniensu sutoa no chishiki*. Nihon Keizai Shimbunsha.

Maruko, M. (2000): *1,000 yen shops offer customers discount-shopping thrills.* The Japan Times, November 30, 2000.

Miwa, Y. and J. Ramseyer (2001): *Japanese distribution: Background, issues, examples.* Discussion Paper No. 312. 02/2001, Harvard Law School.

Nariu, T. And A. Torii (2000): *Long-term manufacturer-distributor relationships.* In Czinkota, M. and M. Kotabe (Eds.): Japanese Distribution Strategy. London: Thompson Learning.

Nihon Keizai Shimbun (2001): *Lawson ga kenkô konbini gennôyaku yasai nado soroeru.* Nihon Keizai Shimbun, July 10, 2001.

Uniqlo Official Website (2007): Downloaded from http://www.uniqlo.co.jp.

Upham, Frank K. (1989): *Legal regulation of the Japanese retail industry: The Large Scale Retail Stores Law and prospects for reform.* USJP Occasional Paper 89-02, Program on U.S.-Japan Relations.

Yoshihara, K. (1986): *The Invisible Link: Japan's sôgô shôsha and the organization of trade.* Cambridge, Mass.: The MIT Press.

Yoshino, M. Y. (1971): *The Japanese marketing system: Adoptions and innovations.* Cambridge, Mass.: MIT Press.

12. Entrepreneurship in Japan

Jeffrey Honma, Kotaro Kinoshita, and Ayano Sakuragi

Japan is generally seen as a country where most individuals prefer to enter a company and stay there for a lifetime if possible, not as a country of entrepreneurs. The reason is a high risk avoidance among the Japanese and administrative hurdles when founding an enterprise. Although Japan is well-known for its post-war economic recovery and was thought to be the next economic leader, recently Japan's "14-year economic slump has led policy makers and corporate leaders to realize that the powerful industrial system that they created is now a handicap." (Hane 2004)

Japan's economy has also moved out of a period of stagnation and has shown signs of recovery in recent years. Lately, there have been "a substantial number of government policies designed to promote entrepreneurship comparable to other industrialized countries." (Yasuda 2004) This led to a number of governmental initiatives, which have been changing the environment in order to motivate contemporary entrepreneurs and to increase the number of start-up ventures.

Historical Development of Entrepreneurship in Japan

Before considering government efforts and the effects, we will briefly summarize theories on the scarcity of entrepreneurs in Japan. A survey conducted by the Global Entrepreneurship Monitor (GEM) shed some light on the low level of entrepreneurial activity in Japan. This survey, conducted in 2006, surveyed the adult population, aged 18 to 64, in 42 countries and recorded the percentage of 1) nascent entrepreneurial activity; 2) new business owners; 3) early-stage entrepreneurial activity; and 4) established business owners. According to the results, Japan's percentages were among the lowest three for the countries surveyed. Just 3% of the adult population polled showed early-stage entrepreneurial activity and 5% were established business owners. Moreover, less than 2% of the population showed nascent entrepreneurial activity and were new business owners (Bosma and Harding 2006).

The percentage of Japanese entrepreneurs is much lower than in rival economies, such as the United States and China, which have some of the highest ratios of entrepreneurial activity according to the survey. In a survey comparing the early stage entrepreneurial activity among OECD countries Japan ranks second last.

Despite low levels of entrepreneurship, in the history of post-war Japan, there have been many capable entrepreneurs. The first boom of venture companies was from 1970 to 1973, the end of Japan's high economic growth period. The "corporate dropout" (*datsu-sara*) was one of the trends in this period, and this boosted new businesses. However, because of the oil shock in 1973, businesses faced a depression and a lot of venture companies went bankrupt. The second boom was from 1983 to 1986. In this period, companies were established in new fields, such as electronics R&D, new materials, and biotechnology. These new fields developed because of the need to save energy following the oil shock. However, the credit relaxation in November, 1983, led to excessive investment in and loans to venture companies. Eventually, the high-yen recession of 1985 caused bankruptcies among powerful venture companies. The third boom was from 1993. After the bubble economy burst, it was thought that entrepreneurs would overcome the long-term stagnation of the Japanese economy. Therefore, the government, local authorities, and the private sector began efforts to support entrepreneurs (Fukuda et al. 2000).

But who becomes an entrepreneur in Japan? Some 37.8% of entrepreneurs in Japan are between 41 and 50 years old and 29.6% between 51 and 60. The percentage of entrepreneurs younger than 40 is only 27.8%. It is obvious that a percentage of start-ups classified as entrepreneurial start-ups include those established by older people who have no intention of growing their businesses. These start-ups are not the main target of entrepreneurial support provided by the government.

Barriers to Becoming an Entrepreneur in Japan

So why does Japan have such a low number of actual start-ups? There are many other challenges that make it difficult for aspiring entrepreneurs to take the first step. These challenges include finance, finding high-quality employees, and finding consumers for the products. The biggest problem encountered by aspiring entrepreneurs is funding. The Applied Research Institute conducted the *Survey of the Environment for Startups* in 2001 and 2006. This survey uncovered various data concerning the challenges faced by entrepreneurs. It showed that some 50% of entrepreneurs had difficulties procuring funds for their start-up and 48.6% of entrepreneurs had difficulties in procuring funds for their business. The problem of finding finance for start-ups is faced the most by entrepreneurs in their 40s or younger (SME Whitepaper 2007). Most start-ups are funded from personal investments by the entrepreneurs themselves. This makes it extremely hard for entrepreneurs who have ideas, but do not have the means to procure the finance. Another aspect of this data shows that venture capital investments are nearly non-existent. "Japanese capital owners are unwilling to take on the risk of providing serious backing to leading-edge start-ups. Most venture capital funds put together a highly diversified portfolio of tiny investments and avoid early-stage investing. Rather than sharing entrepreneurial risk and reaping fifty percent returns, Japanese capital owners wall off their backyards and harvest five percent returns." (Miller 2008) It can be noted that "The slow growth of new venture creation in Japan can be attributed to numerous variables, including conventional Japanese business culture, life-time employment, the seniority system, labor unions inside companies, tight regulatory policies of the government, and the group-oriented, risk-adverse orientation of the population." (Helms 2003) All these factors represent a culture that is "entrepreneur unfriendly."

Another cultural aspect that affects the development of entrepreneurship in Japan is the notion of being successful. Japanese culture is generally said to be risk averse and, when it comes to entrepreneurship, this can be seen very clearly. The barrier involved here is the lack of acceptance of failure in Japanese society (Carstens 2007). It is still a strong cultural aspect among Japanese students to go to a good school in order to get into a good college, in order to get into a good company. If, in any part of this process, an individual makes a decision to quit and start up their own business, it is most likely to be against the approval of their parents. In the "United States start-ups attract top talent because they offer the chance for enormous financial rewards with minimal risk." (Feigenbaum and Brunner 2002) In Japan, a good school which leads children to a good job in a large company, which provides success and stability, is the most appealing route. There are even studies that show that the probability of starting up in business is significantly lower the higher an individual's educational background (Small and Medium Enterprise Agency 2007). Other research reports that the effect of failure upon the Japanese entrepreneur is more damaging to their career than in other countries. Some 13% of Japanese entrepreneurs of failed firms become corporate managers again, compared with the corresponding figure for their United States counterparts of 47% (Kyodo News 2002). Therefore, it is extremely rare for parents to be in favor of a son or daughter starting their own business. This is because the parents want nothing but success and stability for their child and their family name, and starting a business is a major risk. This deep cultural aspect of the Japanese family can be blamed for discouraging a major percentage of capable Japanese from starting up their own business.

The next two challenges faced by entrepreneurs are recruiting high-quality employees and finding customers for their products and services. As mentioned earlier, the fear of failure or risk aversion can be blamed. Since Japan is a rather conservative nation, people want "the benefits of entrepreneurship, but want other people to bear the cost." William Miller of Stanford University describes this as "NIMBY entrepreneurship." NIMBY stands for "not in my backyard." This concept of NIMBY entrepreneurship explains the difficulties of finding high-quality employees and finding consumers. "Elite students who take jobs with large corporations and parents that discourage children from joining startups: both are refusing to share the costs of entrepreneurship." The next problem of finding customers for start-ups comes from the unwillingness of Japanese companies and the government to bear the risk of buying new products from startups. "To reduce the risk of costly mistakes, large Japanese institutions are late adopters of new products, emphasizing reliability and relationships over functionality." These characteristics of Japanese companies and the government create barriers for entrepreneurs who want to successfully grow their business.

Japanese entrepreneurs face these types of barriers that make it difficult to or discourage them from taking their first entrepreneurial step. The mindset of the Japanese still appears to be too conservative to embrace naturally risky entrepreneurial activity. In order to encourage a more entrepreneurial culture in Japan, risk-aversion tendencies must change to risk-management tendencies. To develop professionals skilled in management of entrepreneurial risk, the entrepreneurial habitat must motivate individuals to take intelligent risks.

Recent Changes

Japan was forced to create regulations and institutions which were necessary to cope with post-war economic conditions, which "many credit for the country's spectacular industrial rise in the 1950s and 1960s." These institutions "favored large producers over smaller ones, limited 'wasteful' competition, and guided capital investment and labor to chosen sectors." Owing to the stagnant economy or "lost decade" after the burst of the bubble, these traditional institutions have been under criticism for hampering entrepreneurship. Spurred on by criticism and the apparent stagnation of the economy "there has been talk of change for the last two decades, after serious study by numerous government working groups, such as the IT Strategy Council, by METI, by Japan's private and public financial institutions, and by private business groups such as *Keidanren* and *Keizai Dôyukai*." (Rowen and Toyoda 2002)

Government Support

After the collapse of bubble, which extended from 1980 to 1990, Japan suffered a lost decade. In 1990, many new IT companies emerged and new businesses were established, and those companies had a positive effect in many countries all over the world by producing services. Those companies, established in foreign countries and making an impact on the business world, were mostly venture companies, which are a new type of company. Many people explored the new business opportunities in foreign countries as business laws are more supportive of entrepreneurs than in Japan. In 2006, a new policy introduced by the Japanese government had a positive effect on people starting new businesses and becoming entrepreneurs. If there are more companies and the market is competitive, new products and services can be brought to market. In May, 2006, the Company Law (*kaishahô)* of Japan was revised by the Japanese government. The main feature of the new company law (*shinkaishahô)* was to make it easier to start a business.

In the past, there was a restriction on the minimum amount of the lower bond which had to be invested in order to establish a company under the old Commercial Code and Law for a *yûgen kaisha* or limited company. The new company law now states there is no need to invest 3 million yen or more for a limited company, or 10 million for a *kabushiki kaisha* (stock company). The minimum capital restrictions, which were supposed to protect creditors, were an obstacle to venture businesses or entrepreneurs. The restriction has now been abolished and it is possible to establish a company with only one yen – which gives rise to the term the *1 yen enterprise.* However, a new restriction applies to dividends. When equity falls below 3 million yen, the surplus cannot be divided in order to protect creditors.

Under the new company law, restrictions on similar corporate names were abolished. Under the old commercial law, if the company name was the same or similar to another company already registered in the same town, village, or business area; the new venture could not use that corporate name. This "corporate name restriction" prevented ill-intentioned violation of existing companies' rights and confusion in markets in the same area. Besides the abolition of restrictions on similar corporate names, the restrictions on the "purpose of business" have also been deregulated. As it was difficult to judge the clearness, legality, and concreteness of the company, it is no longer required in the new company law.

Moreover, the Certificate of Capital Deposition is no longer required. This certificate was issued by a bank and proved that a person had prepared a certain amount of money as the initial capital for their company. However, it took a long time, and some banks even refused to issue such a certificate. Under the New Company Law, the Certificate of Bank Balance can serve as proof of the initial capital – an important simplification.

Besides reforming company law, the Japanese government introduced the Angel Taxation System in 2008, which is a system that allows investors to invest in venture companies more easily. The expansion of the Angel Taxation System by the Japanese government is aimed at supporting newly established venture companies in Japan. The commencement rate of new companies against the total number of companies in Japan is only 3.5% (2001-04), which is low compared to 10% in the United States and the United Kingdom.

The key problem for venture companies is finance. Therefore, from 2008, by investing in a company established within the last three years, ten million yen will be treated as a donation and subtracted from income tax. This reduces the risk of venture investment by an individual and supports the entrepreneur financially. Under the current Angel Taxation System, owing to its unfavorable tax treatment, in 2006 only 1.3 billion was invested and only 100 companies had directly benefited from investment under the system since its establishment in 1997. However, in the UK, 20% of an investment is deducted from tax and annual investment is over a hundred billion. To improve the Angel Taxation System, the Japanese government decided to better the treatment of investors. The Ministry of Economy, Trade and Industry (METI) assumes that, if the Angel Taxation System becomes as popular as in the UK, thanks to improvements in 2008, an estimated 3,400 companies could find support over ten years, and some 40,000 new jobs will be created.

University-Industry Collaborations and Spin-offs

Universities can play a major innovative role in various industries. They can provide advanced research, help incorporate innovative ideas in new companies, and have excellent human resources. The United States has long had partnerships between universities and industry. In Silicon Valley, some faculty members in salient departments interact with industry as consultants and advisors to companies, serve on their boards of directors, and take short-term leaves of absence to work in industry. Compared to the United States, the number of Japanese university faculty members who interact with industry is fairly low. This is due to the policies set by the Ministry of Education, which limited national university faculties' involvement in companies (Rowen and Toyoda 2002). According to the Nikkei Weekly (2002), Japanese universities produced only 240 start-ups between 1980 and 2001 compared to 2,624 American university start-ups between 1980 and 2000.

University spin-offs (USOs) are a rather recent concept proposed by the government to create more start-ups. USOs can be businesses begun by university students, faculty members, alone, or in conjunction with private industry. They can also be businesses based on extensions of research done in the university by students or faculty. In the past, government regulations limited all interactions between professors and commercial organizations. Recently, government has begun making changes in order to foster university-industry collaborations (UICs). Some of the significant changes made by the government to help UICs were the 1998 law promoting the formation of Technology Licensing Offices (TLOs) within universities, the 1999 promotion of intellectual property management, the 1999 promotion of technology and business incubation facilities, the 2000 Law to Strengthen Industrial Technology, allowing faculty to take leaves of absence for business reasons, and the 2004 change of the organizational form of national universities, which enabled universities to become independent of the government (Rowen and Toyoda 2002, Hane 2004, Kazu 2007).

Before the formation of TLOs within universities, faculties of universities made informal arrangements with companies and usually did not bother to apply for invention patents, which gave exclusive rights on ideas to the companies. In this old structure of university-industry collaboration, university personnel were often bound exclusively to companies, which made it difficult for other interested companies to acquire opportunities the original company had decided not to pursue. After the 1998 law passed, many universities started to establish TLOs. The Law to Strengthen Industrial Technology in 2000 made it possible for faculty members, under certain circumstances, to be actively involved in working in a company or starting one up (Rowen and Toyoda 2002).

There is data supporting the claim that the loosening of rules and regulations that had once restricted UICs has been effective in creating an environment in which UICs can prosper. The improving environment has created a substantial rise in venture entrepreneurship, from invention to application (Hane 2004). The number of invention disclosures was particularly boosted in 1998 when the TLO law was introduced.

Another study concerning the development of USOs states that emerging R&D spin-off start-ups in Japan will play a key role in the long awaited paradigm change. These studies revolve around an interesting premise which states that Japan is being forced to change from the "how" mindset to the "what" mindset (Maeda 2004). The "how" mindset explains how the Japanese people were forced to deal with the question of "how" to re-build the economy after World War II. After the well-known success of the Japanese economy, the "how" mindset must change to "what" to do for the economy.

Recently, more analysts are emphasizing the need for university spin-offs especially in high-tech industries. The current situation in Japan can be compared to that of the United States in the mid-1970s to 1980s, when a rise in the number of entrepreneurs gave the United States economy a boost thanks to a "launching of many technology-based venture firms, in such fields as software, networking and telecommunications." (Lynskey 2004) As mentioned earlier, Japan has had three start-up booms that have lifted the economy after World War II. The boom from 1945 initiated many manufacturing start-ups, such as Sony and Honda, the boom in 1970 created service start-ups, and in the 1990s there were internet start-ups (Maeda 2004). The "what" mindset calls for the next series of start-ups to be in high-tech industries, that is, R&D start-ups. High-tech start-ups were not needed in the development of Japan's industries after the war and highly educated personnel were not interested in beginning their own start-ups or joining a start-up company.

The trend towards UICs and USOs has had a visible effect on the start-up environment of Japan. Studies estimate that

USOs will have an impact upon the economy amounting to some 364.2 billion yen and that they will create 25,858 jobs (Tsukagoshi 2007). A 2005 report by METI stated that Japanese USOs total 1,503 companies, some 25% in IT software, 23% in machinery & equipment, 10% in IT hardware, and 10% in material science (METI 2006).

Efforts by the government to increase the number of university spin-offs have proved to be effective as well. While in 1996 there were virtually zero USOs, 2003 ended with 190 recorded ventures. There was a rapid increase between 2000 and 2001 due to a government policy, which was implemented in 2001 to create 1,000 new USOs (Debroux 2007). In addition, METI granted 43.4 billion yen in 2003, 45.1 billion yen in 2004, 50.9 billion yen in FY2005, and 52.8 billion yen in 2006 (Tsukagoshi 2007).

There are many studies on the current trends for USOs. Most USOs have so far been unprofitable and some are not making any money at all. Other studies explain how Japanese university spin-offs are unlikely to play an important economic role in the short and medium term, but that their emergence is symptomatic of a number of deep changes in Japanese society and the economy (Debroux 2007).

New Image for Entrepreneurs

In 2004, the news was dominated by the struggle to purchase Kintetsu Baseball Team between Takufumi Horie, CEO of Livedoor, and Hiroshi Mikitani, CEO of Rakuten. This was the start of a media fascination with entrepreneurs. Besides competition to buy the team, the media also focused on the lifestyles of these successful entrepreneurs. Thus, the public became aware of the extravagant lifestyles and the revolutionary attitude of these businessmen.

Takafumi Horie, Hiroshi Mikitani, Susumu Fujita, CEO of Cyberagent, and Kaoru Uno, CEO of USEN, are major entrepreneurs in Japan today. They are all charismatic managers and have influenced Japanese society a great deal. Their entrepreneurship and ideas have spread among young people by means of the media. They contribute to the Japanese economy by producing a variety of IT services, such as internet shopping, internet access, web hosting, etc. The positive and revolutionary ideas of these entrepreneurs were reported on by the media on a daily basis, thus creating an entrepreneurial boom in Japan. However, a turning point came when Livedoor CEO Takafumi Horie was arrested for window-dressing financial results. The arrest of such a famous entrepreneur shocked Japanese society, and the media started to focus in on the negative side of entrepreneurs who were doing business in grey areas of the law. This negative business image of major Japanese entrepreneurs demolished the previous positive image and they started to be seen in a negative light. However, new entrepreneurs such as Kenji Kasahara, CEO of Mixi, have appeared and they are seen as the forerunners of a new wave of entrepreneurs. The newcomers will be scrutinized and provide an opportunity to regain trust back from society, as well as play an important role in the Japanese economy.

Mixi
Case Study

Mixi was established by Kenji Kasahara. It holds the largest market share in SNS (Social Networking Service) in Japan today. The service started in February, 2004, and it is one of the first companies to enter the SNS business in Japan. Social Networking Service is a service which allows people to communicate easily on the internet. It originated in the United States in the form of Friendster, which was created by a group of Stanford University graduates. The name

"Mixi" is a neologism that comes from "mix," which means to communicate, and "i," which means a human being. The special features of "Mixi" are blogging and the possibility of commenting on blogs. It is different from previous social networking services and the number of users is increasing rapidly.

Kenji Kasahara was born in 1975 in Osaka and graduated from Tokyo University's Faculty of Business Administration. When Kasahara was a junior at Tokyo University in 1997, he joined a management strategy seminar and studied the methods of several leading companies in the U.S. market. At that time there was an IT company boom and the case studies in his class concentrated on "Windows vs. Mac OS" and "Intel vs. AMD." Kasahara was interested in the strategies and the competition between the IT companies. Therefore, he read many books about the IT market at this time. Kasahara was fascinated by the IT market and especially by Microsoft. However, he knew nothing about computers. Therefore, he bought his first computer in his junior year, which is late compared to the other CEOs of venture companies. It is interesting that his encounter with IT was not through an interest in the technology, but from the study of a business model of a U.S. IT company.

From 1996 to 1997, there was boom among IT companies in Japan, such as Yahoo! Japan, Rakuten, and Amazon.com. At this time, Kasahara realized that he had to create a company brand. Therefore, he started to make a web site for his company called "Find Job!." Kasahara thought the advantage of the internet was the ability to locate specific information from a large number of sources and in real time. He thought these features could be best utilized by offering information on vacant positions. Actually, Kasahara did not receive any e-mails during the first month. However, he put more effort into the selling side and gradually the number of customers increased, which made him realize that this business would definitely grow. Kasahara established "eMercury" in 1999, and it launched him on the path to becoming an entrepreneur.

By making a profit from a business which offers job positions, he felt uneasy about the core business of his company. The number of companies registered could be increased by expanding sales. However, it is not easy to guide an applicant to the web site. If there are fewer applicants, then the number of companies registered will gradually decrease. Therefore, he started to work on making different web sites with the power to pull in applicants. In 2003, Kasahara turned his attention to social networking service (SNS), which was popular in the United States.

First, Kasahara started his SNS by making his own account at a United States SNS, and he noticed that it is an interesting way to develop real human relationships on the internet. However, he could not find the point of using this service continually after realizing that the fun of inviting people he knows fades after just one week. What prompted him to start "Mixi" was the idea of enriching the communication function so that people could communicate on a daily basis. Then, this service would have a big impact on society. He was fascinated by the attractiveness of such a service.

"Mixi" was started in February, 2004. There were only about six hundred registered users, most of whom were male. The first year was challenging, but the numbers drastically increased and reached 5 million in just two and a half years. In 2006, there were 5.2 million users and 2.8 billion hits a month.

"Mixi" is a free service and to join needs only an invitation from a current user. Kasahara and his team often make changes to satisfy the needs of the users. For example, they have added the "Mixi Premium Service," which provides a user with a larger capacity in order to upload pictures and files and save more messages on their Mixi account for a monthly fee of 315 yen. Furthermore, Mixi can be accessed from mobile phones using a service called "Mixi mobile." In September, 2007, there were some 63.4 billion hits. The number of Mixi mobile users is now higher than PC users, therefore, Kasahara is looking to increase advertising revenue from the mobile service. When Kasahara established "Mixi," there were just three people involved, including the CEO and the engineers. Today there are 194 employees. Kasahara has the philosophy that "good service and profit will coexist."

Woman Entrepreneurs

The role of women in Japanese society has shifted. There are studies showing the number of women joining the workforce. Tatsuyoshi Masuda (2006) found from research in the *Employment Status Survey* that there has been a steady increase in the number of female workers. He claims that this increase in female workers has "had a positive effect on latent entrepreneurship. Female workers have a strong willingness to take higher risks to be entrepreneurs in the near future."

Japan is currently suffering from a low birth rate and labor shortage due to an aging population (Brown 2007). The solution calls for women who have good educations and are capable of doing quality work. Public authorities have become aware of female entrepreneurs and their potential to stimulate the economy. Japanese women from 1997 to 2002 have started their own businesses at twice the rate of businesses initiated by Japanese men (Kanbayashi 2002).

In fact, 62.8% of start-up founders are men, whereas 37.2% are women. The number of "would be start-up founders" or prospective job-changers, and job seekers who want to be self-employed is even lower: only 31.6% are women, compared to 68.4% men (Small and Medium Enterprise Agency 2007). Reasons explaining this trend toward a higher number of female entrepreneurs include the idea that women in Japan have little obligation to give financial support to their families. This secondary societal position gives women an advantage in taking risks and taking on new challenges. Another explanation is that, since women are the main consumers in Japan, they understand the demands of consumers, which gives them business ideas from their daily lives (Brown 2007). Moreover, internet and mobile internet technology have made it easier for women to start businesses and manage their families at the same time. The topic of women entrepreneurship is grabbing a lot of attention and is considered to be one of the key factors changing business institutions.

Impact on the Economy

We believe that Japan has the necessary drive to cope with these changing times and, within the next two decades, will successfully build a framework similar to the United States, which supports and motivates elite members of society to work for start-up companies or to become entrepreneurs themselves.

There is already data existing supporting the claim that start-ups are increasing. Mentioned earlier was the increase in university-industry collaboration based start-ups. High-tech start-ups have also begun to emerge and are showing early signs of success. There are also estimates which claim that there will be more than 450 high-tech R&D start-ups alone by the year 2010. More and more elite human resources are deciding to be involved in these start-up companies to gain early stage development as a business specialist who is free from lay off. To cope with these changing times, there are indicators that companies are finally beginning to embrace the idea of spin-out entrepreneurs (Maeda 2004).

The current situation of Japan's entrepreneurial environment could be encapsulated by the phrase "time of change." As stated in this chapter, the government has undertaken efforts to improve the business environment and cope with Japan's long term economic stagnation. There have been positive effects from these measures to promote entrepreneurship, and individuals and organizations are responding to changing incentives to take new risks (Hane 2004).

Bibliography

Asahi Shimbun (2002): *Can Japan build up knowledge oriented country?*. Asahi Shimbun July 9, 2002.

Bosma, N. and R. Harding (2006): *Global Entrepreneurship Monitor GEM 2006 Summary Results.* BABSON, London Business School.

Brown, C. and Oakland, N. (2008): *Entrepreneurship; There are indications of global changes in venture businesses in Japan.* Downloaded from Graziadio Business Report 10(1), 2007.

Carstens, A. (2007): *Exploring Japan's true entrepreneurship potential.* Downloaded from http://globis.jp on January 30, 2008.

Debroux, P. (2007): *Innovation in Japan: what role for the university spin-offs?*. Research Paper, unpublished. Tokyo: Soka University.

Feigenbaum, E. A. and D.J. Brunner (2002): *The Japanese Entrepreneur: Making the desert bloom.* Tokyo, Japan: Nihon Keizai Shimbunsha.

Fukuda, M., Kasahara, E. and Teraishi, M. (2000): *Venture sôzô dainamikusu.* Tokyo: Bunshidô.

Hane, G. (2004): *Venture entrepreneurship in Japan.* Asia Program Special Report. Research Paper, Woodrow Wilson International Center for Scholars. Downloaded from http://www.wilsoncenter.org/ on February 15, 2007.

Helms, M. M. (2003): *Challenge of entrepreneurship in a developed economy: The problematic case of Japan.* Journal of Developmental Entrepreneurship, December 2003.

Kanbayashi, T. (2002): *Women work way up in Japan; Entrepreneurial spirit helps lift ailing economy.* The Washington Times, July 26, 2002.

Lynskey, M. (2004): *Knowledge, finance and human capital: The role of social institutional variables on entrepreneurship in Japan.* Industry and Innovation, December 2004.

Maeda, N. (2003): *Japanese innovation system restructuring with high-tech start-ups.* Working Paper, Stanford Japan Center.

Masuda, T. (2006): *The determinants of latent entrepreneurship in Japan.* Small Business Economics 26 (3), p. 227–240.

Motohashi, K. (2007): *Growing R&D collaboration of Japanese firms and policy Implications for reforming national innovation systems.* Asia Pacific Business Review, 14(3), p. 339-361

METI (2006): *Research report on growth support for USOs.* Ministry of Economy, Trade and Industry, Research Report.

Nikkei Weekly (2002): *University-origin start-ups aim at eventual listing.* Nikkei Weekly 2002.

Rowen, H. and A. M. Toyoda (2002): *From keiretsu to start-ups: Japan's push for high-tech Entrepreneurship.* Working Paper, Stanford University.

Small and Medium Enterprise Agency (2007): *White Paper on Small and Medium Enterprises in Japan.* Ministry of Economics, Trade and Industry of Japan.

Tsukagoshi M. (2007): *Expected role of business angels in seed/ early stage university spin-offs in Japan.* Unpublished.

Yasuda T. (2006): *Programs to stimulate start-ups and entrepreneurship in Japan: Experiences and lessons.* Presentation at the National Institute of Science and Technology Policy.

13. Employment Conditions of Japanese Women

By Yuuko Shimizu and Asako Washizu

This chapter discusses the employment conditions of Japanese women in the 21st century with reference to different secondary sources. Even as the world's second largest economy, Japan lies behind the rest of the industrialized nations in terms of the empowerment of women. This fact makes it important to conduct in-depth research on this topic. In the workforce, there is strong sexual discrimination against women, which makes it harder and more complicated for women to work as equally as men. The government of Japan is trying to change the laws to help ameliorate the harsh current conditions for women in the workforce, but the reality is that people's discriminating attitudes, which are deep set inside their minds towards women, haven't changed much. By looking back at the historical role of women role in society and the labor force, and how it has changed over time, the chapter answers the research question about what challenges Japanese women face. Moreover, it discusses the future outlook for women.

Traditional Employment Conditions of Japanese Women

Traditionally, Japan was a country that was not aware of the different roles men and women were to play in society. The enactment of a law by the government around the end of the 19th century to the beginning of the 20th century changed views on gender roles. This law is based on Confucianism, which believes that the leader of the household is the first son, and the rest of the members need to follow him. Moreover, it also believes that women have a lower social rank than men and are responsible for supporting the household. Thus, after the establishment of this law, society's understanding of gender roles changed so that males were the dominant part of the household and women were there to help. Yet, in the 20th century, when Japan was still an agricultural nation, both men and women needed to work together equally to support the household economy. After World War I, people were better-off and new attitudes entered society. Being an *okusan*, a full-time wife of a *salaryman*, a typical Japanese businessman working in the big cities, was a desired status for women. Girls and women were educated by their mothers to become more feminine so that they could get married to a *salaryman*, who would take care of them financially so that they could stay home and take care of the household. When the oil and dollar shocks hit in the early 1970s, women started to work outside the household again as part-timers to boost the family's income. Because housewives could not depend only on their husband's income anymore, the occupation of a *salaryman* degraded to being a normal and common status, and consequently being a housewife was no longer considered special or ideal (Masataka 2003).

Yet, the traditional view of women supporting the family still exists in society even in the 21st century as the Japanese word *kanai* suggests. *Kanai* is usually used by men to introduce their wives, meaning "in home," indirectly re-enforcing the idea that women are to stay home. On the other hand, when women refer to their husbands in public, they usually use the word *shujin*, which literally means the "master." The master is responsible for protecting and taking care of his wife and children economically and socially throughout his life. The social concepts of men and women are engraved in the Japanese language itself, which proves how people still accept these ideas as common understandings.

However, more women started to receive a higher education in universities, and they wanted to pursue a career. "There has been a shift in the enrolment of women in higher education away from two-year college programs to four-year university courses, and much of this shift occurred after 1986" (Rebick 2005, p. 115), which is the time since the Equal Employment Opportunity Law (EEOL) was established. However, what made it hard for these women to work was, first, the corporate culture that makes people work from the morning until midnight, requiring women, even those with children to take care of, to work the same amount as male colleagues. Second, "except for a few Western societies, in the rest of the world females are not granted the same opportunities as males, and do not enjoy the same privileges. The Japanese society, by all accounts, is still a strictly male society." (Fatehi 1996, p. 175) Thus, these social and corporate customs made prejudice against women in the workforce rise to the surface. The desired employment conditions of women and the corporate culture do not match, causing conflict between women's careers and their personal lives. Today, an increasing number of Japanese women enter the Japanese workforce and wish to establish successful careers, and they hope for changes in the harsh employment conditions that restrict their career paths.

The Equal Employment Opportunity Law

Japan has been facing the problems of a declining birth rate and an increasing number of aging workers who will soon be retiring. As the number of people aged sixty-five and up is growing rapidly, a good number of the labor force will be lost within the next decade. Another demographic issue is the falling fertility rate, which affects the pension system, as the labor force required to sustain the economy and retired workers will be reduced. In response to the demographic shifts, the government addressed the importance of increasing the fertility rate, to keep the nation from depopulating, by emphasizing the importance of female participants in the workforce. The government started to support females by implementing policies at firms and in public services to encourage childrearing and employment opportunities. Therefore, these measures boosted gender equality as more women entered the workforce. However, as analysts point out as essential to fixing the problems, a balanced private and work life as well as improvements in the working conditions of women are needed.

Since 1970, the number of women entering the workforce has increased. More and more women prefer to take a four year university degree instead of going to a traditional vocational school (*senmon gakkō)*, which was supposed to prepare them for marriage. Aiming for a degree in higher education meant that women started to build stronger ties between work and life, rather than the traditional roles that restricted them to family and household tasks. The improvement in women's roles indicated a change in the labor market as many headed towards higher employment opportunities instead of the simple tasks of photocopying and serving tea for men. In order to allow female participants to work even after marriage, there was a need to revise policies because there were limitations set upon female workers. As the current economic problems point out the need for improving working conditions for women, the issue has encouraged the Japanese government to support some employment policies.

Following the United Nations' Convention on the Elimination of all Discrimination against Women (CEDAW), the Equal Employment Opportunity Law (EEOL) was passed in Japan in 1986 to fulfill the purpose of having women join the workforce without being discriminated against due to their sex. The law was meant to improve the conditions of those seeking to pursue a career in the workforce, while serving the purpose of supporting the future economy of Japan. Frequent problems that arose in Japanese corporations were the wage gap and the meager opportunities for promotion as females were subject to discrimination. For the United Nations, CEDAW promoted the equality of women by drawing upon the importance of the participation of all workers in striving towards equal rights in society. Similar to CEDAW, the goal of EEOL was to enable females to feel secure about working at a firm by eliminating inequalities within the firm. By enforcing the labor law, the government hoped to provide better conditions for women as it tried to eliminate the differences created by the gender gap.

In Western nations, CEDAW had been responsible for strengthening the position of women. After the enactment of the policy, more females entered the workforce, achieving higher management positions in corporations. Western people have incorporated the policy into their lifestyles by reflecting on traditional work patterns; however, Japan has showed little improvement since the input of EEOL because of the closed nature of the employment system in Japan (Rebick 2005, p. 114). Even with the adoption of the policy, EEOL was not strictly enforced in companies and was initially considered a guideline rather than a requirement (Faiola 2007). According to the research findings of Tachibanaki (2005), the issue of discrimination is analyzed using two variables. First is the size of the wage gap between men and women. Second is the gap in the promotion between men and women. Therefore, identifying the problems of "female labor force participation" was important to understand why it is difficult to promote female participation in the workforce. One of the reasons why promoting women to certain positions is difficult is because EEOL had little effect on improving working conditions. Even if companies were not allowed to discriminate against participants by gender, Japanese companies worked around the law by distinguishing their workers through adopting a management system that categorized workers as *sōgōshoku* or *ippanshoku*. *Sōgōshoku*, the "career track," is usually reserved for men. The other option is *ippanshoku*, the "administrative track," that is usually offered to women, who are expected to quit their job after several years when they find a suitable partner to get married to. Although this "dual-track system of hiring" (Rebick 2005, p. 114) opened up more choices for women, other than working part-time, women working along this track never get promoted and their jobs include all the simple work, such as copying materials and serving tea for the male employees. This hiring system was designed for women, thus, these *ippanshoku* women were usually referred to as OLs, the office ladies. Evidently, this is unequal treatment that separates what men should do from what women should do in their jobs.

When observing the ratios of male to female employees working in *sōgōshoku* and *ippanshoku* tracks, it becomes obvious that most of the positions offered by Japanese companies are selected on the basis of gender. *Ippanshoku*, or in other words the "administrative track," is almost exclusively offered to women. The positions involved are secretarial or clerical in which they only do subordinate tasks. Females find the situation to be dead-end, as being placed into the *ippanshoku* track only makes the wage gap wider and restricts the possibility of receiving pay raises or promotion. Some of the discrimination is visible during the recruiting processes for college students, when meetings are held or information distributed by gender. In comparison, *sōgōshoku,* or "career track" jobs, are often taken by male workers who pursue long term careers in the company. Men are given opportunities to climb up to executive roles and the chances of receiving promotion are much higher than for women because it is an accepted social phenomenon that women will leave the workforce after marriage. Thus, most companies will refrain from placing women in higher positions, or even training them, because women are likely to quit. Therefore, very few women reach managerial positions because there are limited numbers of candidates who pursue that career track. Thus, the gender gap still prevails in Japanese companies as *sōgōshoku* positions are mainly given to men and *ippanshoku* positions to women in order to separate the workers.

Despite efforts to improve the position of women, EEOL did not immediately fix the gender gap problem as discrimination was openly accepted within the corporations. Workers were not selected equally based on capabilities and knowledge, and, therefore, it failed to serve its purpose of improving the working conditions of females as there were no penalties for violators. The problems with the law led to a revision of EEOL in 1997, when an attempt was made to fix some of the problems that the companies overlooked. More importantly, EEOL was revised once again in April of 2007, when it focused on both genders rather than on protection for women only. The revised law prohibited sexual harassment against both genders and discrimination through setting physical standards such as weight and height. It also continued to support women by prohibiting discrimination practices against pregnant mothers and mothers with babies in the form of wage cuts. As opposed to the earlier form of EEOL, which did not penalize violators, the revised law actively prevents firms from acting against the law.

The gender gap seen in working conditions proves that the labor law needs more time to take full effect. Even though 27 million females work at Japanese companies, pursuing a career is difficult when Japan still has stereotypical images of women assisting male workers. As there is substandard pay and fewer opportunities for promotion, pursuing a career has been difficult because men ultimately have had more opportunities to succeed. Wage levels between women and men appear unequal as overall wages for men are higher than for females. A possible interpretation for this is the difference in education, although more women are getting higher education, men still have higher degrees from university education than females, and, therefore, have better opportunities for promotion and salary increases. The types of jobs most commonly performed by females are clerical as opposed to males who take on high-level white collar and physical jobs (Tachibanaki 2007).

The United Nations Development Program (United Nations Department of Public Information 2008) has a method for measuring the inequalities between males and females using the gender empowerment measure index. The percentage of women taking senior corporate and political positions after the passage of the Equal Employment Opportunity Law in 1985 was 10.7% compared with 43% in the United States. According to the WEF (World Economic Forum), which released the 2006 Global Gender Gap Report, Japan dropped from last year's 38th to 79th place out of 115 nations surveyed. The survey shows that Japan ranks below other Asian countries such as China, Thailand, and Indonesia. Japan ranks low compared to the rest of the industrialized nations which have women holding high positions in political and managerial fields. Women lack economic participation and political empowerment and Japan ranks below other advanced nations (Ichimura 2007).

Compared with North American or European discrimination laws, Japanese laws are not strict about punishing companies that discriminate against their workers. Although the government wants to tackle the problems of a declining birth rate and increasing retirement, which is eroding the labor force, traditional attitudes still prevail as many older people with traditional minds have trouble removing stereotyped images of gender roles in society. Hakuo Yanagisawa, the health minister for former Prime Minister Abe, once publicly described women as "baby making machines," thus openly disrespecting the rights of women (BBC News 2007). The country wants to shift towards feminism, however, like Yanagisawa, there are people, usually older men with the most corporate power, who find it difficult to move away from the traditional Japanese roles in which men work and women stay at home.

Difficulties in Combining Family and Career

Working as a full-time employee at a Japanese firm means working long hours, starting from early morning, until late at night, in order to finish tasks. Especially in highly competitive and demanding workplaces, females will be treated equally. However, Japanese companies are hesitant to hire women into *sōgōshoku* positions, which pay higher salaries, because most women quit in the middle of their careers after marriage. Recruiting processes and training are expensive and time consuming so that men are better candidates because companies have to worry less about finding coverage. For women, this means that combining a successful career and a family is almost impossible. Women with a higher education, therefore, often delay marriage because leaving work would lower their standard of living. Having high paying jobs and working full-time, they do not have to depend on men because of their high incomes. The demanding working hours are a reason why most women cannot fulfill their dream of moving up to a managerial position because marriage, childrearing, and childcare require them to be committed to family duties more than work. Therefore, the average age of marriage is increasing as working women are aware that marriage and childrearing mean that they are less likely to return to work or maintain the same position in the job that they worked hard to achieve before (Nagase 2006). Thus, more women are postponing marriage until they reach a certain age, or staying single. This contributes to the decline in the fertility rate. Career lifestyles of Japanese women have changed the traditional patterns of marriage.

Still, the generally accepted idea is that men work and women protect the family. Thus, men are granted better treatment because the working hours for a full-time worker are long and tough on the worker. As a worker moves up the hierarchical chain of promotion, there would be more chance of being transferred to a different environment, which disrupts a person's private life. Moving with the family becomes very difficult, especially when a child is born. These obstacles stand in the way of married women because it blocks the path to maintaining stability in their lifestyles.

Economic pressure forced many women to take up work during the economic crisis. Many female workers were hired as part-time or contract workers after the bubble burst in the early 1990s as companies hired women as a cheap source of labor. Many thought positions would eventually improve into full-time jobs; however, today, Japan has a record 8 million part-time workers, more than 90% of whom are women (The Japan Times 2006). Rebick (2005) explains that there is a wage and opportunity gap between regular and non-regular participants. The part-time or temporary jobs common to females have fewer hours than full-time workers, and they have a lower hourly wage. The treatment of regular and non-regular workers is different in that career development is not promoted among non-regular employees, and it reproduces the old traditional system of distinguishing workers. The regular employee gains job security and is blessed with benefits, such as company housing, pensions, health coverage, and family benefits. However, non-regular employees, such as part-time workers or contract workers, need to renew annual contracts. Contracts for temporary workers could be terminated at any time so workers constantly face anxiety problems. As pay becomes a substantial difference between the employees, promotion and pay raises are given only to regular workers, some of whom are also granted bonuses.

Therefore, many women are committed to staying at home and raising the children until they reach a certain age, unless there is the cooperation of the spouse, which would allow the female to continue working as a full-time employee. When a family decides to consider childcare, the male spouse hardly ever takes leave because doing so could jeopardize his career prospects. Those women that desire to return to work after child rearing are interested in having part-time work because it is easier for them to balance work and family because of flexible working hours. According to a survey conducted by Erukomi, a popular Japanese website for women, in 2004, 85.6% of married women wanted to return to work. Common reasons were financial factors to support the family, increasing leisure time and obtaining freedom (Erukomi 2007).

As more females plan to return to the workforce, a good number of women in their late 20s and 30s prepare for new lifestyles. Many start attending classes so there would be a smoother transition in career change if they are unsatisfied with their current career. This trend has helped build up confidence among women as they concentrate on specialized areas of interest. It was common for people to take lessons, such as cooking and beadwork for self-improvement, or as a hobby in earlier times, however, licensed skills could help them get better positions. Strengthening skills would help women be in control of their future even after marriage when they go back to working (Maruko 2000). When a spouse is in control of their own life, they do not have to rely so much on the partner. The family could prosper more if the partner is able to support financially as well. It takes away pressure from the other partner. As Japanese people are slowly shifting attitudes towards gender roles, younger generations feel that women should work and not stay as housewives. Gender-based roles are slowly diminishing in that women also rely on their spouse for childrearing as well. If more women are able to strengthen their skills, it would help a great deal with their careers. This would continue to build a stronger image of women and their independence.

Japan's Tax Laws Prevent Women from Returning to Work

However, one barrier that keeps women from returning to the workplace is the "closed internal labor market and the tax and benefit system" of the Japanese firm, which is considered a way to keep women in part-time jobs, or positions that have lower wages (Rebick 2005, p. 121). A family is exempted from making payments to pension and health insurance if a spouse works a fixed amount of hours that is shorter than full-time work. If the part-time spouse's income exceeds 1.3 million yen, they would need to pay a fee for social insurance cover that is estimated to be around 200,000 yen. The fringe benefits that the full-time worker benefits from could also be taken away if a company finds out that the spouse working part-time is making more than the set amount. Therefore, many women are discouraged from become full-time employees because of the burden it enforces on the family. This system becomes problematic as it works against women's desire to work again.

There has been slow progress in making improvements in the working conditions of women. However, since labor is needed to sustain the economy and the government hoped that women would return to work, or stay in the workforce while raising a child, the government needed to come up with solutions. As in many industrializes countries, Japan still holds dear the ideal of a full-time mother and housewife. Japan needed to realize more measures to create systems where women could have childcare services that accompanied their working time so that a balance between private and work life could be arranged. In response to the problems, the government passed the Childcare Leave Law in 1992 to let a spouse concentrate on raising a child. Also, it allowed women to return to the workforce without having to worry about the consequences of being absent because they are excused. The system allows a member of a family to take leave from a company for up to a year to care for a child. Also, women with pre-school age children can be exempted from night work between 10 p.m. and 5 a.m. Under this policy, the government supports workers by providing up to 40% replacement earnings if the worker is covered by insurance: "Women who worked in firms that were covered by childcare leave were twice as likely to return to work at the same company, as those who were not, with 80% returning after a break." (Rebick 2005, p. 122) Another supportive policy that the government instituted was a policy known as the "Angel Plan." The purpose of the plan was to increase the availability of daycare centers for full-time working mothers by providing long opening hours. As there were many shortages in urban areas at the start of the plan, by 2004, the number of facilities had increased and it had become much affordable than before. The implementation of the laws encouraged shorter, more flexible working times at companies. Therefore, working conditions have become much more tolerable for people with children.

As the traditional roles of females have undergone many changes, so has their ability to participate in the labor force along with men. Some of the problems for working mothers are daycare programs that do not assist them as their closing time is too early. Most women find that the well-being of the family is left to females. However, juggling both a career and a private life is difficult as working in a Japanese company means that a worker must be dedicated to their work. Traditional Japanese society had strong relationships between neighbors and families, and it enabled females to go out to work while a child was being cared for by a member of the community. However, nuclear families have become increasingly common in today's society and more and more people have trouble depending on other people. Now that more companies are implementing services that offer childcare or rehiring women who leave to get married, not only does it respond to labor shortages, it relieves financial worries as well. Some companies, such as Nissan, have taken measures to improve working conditions by introducing flextime (Suzuki 2006). It would be a waste of labor if a company cannot recruit highly educated women. Thus, firms are appealing to mothers who have the desire to work again through better working conditions (Rebick 2005).

Challenges in Pursuing a Career

Despite all these barriers, more and more Japanese women are entering Japanese companies with the aim of building successful careers. According to surveys by the Japan Productive Centre for Socioeconomic Development, the ratio of female workers who upon joining a company aspire to take up executive positions has increased. It has jumped from 8% in 1976 to 21.2% in 2005 (Kitazume 2007). Since the 1980s and 1990s, the number of working women in the potential female labor force has increased steadily. Among those women under the age of sixty-five, 60.3% were working in 2004, which is an increase from 52.5% in 1980. The ratio of women with children from age zero to three who work has increased too, from 29.3% in 1990 to 32.5% in 2004. These statistics show that support for women, such as EEOL, which was implemented in the 1980s and 1990s, has helped to increase the number of women entering the workforce (Ministry of Economy, Trade and Industry 2005). This proves that barriers still exist in male dominated organizations to women pursuing a career. The present state of job hunting among prospective graduate students for new graduate enrollment in companies also shows the increasing desire to work. The number of female students in their senior year of university receiving a *naitei*, which is an informal notice of a hiring decision by a company, topped that for male students. According to the career centre at Rikkyo University in Tokyo, the increase in the female intake by corporations has motivated university students to enter larger enterprises (Nihon Keizai Shimbun 2006). However, pursuing a career is not an easy task and there are numerous challenges that need to be overcome in order to pursue a career in a Japanese corporation.

Lack of Support for Child-Rearing

There is a desperate need for female labor in Japan. However, what makes it hard for women to work continuously is the lack of support from the government for child-bearing and child-rearing. Although the Japanese government passed the Angel Plan in 1994 and the Child and Child-Rearing Support Plan in 2004, hoping to increase the fertility rate, there has been no obvious effect so far. There is a conflict between work and private life that restricts women from having both work and family. In the current situation, it is predictable that working women with children will have a rough time trying to figure out how to balance work and time with children, especially when the number of childcare centers does not meet demand.

The government mentioned in 2001 that, "While there are currently 33,000 children on day-care waiting lists, the number actually needing the service could be as high as 100,000 because many parents have given up applying." (The Japan Times 2001) This suggests a need for more supportive plans, particularly a higher number of childcare centers with flexible opening hours and with reasonable fees. Also, companies need to protect employment positions or posts during maternity leave. The lack of support for maintaining a career and child-rearing is the most common reason why women feel a barrier to continuing their work (Ministry of Health, Labour and Welfare 2002).

Traditional Assumptions about the Labor Division

As emphasized above, the labor environment in Japan is still based on tradition and on the assumption that men work and women stay home to take care of the family. Thus, the new era of women working together with men contradicts this rigid stereotypical cultural thinking and, hence, the rules that governed companies for decades. Because of these contradictions, women face several challenges when pursuing a career. Thus, pursuing a career means working on the *sōgōshoku* track, while working up the hierarchy in management. A survey conducted by the Ministry of Health, Labor and Welfare among women in the *sōgōshoku* track, showed that 35.0% of subjects were "somewhat unsatisfied" and 7.1% were "very unsatisfied" with their work. The main reasons for this are they are not challenged by or rewarded for their jobs, and they can not hope for future promotion and wage increases. Moreover, the survey showed that 60% of women feel a gap between themselves and their male colleagues in terms of promotion, pay, and the jobs given (Ministry of Health, Labor and Welfare 2002). This traditional barrier leads to the further problem of a glass ceiling.

Glass Ceiling

There is a glass ceiling when pursuing a career, which is clearly shown by the Gender Gap Index measurement that was conducted worldwide. According to the World Economic Forum, the Gender Gap Index assesses countries on how well they are dividing their resources and opportunities among their male and female populations, regardless of the overall levels of these resources and opportunities (World Economic Forum 2008). In 2007, Japan was ranked 91st out of 128 nations measured. Moreover, Japan dropped in the rankings from 80th in the previous year, especially because of several categories regarding labor conditions that scored very low. The four major categories are: first, Japan has a low ratio of women participating in parliament; second, there is a low ratio of women working as assembly members, executives, or managers; third, there is low participation of women in the workforce; fourth, women earn lower incomes than men for the same job (Ichimura 2007).

As the Gender Gap Index proves, Japanese employment conditions are still unequal, thus confirming that, "females are not given prominent roles in business and government." (Fatehi 1996, p. 175) This also leads to limited promotion and a wage gap between the two genders in the same country. Kazuo Koike, a former professor from Hōsei University, says that, although there are exceptions, continuity of work is lower for women than men on average. To be able to know whether a particular woman would stay and work long in a company would be difficult and costly. Thus, realistically, men stay longer in one company, allowing them to take part in long-term, on-the-job training courses. Thus, differentiation between men and women occurs, and a wage gap is created. He concludes that companies prefer to hire men more than women based on the good of the company (Nishiyama 2007).

Sexual Harassment

Women also face sexual harassment in the workplace. Although views toward sexual harassment, which includes speech and action against women's wellbeing, have changed in recent years, many women are still unable to speak out and get help. Professor Noriko Hama, economics professor at Kyoto's Doshisha University, commented about a harassment suit "…the older generation of salarymen, who in the past tended to be pretty blinkered and knew that as long as they remained loyal to their company, then nothing else mattered and they could get away with almost anything." (Ryall 2006) This was the traditional way of thinking before the word "sexual harassment" spread in Japanese society in 1989. The word is now used familiarly in Japanese in the abbreviated form *sekuhara*. In a government survey conducted in 1997, "more than 60% of women claimed to have witnessed sexual harassment in their workplace. Sixty per cent also claimed to have been the recipient of unwanted speech or actions (usually from a superior) at some point." (Rebick 2005, p. 119) After the introduction of the new word and the concept, women were inspired to stand up for their rights and equality. There have been cases where women sued the harasser. According to a survey conducted by the Tokyo Metropolitan Government (2006), 21.5% of women had experienced sexual harassment, 14.9% had experienced something similar, but were not sure, and 31.7% had seen or heard about such harassment in the workplace. These three different answers total up to 68.1%, which is higher than the 41.8% of workers who had never seen or heard of sexual harassment. On the other hand, only 3.6% of male workers have experienced sexual harassment. These statistics show that women are more likely to be harassed as the harasser believes that women are in a weaker position and that they are unable to fight against it. If they do speak up, it may affect their potential promotion and work, especially when the harasser is the boss or manager.

Current Developments of Female Employment in Japan

As explained above, it is difficult to combine career and family in Japan. While trying to reform some working conditions for women, the Japanese government is also attempting to fix the two major problems that it faces now: the low fertility or birth rate and the fall in population.

The Low Birth Rate Improves Working Conditions for Women

Since the declining birth rate causes shortages in the labor supply, working conditions for women are to be improved to bolster the labor force. The fertility rate shows the number of children a woman will bear in her lifetime. While the rate was 2.13 in 1970, the lowest level in recent years was only 1.26 in 2005. In 2006, the rate increased to 1.32 due to economic recovery in Japan. Yet, the rate is still insufficient to maintain former population levels. Here, we will discuss the fertility rate and suggest some solutions to this social and economic problem.

There has been an argument that an increasing number of working women leads to a declining birth rate. It is believed that an increasing number of working women means these women are not going to marry or that they will marry later in their lives, and, thus, have less time to spend on child rearing, or will not have a child at all. It is partially true that career-minded women could contribute more to the birth rate. However, it is easy to counter this argument if we look at the examples of France and Sweden, countries which have seen a recovery in their birth rates, despite increasing numbers of working women, because of reforms conducted by the government and corporations. These two countries are also known for achieving equal rights for both men and women in the labor force. In France, the fertility rate rose from 1.66 in 1994 to 2.0 in 2006 as the government started to support working mothers as from the 1990s. France also allowed maternity leave of up to three years, with the protection of one's position in the company before leave, and maternity payments based on regular income (Hokkaido Shimbun 2008). There are many other reforms France conducted in bringing the fertility rate to 2.0, putting less pressure on working parents as regards child-rearing and effectively balancing out work and family life. Japan needs to work towards such reforms.

Maruo (2006) summarizes three reasons behind the increase in fertility rates in countries that have been suffering from low rates for years. First, the changes in market economies, systems, and public consciousness that occurred after more women were involved in the workforce are integrated into the society. Thus, conservative nations like Japan that "stick to traditional status relations and gender-based roles" will have low fertility rates that are likely to continue dropping. Second, the rate goes up when the government "spends a larger share of gross domestic product on support of child care." For example, "North European countries spend 2.9 to 3.8 percent of GDP on support of child care," but Japan only spends 0.6 percent. Third, another major contribution to the fertility rate are the prospects for the economy. If people are optimistic about the economy and employment, more couples will have babies as they think they can afford the money needed to raise their children. Thus, considering these three inter-related reasons, it is crucial to improve the economic situation as well as the emotional burden of child-rearing for working women. Supporting these women through government spending to create a better system is needed in order to increase the fertility rate again (Maruo 2006).

Concerns can also be observed among members of the Japanese government. Kuniko Inoguchi, the former cabinet minister in charge of gender equality, commented that "birth rates here are declining because of the lack of equality for women" and also company representatives such as the management of Teijin (see case study below) refer to studies "showing that nations with greater workplace participation, like the United States, actually have higher fertility rates." (Fackler 2007b) Thus, the fertility rate has not been decreasing because of more participation of women in the labor force, but because of a lack of understanding in the government for women who have dual lives at work and in the home. Learning from countries such as Sweden, which has successfully turned around its birth rate, is necessary to improve the situation in Japan. Among the many reforms that helped Sweden and France to increase the birth rate, while reinforcing equal working rights and opportunities for women, was that of flexible child care, which Japan lacks. This is one of the solutions that will solve both women's problems when having a child and the country's decreasing population. The main reason for quitting a job is child-rearing. Research conducted by The Cabinet Office showed that in double-income households, between the ages of twenty to thirty-four, women do most of the housework and child-rearing, while men depend on their family to do such duties (The Cabinet Office 2003). Thus, when a working woman has a child, it is important to support her by giving her a hand in taking care of the child.

The traditional reason behind the statistics mentioned above is the assumption that men work to bring in the income to support the family, while women take care of the household and perhaps work as a part-timer for additional income. However, this assumption does not fit the current situation in

Japan, as more people, including both men and women, are working as part-timers, and women are taking full-time jobs. When it comes to having a child, time becomes extremely valuable. While the traditional mode of operation of Japanese companies requires workers to work long hours, being a parent would not allow you to do so. Therefore, more effective working styles are required and need to be implemented, such as working at home, flextime work, longer childcare leave, and a more acceptable job-return system.

Labor Shortages Increase Women's Career Chances

Another fear that Japan faces is the labor shortage resulting from a decreasing population. Moreover, Japan is a country that does not accept immigration, which limits the labor supply further. Currently, there is a strong anti-immigration policy. Foreign workers only account for 1% of the overall Japanese labor force. According to the Organization for Economic Cooperation and Development (OECD), the number of foreigners working in Japan in 2004 was 192,000. Compared to other advanced nations, this number is very low. For example, in the United Kingdom, although its population is only half that of Japan's, the number of foreign workers is seven times greater (Maruyama 2007). If Japan does not change its immigration policy, the labor force will keep on decreasing if the fertility rate does not drastically change within a few years—which is unlikely to happen.

With a decreasing population, the Japanese economy would be in jeopardy. Since 1998, there has been a marked decrease in the labor force (Ministry of Economy, Trade and Industry 2005). The Health, Labor and Welfare Ministry estimates that by 2030 the labor force will decrease by 10.7 million (The Japan Times 2007). The number of workers or those looking for a job aged 15 and above will decrease from 66.57 million now in 2006 to 55.85 million in 2030. This estimate suggests a dreadful economic situation in Japan. That is, due to less labor, pension payments will decline and as fewer people earn income, consumption will fall causing financial difficulties. Hence, government will increase taxes and decrease administrative services to bridge the gaps (Nihon Keizai Shimbun 2007b). Along with the estimated decrease in labor, the ministry also announced shortfalls in economic growth of 1% every year. The Japanese government is now trying to improve working conditions for women in order to avoid shrinkages in the labor force. The fact that 70% of women quit their job at the time of giving birth re-enforces the importance for companies to take some measures to return those women to the workforce after child-bearing and child-rearing. If helping working women increases the fertility rate in the future, it would automatically increase the population. Thus, improvements in working conditions must be quickly enforced.

Teijin
Case Study

Teijin is a polyester fibers business group with head offices in Osaka and Tokyo. The corporate philosophy of Teijin is to enhance the quality of life through a deep insight into human nature and needs. It does this successfully by delivering a message that there are ways in developing chemical technologies that are both people and environmentally friendly. Teijin actively supports the promotion of female employees. The company aims at recruiting at least 30% of university graduates to join the workforce and hopes to add more diversity to the company. It also sets goals in tripling the number of females in managerial positions. It currently sponsors forums that promote awareness of the work-life balance in order to support the fertility rate.

According to a survey of firms in 2007, Teijin ranked 13th, up from 27th in the previous year, as it improved services for people with children. It encouraged women to take maternity leave without taking away their benefits. Teijin also focused on encouraging male workers to participate in childcare and it started to pay workers during the days they were absent. It also allowed its workers to build strong family ties as Teijin implemented a system where, in case of transfer, the spouse is also found a job. Transferring makes it difficult for a spouse to work and some families live separately because of the problems. Therefore, Teijin tries to minimize the stress on both the worker and the spouse.

In 2001, Teijin introduced a policy called "Hello Again," which attempted to bring back workers who had quit to have children. Since its introduction, four female workers were assigned full-time positions. Teijin will not only focus on female participants, but also try to apply principles that would incorporate foreigners, the elderly, and the disabled. As xenophobia and bias still exist in Japanese companies, Teijin's principles would open the doors for many as they hire people from diverse backgrounds. With this strategy, Teijin tries to portray that the firm is openly creating an environment that would encourage the development of both workers and company as they introduce principles to create a good working environment.

Increasing Company Awareness

Many diversification systems have been suggested and more companies are incorporating them, such as Nissan Motors, P&G, and Teijin. However, there are many other companies that have not taken any action. One solution would be abolishing the dual-track hiring system. There are several jobs, such as construction work, which are more efficiently performed by men, but labeling women as *ippanshoku* is discrimination towards women as it segregates men and women in work and limits those women to simple tasks. Mitsui Sumitomo

Bank, as the first main bank in Japan, announced that would abolish *ippanshoku* from summer 2008. The bank decided to hire two thousand temporary staff working in branch offices as full-time workers. These workers will be categorized in a new division, the "Business Career" track, doing mainly office work as done by *ippanshoku* track workers. Of course, those already in the *ippanshoku* track may remain there and be categorized as "Business Career" track workers. The company is also offering a further full-time category known as the "Consumer Service" track, in which the salary could go up yearly depending on the knowledge the worker has, and there is also possible promotion to managerial posts. If more companies decide to install a new system to increase motivation like Mitsui Sumitomo and abolish *ippanshoku*, it would create greater opportunities for working women. This is only the first small step taken by the company and more time will be needed to adjust the corporate system in order to accept more career-minded women into the workforce (Asahi Shimbun 2007).

Creating Role Models for Women

Although there are successful women in Japan, who build their own companies and who hold executive posts in major companies, the sad reality is that most women do not feel that there is role model for them. Kahoko Tsunezawa, the founder and president of Trenders Inc., runs workshops helping women to set up in business. She comments, "From now on, women will be required to manage and lead other women. But right now, there is very little know-how in Japan on how women can lead. There are no role models for women." True, there are no strong female leaders currently, as Yumiko Ehara, professor of sociology at Tokyo Metropolitan University, verifies by saying, "The leading female prime ministerial hopeful Seiko Noda has lost her clout, and (ex-Foreign Minister) Makiko Tanaka is out of the picture, I don't see anyone rising to the top post within the next 10 years." (Otake 2006)

The article above emphasizes the fact that there few female leaders in Japan to positively influence other women in the country. While Japan waits for a new female leader to appear, Japanese companies should work on building role models within their organization to motivate the workers. In Mizuho Financial Group, the number of prospective female graduates wishing to work as *sōgōshoku* has increased by 50% over the previous year, showing the changing attitudes of women towards their working styles. Shuzo Haimoto, corporate officer and personnel manager from Mizuho Financial Group, commented that it is important for new employees to improve themselves by observing their *sempai*, the seniors working in the company. Thus, there is a need for female role models for new employees to follow. He, therefore, stated that training to understand career women is needed. Overall, he plans to promote his "4R" plan, which stands for "recruit" women, "raise" them, "retain" them in the company and "relate" them to their *sempai* and bosses, in order to push for efficient acceptance of more women in the workplace (Nihon Keizai Shimbun 2006). Besides Mizuho, there are other companies that are trying to build role models within the organization.

Conclusion

Changes happen slowly within Japanese corporations and society. Looking back at the time before the first EEOL was established until the current day, conditions have not changed drastically in a way that women are more comfortable and capable of working in the Japanese workforce. "The government hopes to increase the percentage of women in managerial positions at private and public organizations, and in professions such as doctors, to 30 percent by 2020." (Nakamura 2007)

First, it is important to notice that views on marriage and work need to match the actual reality of society. Labeling different tasks and work for men and women is the first step in creating inequality between the two genders. As for the employment conditions of Japanese women, it is not easy to change corporate and social views. Thus, second, what is needed in today's society is a gradual change towards diverse working styles and choices.

The economic situation in the future is unpredictable. Data from the Ministry of Public Management, Home Affairs, Posts and Telecommunications on the satisfaction rate in Japanese society in 1999 shows that only 35.2% of people are satisfied, down 8.3% in five years. The Japanese satisfaction rate is ranked third bottom among the eleven countries surveyed worldwide, showing a pessimistic view among Japanese towards their country (Ogi 1999). The increasing number of late marriages and double income families are also an indication of women not being dependent on men for their living income. Women earn their own income, and are also capable of supporting the family, which is a drastic change from the past. Despite stronger independence, it is interesting to see that an increasing number of women in their twenties see advantages in marriage, while fewer women from age thirty to thirty-four do so according to a survey conducted by National Institute of Population and Social Securities Research (Shimizu 2007).

However, the focus of this chapter has been the working women who wish to establish a career. It is important for a company to support the career tracks of these women so that they can reach managerial posts, as well as for the government to support them in achieving equality in the workforce and maintaining a balance between work and life. As Carlos Ghosn, CEO of Nissan and Renault, stated, "Companies make better decisions when women are involved in decision-making." (The Japan Times 2006) As the fertility rate improved in 2006, there is hope that it will continuously grow to keep the Japanese economy and employment stable in the next decade. Moreover, it is crucial for the government to support not only women's welfare, but also the welfare of male employees in order to aim for the diversification of work and life in the future.

Because great attention has been paid to the problems that Japanese working women are facing, conditions will slowly, but gradually improve in the future so that a balance between work and lifestyles is achieved for working women. Although this change in society is not for feminist reasons, but for demographic reasons, more studies on balancing work and personal lives must be conducted to open up the narrow career path for ambitious women in business. Women are not trying to compete against males in this gender-based society. Instead, they are hoping for culture and corporations to change to allow them to achieve a balance between work and personal lives. The need of Japan to become like other industrialized countries must be stressed. We hope Japan will gradually achieve a gender-free society in which there is no discriminatory division of work between men and women, as well as improving on problems such as a low fertility rate and decreasing population. When these problems are all resolved, the future will be brighter for Japanese women.

Bibliography

Asahi Shimbun (2007): *Haken nissen nin o seishain ni mitsui sumitomo ginkô -ippanshoku-wa haishi e.* Asahi Shimbun, December 7, 2007.

BBC News (2007): *Japan women called child machines.* Downloaded from http://www.bbc.co.uk on January 27, 2007.

The Cabinet Office Japan (2003): *Defure shita de kawaru jukunen no katei seikatsu.* Whitepaper. The Cabinet Office Japan. 2003.

The Daily Yomiuri (2007): *Japanese women "still seen as cheaper labor."* The Daily Yomiuri, August 2, 2007.

Erukomi (2007): *Hatarakitai onnatachi e kaji-ikuji to no baransu ga kimete.* Sankei Living. Downloaded from http://www.lcomi.ne.jp/.

Fackler, M. (2007a): *Career women in Japan find a blocked path, despite equal opportunity law.* The New York Times, August 6, 2007.

Fackler, M. (2007b): *Japan's glass ceiling held firmly in place; Toothless law no match for traditions.* The International Herald Tribune, August 6, 2007.

Faiola, Anthony. (2007): *Japanese working women still serve the tea; despite hopes for change as their ranks have grown, discrimination persists.* The Washington Post, March 2, 2007.

Fatehi, K. (1996): *International management: a cross-cultural and functional perspective.* Prentice Hall.

The Hokkaido Shimbun (2008): *Furansu Shôshika taisaku.* The Hokkaido Shimbun Press. Downloaded from http://www5.hokkaido-np.co.jp/motto/20060812/ on January 30, 2008.

Ichimura, K. (2007): *2007 nen no danjo byôdô shisû nihon, 91 kurai no kôtai.* Nihon Keizai Shimbun. November 9, 2007.

Ikeda, D. (2006): *Equal rights for women.* The Japan Times, June 13, 2006.

Japan Times (2001): *15,000 more day—care centers vowed.* The Japan Times, May 24, 2001.

Japan Times (2006): *Unfinished business for women.* The Japan Times, March 20, 2006.

Japan Times (2007): *Workforce may shrink by millions by 2030.* The Japan Times, November 29, 2007.

Kageyama, Y. (2007): *Diversity at Nissan; what's driving women at Japanese carmaker.* Newsday, July 29, 2007.

Kitazume, T. (2006): *Population Symposium—Environment, not career major hurdle to big families.* The Japan Times, November 9, 2006.

Kitazume, T. (2007): *Population woes said best served by adding women.* The Japan Times, October 2, 2007.

Mami, M. (2000): *Young women study up for the future.* The Japan Times, May 11, 2000.

Maruo, N. (2006): *Birth rate born of optimism.* The Japan Times, November 6, 2006.

Maruyama, H. (2007): *Nihon kigyô gaikokujin saizô wazuka 1%.* Nihon Keizei Shimbun December 3, 2007.

Masataka, N. (2003): *Keitai o motasu saru.* Chûô kôron shinsha.

Mees, H. (2007): *Countries pay high price for gender gap.* The Japan Times, September 3, 2007.

Ministry of Economy, Trade and Industry (2005): *Danjo kyôdô sankaku ni kan suruchôsa – josei ninzai katsuzô to kigzô no keiei senryaku no henka ni kan suru chôsa.* Research Report on Gender Equality, June 2005.

Ministry of Health, Labor and Welfare (2002): *Heisei 14 nenban—Hataraku josei no jisseki.* Research Report on the Contemporary Situation of Working Women.

Nagase, N. (2006): *The changing Japanese family.* Routledge.

Nakamura, A. (2007): *Work-life imbalance said birth rate's key foe.* The Japan Times, September 6, 2007.

Nakamura, M. (2006): *Time to end indirect discrimination.* The Nikkei Weekly, March 13, 2006.

Nakamura, A., Matsubara, A. and Ueno, Y, (2007): *Work to raifu chôwa o motomete ikukyô mama ni shanai jôhô.* Nihon Keizai Shimbun, November 9, 2007.

Nihon Keizai Shimbun (2006): *Hirogaru jôsei saiyô kigyô no honki mikiwametai —katsuyôsaku, kakegoe yori nakami.* Nihon Keizai Shimbun, October 23, 2006.

Nihon Keizai Shimbun (2007): *Nisodate shien taishô tokushû.* Nihon Keizai Shimbun, December 12, 2007.

Nihon Keizai Shimbun (2007): *Shôshika rodô shijô kaikaku.* Nihon Keizai Shimbun, November 9, 2007.

Nihon Keizai Shimbun (2007b): *Rodôsha jinkô 2030 nen ni 1000 man ningen.* Nihon Keizai Shimbun, November 29, 2007.

Nihon Sangyô Shimbun (2007): *Hatarakiyasui kaisha 2007 sôgô jôi yakushin kumi ni kiku teijin.* Nihon Sangyo Shimbun, September 2007.

Nishiyama, A. (2007): *Jôsei sabetsu no kongen wa koko ni aru.* Nikkei Business, September 19, 2007.

Ogi, N. (1999): *Gakkyû hôkai o dô miru ka.* NHK Books.

Otake, T. (2006): *Equality still has a long way to go.* The Japan Times, March 12, 2006.

Pesek, W. (2007): *A failure to innovate.* The International Herald Tribune, February13, 2007.

Rebick, M. (2005): *The Japanese employment system.* Oxford: Oxford University Press.

Ryall, J. (2006): *Harassment suit puts salaryman on notice; A new generation of Japanese working women won't tolerate "high jinks" of old.* South China Morning Post, May 4, 2006.

Sakakibara, N. (2007): *Birth rate lessons from Germany, Italy.* The Daily Yomiuri, May 10, 2007.

Shimizu, O. (2007): *Dansei erabi yori ikikata.* Nihon Keizai Shimbun, November 10, 2007.

Shoji, K. (2007): *Allure of cakes too much for housewives to resist.* The Japan Times, July 10, 2007.

Suzuki, J. (2006): *Companies court women with children as workforce shrinks.* The Japan Times, April 14, 2006.

Tachibanaki, T. (2005): *Why do government policies fail to promote female participation?.* Research Report. Research Institute of Economy, Trade and Industry. Downloaded from www.rieti.go.jp.

Tokyo Metropolitan Government (2006): *Kigyô ni okeru josei koyô kanri to sekusharu harasumento no torikumi nado ni kan suru chôsa.* Report on Sexual Harrassment Tokyo Metropolitan Government 2006.

United Nations Department of Public Information (2008): *Short History of CEDAW Convention.* Downloaded from http://www.un.org/womenwatch/daw/cedaw/history.htm on January 29, 2008.

World Economic Forum (2008): *Gender Gap Index.* Downloaded from www.weforum.org on January 30, 2008.

14. The Japanese Firm as an Intercultural Workplace

By Nodoka Kobayashi, Kaoru Miki, Delphine Pilate

Looking back at the history and the current situation of foreign workers in Japan, the working environment on these small Asian islands has changed gradually, and today there are many foreigners working in Japan who have steadily diversified their tasks. In this chapter, we aim to examine Japan as a multinational workplace and analyze the current situation and changes being observed. This topic is particularly interesting as today more and more workers are recruited from overseas to work in Japanese companies. While many aspects concerning this phenomenon have changed, the prime motivation for attracting foreigners still remains the increased push towards internationalization, bringing in language skills, or just for the transfer of job-related skills. Although it is easier to hire a Japanese mid-career manager these days, due to the recession and a growing labor shortage, and the fading tradition of lifelong employment in Japan, a mid-career foreigner will be able to fulfil the expectations without doubt. Today, such people do not only work for foreign companies, but they are also commonly recruited as non-regular employees in Japanese companies. Indeed, as it is often assumed that they will leave the company after a certain period of time, they might be treated differently as regards working conditions and pay. However, if they are expected to stay, they will be recruited as regular employees (*seishain*), which will give them the possibility of promotion to management positions. Nonetheless, a person from abroad will often have the feeling that the Japanese company has no idea of how to take advantage of the qualities they provide. The fact that the overseas employee does not experience any involvement in the workplace, especially in all the general management decision-making, will often lead to frustrations, which will also be discussed in this chapter. Although foreigners can still typically be found in English-speaking jobs (e.g. English teachers, tasks involving correspondence, translation, or rewriting), we will discuss all white collar workers.

First it is necessary to trace the entry of foreigners into the Japanese market in order to talk about the multinational workplace and foreigners working in Japan, since Japan comprises four large islands and is almost a mono-ethnic nation-state. According to Japan Times Job, the history of foreign companies starting businesses in Japan dates back to the end of the Edo period and the mid-19th century. At that time, Japan had finally opened its doors to foreigners after more than 200 years of a closed-door policy in the Tokugawa period. Fearing the threat of foreign powers trying to enter Japan, it had isolated itself from the rest of the world. This period helped to develop Japanese culture and its way of thinking. In 1859, a British trading company importing alcohol, such as whisky, established an office in Yokohama. Also, the forerunner of the Dutch Bank, the Dutch Trading Chamber of Commerce, opened an office in Nagasaki. After that, many foreign companies followed, and, during the Meiji period, in 1902, City Bank started business in Japan with an office in Yokohama. Food companies such as Nestle and chemical companies such as Bayer entered Japan around that time as well. From the Taisho to the Showa period, at the beginning of 20th century, large companies such as American Express, Ford and General Motors entered the Japanese market. Still, it has to be noted that those companies were exceptions, as the fraction of worldwide FDI that Japan acquired at the beginning of the 20th century was extremely low, being barely some 0.2% (Yuzawa 1990). In 1937, IBM Japan was established as the largest foreign company ever. At the start of the Pacific War, foreign companies stopped entering Japan for a while, but as soon as the war ended, the trend resumed. Between 1950 and 1960, global companies such as Coca Cola, General Electric, and Philips established Japanese corporations, one after another. Especially after the Japanese government announced the liberalization of stocks, the number of foreign companies entering Japan increased, and in 1973 McDonald's opened its first restaurant in a big department store in Ginza. From 1970 to 1980, IT companies such as Intel, Apple Computer, and Microsoft began entering the market, and, later, at the time of the Japanese bubble economy, foreign banks opened offices in Japan in quick succession. After the bubble burst, service and retail companies also entered the Japanese market, for example, Toys-R-Us and HMV. This brought a new culture to young people as many mega-retail outlets, fashion brands, and restaurant businesses opened new stores all over Japan (Japan Time Jobs 2008). As mentioned above, from a Western point of view, foreigners and especially foreign companies were motivated to come to Japan because most were conducting very successful business operations. However, investing in Japan was considered a challenging task, even before the economic crisis. Many companies and governments were certain that investing in Japan would just be too difficult and hazardous, and preferred to neglect the country. Nevertheless, empirical data from the mid-1990s proves the contrary, as a huge majority of foreign companies were doing great business and most of them were planning to increase their activities in Japan. More precisely, 72% of the surveyed foreign companies classified themselves as "successful" or "very successful," while only 6% described themselves as "failures" and 22% as "as expected," having average results (Khan and Yoshihara 1994). But Japan was not only very interesting just in financial terms. While the initial plan often was to apply the technology of the parent company in Japan, frequently the contrary occurred and new products and innovations were brought back home. Almost two-thirds of foreign companies could pass research and development (R&D) results back to the parent company, situated outside Japan. Statistics confirm this, as 64% of companies acknowledged the transfer of R&D results to the parent company or other subsidiaries (Khan and Yoshihara 1994). This was also the case for know-how and patents, which proved to be very beneficial to foreign investors. However, in reality the number of foreign companies entering Japan only rose at a very slow rate. Japan's circumstances and surroundings were perceived as unfavourable for global business until the late 1980s, the overall Western view of Japanese management being very negative. In fact, at that time, it was generally believed that the unusual Japanese style of management could not lead towards a modern society, and the general public showed very little interest in it. In addition, the overseas job opportunities were very few back then. However, people gradually started to realize how successful the Japanese management model in reality was, and set up studies with the intention of understanding and copying the "secret factors" that had led to success. Control without motivation, technology without investment, research without application of its results, and marketing skills without the benefit of a constructive long-term strategy were features that fascinated the West (Trevor 1986). The Western approach was no longer seen as the only accurate way to manage businesses, nor was it any longer implied that Japan would eventually have to adapt if it wanted to catch up with the West. Thus, it was only a matter of time before large numbers of enterprises started to move to Japan. When a foreign firm was set up, in many cases not only the key management positions, but the entire staff, too, would largely consist of outsiders. Initially, foreigners would also have a higher salary than Japanese and would encourage and expect their Japanese co-workers to learn their language. Over time, the top management would learn Japanese, hire more Japanese staff members and start working with Japanese dealers. As companies became more Japanese, they also hired more Japanese staff.

Foreign Employees in Japan

From the Japanese point of view, it was an advantageous idea to develop traditional Japanese companies into international workplaces. In fact, it became a necessity for them to recruit foreigners, as they were struggling with English negotiations and formalities due to globalization. As Japanese people who had completely mastered the English language were rather few at that time, it was easier and cheaper to hire someone from overseas. Also, the best and most inexpensive way to bring in new ideas and customs into the company was through the employment of foreigners. The historical reason for this is that "Western talent with Japanese spirit" (*wakon yôsai*) was a much appreciated principle among Japanese business managers. Nonetheless, they had highly national Japanese interests, and they wanted to be taught Western skills and adapt their management style. The Immigration Bureau of Japan announced that at the end of 2006 there were 2.08 million foreigners registered in Japan, which was 50% more than a decade earlier. Considering that the Japanese population as a whole increased by only 1.5% during the same period, this represents a huge increase. According to Nikkei, this trend is expected to continue for some time because of the ongoing population decline necessitates bringing in and relying heavily on foreign workers (Nikkei Weekly 2007b). We can see that in Japanese society, despite its reputation for being closed to foreigners, long-term residents have gradually begun to play a bigger role. Some foreigners say Japan has become more open, which is a significant change over the 15 years since the collapse of the bubble economy (Nikkei Weekly 2006). The managerial mix of foreigners and Japanese in a multinational company varied largely from firm to firm. About 15 years ago, the number of expatriates in a foreign company was very limited in all job positions. The ratio of Japanese to foreigners was at least four to one, except for CEO positions, 63% of which were held by Japanese. Also, more than 80% of departmental heads were Japanese. This inevitably led to a more Japanese management style and a more "Japanese" foreign company. However, this was only partially true, as usually overall corporate policies and strategies would be imposed by the parent company, the Japanese subsidiary only being in charge of concrete operations and enjoying a limited autonomy (Khan and Yoshihara 1994). In this way, communication and cultural barriers at the local company can be avoided, and a better understanding of the Japanese market achieved. On the other hand, a possible disadvantage might be problems when communicating with a parent company which is unfamiliar with Japan.

Why Does Japan Need Foreign Labor?

Despite all these concerns and Japan's attempt to control the influx of foreign labor, migration will soon be vital for the Japanese economy. Since Japan's population is rapidly shrinking, migration into Japan becomes an important tool to provide labor for the future. For example, according to Nikkei, workers from abroad accounted for only about 1.5% of Japan's labor force based on 2004 government statistics. By way of contrast, it was 15% in the United States, 12% in Germany, 11% in France, and 10% in the UK (Nikkei Weekly 2006). A recent UN report noted that to maintain the size of its working population, Japan would need 17 million new immigrants by 2050. That would represent 18% of the population, compared to today (Yomiuri Shimbun 2006). These figures clearly show the immediate need for more foreign workers, not just as managers aimed at changing traditional Japanese management systems, but also for down-to-the earth jobs, such as waiters at Denny's, which would require using the Japanese language. However, as Japan's birth rate declines and the population ages, there will definitely be a lack of labor and it will become inevitable to recruit people from overseas. According to an article in the Japan Times, Japan is one of the few industrialized countries not to have experienced a high inflow of international migrants, a characteristic of most other industrialized countries. The article also states that, according to the 2000 UN report "Replacement Migration: Is it a Solution to Declining and Aging Populations?," a huge increase in migration is the only way to support a rapidly aging population. The government needs to work on policies which enable the creation of a society in which Japanese and foreign residents can amicably coexist so that there would be equal opportunities for all. But this is not easy. Many Japanese people expect foreign staff to play more than just an English teacher's role, which has been the general model of foreigners' jobs in Japan. Companies want professional foreigners with special skills and knowledge to help them reconstruct their operations in ways different from traditional, established Japanese management styles; they want new, foreign perspectives and new ideas with the potential to solve management problems. The attitude of Japanese people toward foreigners remains mixed, with some welcoming their new neighbours and the rest keeping a vigilant eye on them (Nikkei Weekly 2007a).

Japanese Companies Target Foreign Students in Japan

Although changes in the working environment for foreigners in Japan seem to be slower than one would wish, efforts of companies, government, and society to accept foreigners are increasing. Matsushita Electric, Fujitsu, and other leading Japanese companies have recently been hiring more foreign exchange students studying at Japanese universities. Matsushita already has over 100 foreign workers on its domestic payroll, and plans to hire 100 more over the next three years. One of the main reasons for this action is that a culturally diverse workforce is necessary to expand overseas. Matsushita assumes that a melting pot of various nationalities within the company will be useful for creating and pursuing international strategies. Moreover, for Japanese companies, which are having a hard time attracting talented Japanese students, hiring talented foreign students poses a reasonable solution. Leading Japanese chemical firm Asahi Kasei says that even though foreign students' skills and knowledge are not inferior to those of Japanese students, there is less competition to employ them (Nikkei Weekly 2007b). Sumitomo Chemical began hiring foreign students in 2005, at the same time as they expanded operations in China and South Korea. The company usually hires two foreign students a year, but plans to take in more in the future. Hiroshi Niinuma of the company's human resources department said in an Asahi Shimbun newspaper (2007) interview that they are looking for skilled foreign personnel who can handle international projects in Japan. Sumitomo Wiring Systems is also recruiting 10-15 foreigners each year. They are planning to offer special training programs for foreigners as well. Since leading traditional Japanese companies, which are a model for many companies, are introducing changes, we can expect other companies to follow suit and create a favorable working environment for foreign students. The number of exchange students changing their visa status to work in Japan surged 11.7% to 5,878 in 2005, which is double the figure from five years ago (Nikkei Weekly 2007b). Following this trend, Japanese companies are showing more interest in hiring foreigners. Last year Pasona Global held seminars in Tokyo and Osaka to help foreign students and workers in Japan to find or switch jobs (Nikkei Weekly 2006). Moreover, staffing agency Solver Network has started a free bilingual English-Japanese magazine, which provides job information to Japanese-speaking foreigners seeking work in Japan. It was distributed to students learning Japanese at universities in Japan and abroad (Nikkei Weekly 2007b). This new approach of hiring foreigners as local staff may help to change the working environment for foreigners in Japanese companies and accustom Japanese employees to working with foreign workers. As exchange students are more accustomed to Japanese culture, and, since they are usually young, they are more flexible at adapting to foreign business environments.

Government Supports the Hiring of Foreigners

The government is also requesting changes to make it easier for foreigners to work in Japan. The Japanese Business Federation, known as Nippon Keidanren, recommended that the government make it easier for foreign engineers and other people with advanced expertise to work in Japan. They believe that this will help Japanese companies obtain the workers they need in order to react to a declining population, and boost their global competitiveness. Keidanren also found out in the survey that there is a growing demand among IT firms for foreign-born specialists, as well as those engaged in cutting-edge R&D and international operations, and proposed easing the visa requirements for foreign mechanical engineers, translators, designers, and other people with advanced skills. Under this proposal, foreigners with at least four years of experience in their areas of expertise would be allowed to work in Japan.

Currently a minimum of ten years of experience is required. On the other hand, to prevent an excessive flow of foreigners into Japan, Japan's most influential business lobby will also recommend the implementation of some measures, including Japanese language requirements, and conduct surveys aimed at determining the extent of labor shortages in each industrial area. Keidanren also proposes that central government join forces with regional authorities and private business to ensure these foreign workers have proper housing and educational opportunities for their children (Nikkei Weekly 2006). Although a smaller number of years of experience may open more doors for foreigners, the language requirement is a big obstacle for foreigners. Whether Japanese people truly perceive an urgency to invite foreign workers is questionable. Initial measures have been discussed and may be implemented at the government level, step by step, and not radically.

Integration Activities

At the prefectural level, efforts to welcome and communicate with foreign workers can already be seen. A town called Oizumi in Gunma prefecture, in the Kanto area of Japan, holds the distinction of having the highest percentage of registered foreigners, mostly Brazilians, of any municipality in the nation. A non-profit organization, known as the Oizumi Centre of International Vocational and Training, hosts a free Latin rhythm dance class every Friday night, and, sometimes, more than 100 people come to participate. This serves as a place for foreigners to work off their stress and deepen their interactions with Japanese. This center also offers consultations on a wide variety of issues, ranging from garbage issues, which is one the biggest problems of conflict between Japanese and foreigners, down to dealing with cold treatment at work. In Oizumi, since 1992, public relations brochures have been printed in Portuguese every month, and efforts have been made to explain differences in customs, but overcoming those differences is not easy. In Kanagawa prefecture, which is adjacent to Tokyo, the concentration of foreign residents is highest in an apartment complex owned by the prefecture. In order to deepen mutual understanding, neighborhood councils, government organizations, and volunteer groups have cooperated in holding summer festivals. Multicultural festival workshops aim to create an enjoyable living environment by offering Japanese classes for adults, and by hosting supplementary lessons for elementary school students (Nikkei Weekly 2007b).

From the Perspective of the Japanese Trade Union Confederation

The Japanese trade union confederation Rengo has a three-tier, hierarchical structure comprising enterprise-based unions, industrial federations, and the national centre at the top. According to Rengo, the primary goals of trade unions are to defend the employment and livelihood of workers, and to build democracy in the workplace, community, and society as a whole. In Rengo, there is a section which deals with foreign workers. It aims to cooperate with organizations such as Non-Profit Organizations, and to protect all foreign workers' rights by supporting them. In 2004, Rengo announced that it would tackle the situation of foreign workers in Japan. Among the issues was the use of the foreigner trainee system in Japanese companies. According to Rengo, companies are using foreigners as cheap labor, and the goal of the trainee system, as an international contribution to developing foreign workers' skills, is not being achieved. Thus, Rengo has been urging the government to take action. However, there has been no significant action yet, and the situation regarding trainees is unchanged. Rengo says that in a survey in 2005, 80% of companies using this system in Japan admitted to having employed foreigners as cheap labor. To tackle this issue, Rengo is urging the abolishment of the system, or the setting of stricter qualifications on the selection of companies which may use this system. Besides the trainee system, Rengo is also working on matters such as the care of the children of foreign workers and welfare for foreigners. Although many concerns are being discussed, and the need for change is recognized, movement is very slow and no radical action is being taken (Japanese Trade Union Confederation 2008).

More Foreign Workers Especially from Asia

There were 5,878 foreign students who requested a working visa in 2005. Of these graduates, 4,186 were from China, and 747 were from South Korea. These figures can be attributed to the rapidly increasing number of companies that have an interest in operating new businesses in Asia. The Ministry of Economy, Trade and Industry (METI) conducted a survey in the spring of 2008 asking listed companies about their plans to recruit graduates who can function in a global environment. Of the 289 companies that responded to the questionnaire, about 40% said that they hoped to hire foreign students who have studied in Japan. Overall, there seemed to be more opportunities for foreigners to pursue a career in Japan than expected. Also, it is now a massive trend for companies to specifically employ Asians in order to expand their business. This is illustrated by the following examples. A Vietnamese woman who graduated from Toyohashi Technology and Science University in Aichi started to work for the Asahi Kasei group. She is now involved in the LSI development business. Her bright personality and determination were appreciated. Her dream is to form a bridge between Japan and Vietnam as a technician. Another woman from Sri Lanka graduated from Ritsumeikan Asia Pacific University in Oita, and is now working for Fujitsu. She explains that Fujitsu is expanding its business to become a worldwide player, and that, from the recruiting process on, much attention was paid to her future career. A Chinese graduate from Tokyo Industry University worked for Sumitomo Trust & Banking. The company set up branches in Beijing in 2004 and in Shanghai in 2005. Sumitomo Trust & Banking now wants to train Chinese employees in Japan in order to transfer them to Chinese branches afterwards. Fujitsu plans to recruit 30 foreign graduates out of a total of 585 new employees. But these are just a few examples of actual international students, many of whom wish to pursue careers in Japan.

Foreign Employees Enter Japanese Multinationals Locally

Many foreigners think that companies need foreigners because of their skills, skills that many Japanese people do not have, such as engineering and language skills. However, some companies hire foreigners as they would hire normal Japanese employees. Uniqlo, a clothing company, also recruits foreigners. As they do not distinguish between Japanese and foreigners particularly, there is no specified quota. However, foreigners are treated fairly during recruitment procedures. Foreigners have their contracts updated yearly because of the visa issue, but other factors such as salary and vacation are identical to what Japanese workers receive. They have to work at Uniqlo stores in Japan just as other Japanese employees do. Subsequently, they will have opportunities to work in their home countries, as well as form a bridge between Japan and their home cities. There are many foreign students hoping to find a job within a big company that has subsidiaries in their home countries.

Foreign Women in Japan

Women used to think it would be difficult to pursue careers in Japan. Since being a foreigner already is a challenge, one would imagine that it is almost impossible for women to work like normal business men in a Japanese company. However, there are many foreign women achieving their goals as professionals by coming to Japan. The trick is to turn around the seeming challenges and apparent problems in order to take advantage of their gender and nationality. Usually, it does not even matter if a woman is Japanese or a foreigner, as the main problems in the workplace are credibility and responsibility. For foreigners, interpersonal skills are perceived as an additional weakness. Gaining credibility is much more difficult in Japan compared to other foreign countries. Having had an established position and title at a previous workplace, and being older will automatically create respect and credibility even though no one in Japan knows the applicant personally. This is indicated by the story of how a young American attorney was rejected by a Japanese client. However, after her boss introduced her with a long list of praise for her credentials and her outstanding background and education, the client accepted her. It is indeed crucial to get credibility in Japan by showing one's skills and knowledge (Rutledge 2001). Although there are difficulties, there are advantages as well, as already mentioned. First, foreign women are more visible in a business setting and they, therefore, will be remembered more easily. Japanese will be curious about them, instead of perceiving them as odd, as they do with foreign men. Therefore, foreign women have more opportunities to come in contact with highly ranked men than they would have had at home. Another benefit for foreign women is the high interpersonal skills they tend to have. Because women tend to be better listeners, being interested in others and trying to interact with people positively, it makes it easier for foreign women to adjust to different cultures than for foreign men. Rutledge (2001) further quotes an example of a senior foreign female manager who worked at a male-oriented engineering firm. She learned to remember co-workers birthdays, to walk back to the elevator in order to say goodbye when a visitor came, and to spend more time on socializing at the beginning of a meeting than she ever did in the U.S. Thanks to this, she was able to enhance her credibility, her ability, and her effectiveness as a manager working in a Japanese environment. As one can see from these cases, there are many opportunities for foreign women since there seem to be more advantages for women than men sometimes. In fact, many leading companies such as IBM aim to have diversity in their companies, which means not only gender, nationalities, and religions, but also disabled people.

Carlos Ghosn – The Most Successful Foreign Manager in Japan

Japanese management style used to be an ideal model for other companies in the world. However, the bubble burst, the economy collapsed and many companies went bankrupt. In other countries, it is often said that many Japanese companies need to be restructured, and that they need foreigners to rebuild their management style from the ground up. The most famous example of such an attempt is Nissan, the well-known Japanese car manufacturer. Nissan is famous for its successful reforms under the leadership of a foreign manager. Carlos Ghosn, the CEO of both Renault in France and Nissan in Japan, is now the most famous CEO to have turned around a Japanese automobile company. When the announcement was made that Carlos Ghosn was to become the CEO of Nissan, the Japanese public was shocked at the idea that a foreign manager would play such a major role in one of the most traditional and famous Japanese companies. Although he was called in to act as a crisis manager, which implies that he had to fire many employees, he is almost treated as a hero now as he rescued the company from its most critical situation ever, facing a 17 billion U.S. dollars debt. When Ghosn was appointed as CEO of Nissan in 1999, his first plan, called the "Nissan Revival Plan," was thought to be impossible to achieve. Presumably, the reason for this disbelief was that it normally takes a lot of time for new managers to gain the trust of Japanese employees, especially when the manager is a foreigner. This was an obstacle that Ghosn would have to overcome immediately. Ghosn knew that maintaining a positive relationship is regarded as the most important factor in Japanese companies; it was, therefore, hard for him to cut the number of employees, close some factories, and reconsider the relationship with subsidiaries. Apart from being oriented towards relationships, Ghosn is also known as a charismatic leader, as well as for having extraordinary communication skills. He, therefore, promotes direct contacts with employees. If an employee actually sends an e-mail directly to Carlos Ghosn, he will read it and reply, even if this e-mail is a complaint, or if it expresses disagreement with Ghosn's vision of the future. Ghosn would visit retailers to make sure that there are no problems with the quality of the cars, asking which one is the best seller and inquiring about what they think of the advertising campaigns. To him, communication is the most important factor for the success of the company. As mentioned before, firstly and most importantly, it is very difficult to gain the trust of Japanese workers, partly because of the language problem, but also because they see the newcomer as an outsider who cannot share inside information with them. However, although Ghosn is not good at Japanese at all, he succeeded in communicating successfully with his Japanese employees. This is because his attitude toward the workers made clear that he considered himself one of them and that saving the company was his primary goal. A typical Japanese company never discloses what has been discussed in a board of directors meeting to employees, but Ghosn believed that it was his responsibility to do so. A foreigner who came from abroad suddenly to Nissan has not only cut costs to increase profits, but also increased the employees' motivation so that Nissan could be a good team, working together to develop the company. A typical foreign manager in Japan is usually depicted as a rationalist, only able to fire employees who are less productive than others. However, Ghosn has probably changed this image a little thanks to his efforts in communicating with everyone in the company. And he proved to be extremely successful. Nissan became profitable, and could forecast growth for the coming years. Nissan realized a 331 Yen billion profit—the largest net profit ever for Nissan—in contrast to the enormous losses the year before. The key contributor to this outcome was the development of operating income, which tripled. The Ghosn/ Nissan story emphatically demonstrates the benefits that can be derived from foreign input at the highest managerial level, in a situation where no other Japanese manager would have succeeded. This could, in fact, be said about most managers from abroad. However, what was so special about Ghosn was that he understood the most important factor for Japanese companies: human relationships. Every business in Japan is based on this. Companies do not establish ties with other companies if there is not a well-established relationship. The same thing can be said inside companies. If workers on the shop floor do not trust their manager, good commodities can not be produced. In fact, Ghosn's interview on CNN made clear that in Japan any change implemented by an outsider will face rejection, unless it is explained very clearly why the change is needed, how the change will be done, and what the result will be. He attributed his success to the process of establishing strong ties with every worker at Nissan. Also, because of the efforts he made to communicate, he succeeded in laying off people in order to revive Nissan. He spent a lot of time explaining why this was necessary to restructure the company. It is true that he cut the workforce by 14% and cut the number of suppliers by half. Five plants were closed, and about 21,000 jobs were lost. Some people criticized his "foreign" style of management, characterizing it as a too capitalistic approach. However, what he did as a leader from a different country, having different perspectives, was to bring in new ideas, which were not considered preconceived because of his multicultural background. Of course, he could have just been considered a capitalist in dismissing so many workers. However, what he did was not just practicing capitalism. He put much effort into building a strong relationship with people, and that is how a great leader, who rescued a Japanese company, was born. Ghosn insists that diversity is the key to survival in the 21st century. Japan needs to open the doors to foreigners so that companies are able to see traditional ways of thinking in a critical light. Because of his success, Ghosn not only has made many Japanese companies rethink and accept foreigners, he has also motivated many foreign workers to pursue a career in Japan (CNN News 2005).

Challenges of Working in Japan

As mentioned before, Japanese companies wish to employ foreigners, mostly in order to improve their internationalization, or to bring in language and other skills. By merging the assets of the two different cultures, a "third culture" company will be formed. As the number of foreign workers has grown over the years, the number of resulting problems has risen simultaneously; language barriers, cultural problems, career opportunity problems, as well as different management styles lead to frictions in a mixed organization. The problems were compounded by many Westerners who had certain stereotypes about the Japanese, and, more particularly, about their organizational culture and their way of doing work. These beliefs were oversimplifications of the current situation and were frequently opposed to reality. A more unbiased view of the working environment was needed to comprehend both the advantages and limitations. Even though some might have the impression that the dissimilarities are slowly fading away due to globalization, there are still numerous profound differences in cultural values, and there are still countless mistakes to make.

Communication Barriers

The fact that some 10 to 15 years ago the vast majority of outsiders did not speak Japanese obviously caused countless misunderstandings, confrontations, and general problems. In fact, at that time, barely 6% of the most senior expatriates had some Japanese language ability, 71% spoke English only, and 23% could speak both languages (Khan and Yoshihara 1994). But the language itself represents only a small part of all communication barriers between Westerners and Japanese on the shop floor. That is why even foreigners who do master the language still have serious communication problems on a regular basis. Japanese is very much a multilayered language, where confusing nuances and subtleties reign. This is one of the reasons why expressing any opinion or point of view is a tricky task for Westerners, and why they should carefully choose their words. Another common mistake among foreigners is to state their opinion too resolutely, which could sound too harsh or pretentious, or could also influence the judgment of subordinates on a certain topic or idea. As Japanese dislike being frank when they are not of the same mind, and because contradicting a superior is "not done," this can easily lead to unpleasant situations. Another blunder is not to spend enough time socializing with colleagues after work. Working towards a friendly relationship is very beneficial for good, constructive communication. When this step is skipped or not taken seriously, the foreigner will be shut out. A third and final example of different communication styles is the fact that many workers from abroad do have the feeling that not enough information is being shared with them. As their Japanese colleagues do not intend to behave as translators, and as foreigners often show their impatience whenever they explain something in English, some information might not be passed on.

Cross-Cultural Problems

It is understandable that Westerners will need to go through a tough adaptation process in order to become a useful group member of the Japanese corporate organization, as many cultural differences will arise. There are, for instance, some dissimilarities concerning privacy, overtime, leadership skills, etc., which must be overcome. Most foreigners are truly willing to overcome these barriers, and explicitly want to learn about the "Japanese way," however, some of the older, skilled workers do not intend to or do not have the patience to do so, and just want to do their job in the way they are used to, leading to even more problems. One example of cultural differences is how subordinates are encouraged and rewarded to make any suggestion concerning their job or to communicate day-to-day minutiae straightforwardly to their boss. This is encouraged by treating every member of the company equally, which is visualized by wearing identical uniforms, having one cafeteria, open offices, job rotation, common facilities, egalitarian team symbols, etc. This is fully opposed to Western business culture, where managers react sceptically to bright ideas from knowledgeable subordinates, as they represent a threat to their own position or authority. Another illustration is empowerment in a Japanese company. It is well known that the Japanese, among themselves, can create and implement empowerment very successfully, resulting in employees who "live to work." The problem arises when an outsider enters the company, and the same approaches are used. The pampering of employees is highly disapproved of by expatriates as it makes them feel inexperienced and incapable, and it is regarded as disrespectful.

Career Opportunities

A problem among Westerners, especially among highly ambitious managers, which manifests itself, is the lack of career opportunities in the new job in the foreign company in Japan. Westerners are gradually starting to show some dissatisfaction and to complain about their career prospects as foreign staff. Many mid-career managers and professionals feel like they are working in the lowest positions in the company, and that it is extremely difficult to move up from there due to the very strict hierarchy within the company. Even when expatriates are highly ranked as a CEO, they could also have a hard time trying to take important decisions, especially if their knowledge of Japanese is only modest or non-existent. The corresponding term "*gaijin* ceiling" refers to this immobility of motivated foreigners, who do not get the opportunity for many years, or never, to improve upon the position they initially applied for. Usually, this situation was not expected and not communicated during the contract negotiations, which results in disillusionment. At some point, Westerners might feel betrayed by the company, and regret their decision although they are receiving high salaries. The motive for this is that they believe that their contribution is more often than not symbolic. According to Honyama (2003), a majority of expatriates do not feel respected, and are not perceived of as the heroes they were expected to be, but rather as yes-men under the headquarters' thumb, disliked by many Japanese employees. This problem in a blended organization commences directly with the recruitment of foreign workers, especially as concerns high-ranked personnel. As they are selected merely because they have mastered the Japanese language, it becomes very hard to find candidates who in addition have the necessary expertise, cross-cultural management skills, and who are willing to work abroad. Moreover, Japanese interviewers are not good at picking out such people among the candidates; therefore, to facilitate such recruitment, companies in Japan often use the help of a head-hunter. The problem is that head hunters habitually base their verdict on the candidate's previous working experience in the West, and will understate the importance of flexibility and cultural sensitivity. In addition, the newly hired foreign workers will probably not get the same training as local staff would receive, as the company might worry about the fact that they will leave after a few years. According to March (1992), escaping this vicious circle should be a main concern for foreign companies in Japan. Top priorities should be the recruiting of suitable foreigners, and offering them fair training and promoting them to the decision-making level as if they were regular employees. This process of totally integrating foreigners by adopting new guidelines can be seen today in larger companies since the turn of the century, but it is still very slow in smaller ones (Honyama 2003; March 1992).

Different Management Styles

Overcoming cultural barriers and differences in management philosophies is unavoidable when foreigners are involved. In fact, the principles in Japan are more or less the opposite to those in Western countries. Working in this situation calls for adaptation processes, and cultural openness is necessary. In concrete, the Japanese believe in the power and the will of improving work productivity and quality, they all feel like members of the corporation, and form a family that is very group-oriented. This last feature in particular, conformism, is something especially difficult for Westerners to understand and to adapt to. This is why we will concentrate on group harmony on the shop floor in this section. Western managers will have to get a feel for group harmony instead of insisting on the importance of results. Plenty of patience will be required to take care of team morale and harmony among subordinates, and to achieve group consensus every single time before the actual work can start. This need for harmony can be explained through *amae*, the "psychological condition of dependence on other persons' kindness and goodwill." (Alston 1986) *Amae* should be achieved by reciprocal emotional support on the shop floor, by a leader who is flexible enough to care personally about the specific and individual needs of each group member. A concrete example of this phenomenon is Japanese meetings, where foreign non-Japanese speakers are supposed to be present every single time, even though they do not understand a word and cannot participate. But excluding them from this important group task would shut them out, and this would not stimulate "good vibes" or *amae*. Westerners, in return, would ask for "no Japanese language only" meetings as they would not really understand this concept and still feel isolated from the decision-making processes. But since Japanese meetings are held on almost every topic, stretching over hours, and anyone who could possibly be involved should be in attendance, this regulation is impossible to maintain (Rutledge 2001). One more different management style that is omnipresent in Japanese companies is the power limitations of a CEO. Foreign CEOs should be aware of the authority and power limitations they will inevitably face in a Japanese environment. First, leaders will be held up by the fact that no actual work can be done until the whole group reaches a consensus. Voting for a simple majority does not happen, as this might damage the personal relationship he has with his subordinates, and in consequence damage the *amae*. Pushing your own ideas through will never be a success, even for a highly ranked leader. A second limitation in a Japanese context is the fact that superiors are not supposed to be concerned with day-to-day minutiae, but should only take care of guiding the business in a constructive broad direction for the long term, and should communicate the company vision and the main goals. Details can be further developed by subordinates, who are continuously encouraged to make proposals concerning their own workplace, and the accomplishment of these goals is their responsibility. Finally, the seniority-based system can lead to significant power limitations. These constraints should be considered seriously, as group members have the power to withdraw emotionally from their tasks and obligations, which is a threat to the leader's moral authority.

Dealing with Changes in the Japanese Workplace

Not only have foreign CEOs changed Japanese companies, but recently foreign companies have also changed Japanese individuals' attitudes toward their careers. An increasing number of Japanese employees hop from company to company. They gradually develop some feeling of the Western methods of business management. They understand that staying forever in only one company could impede their personal development. Employers try to combine this with the unique situation of the Japanese market in which workers still yearn for job stability, refraining from any risks inherent in job-switching. However, more Japanese, especially young people, are recognizing the Western management system in which workers are paid according to performance, and they are attracted to this non-Japanese system. This improvement will open the doors to Japan, not only economically or politically, but also as a nation to foreigners. But this is not perceived positively by all. When Japanese think of foreign workers, some will worry about several factors. First, there is the language barrier, and, second, and most importantly, there is serious concern about trusting a foreigner. Trust is one of the most important criteria when recruiting in Japanese companies. They even are cautious when hiring a new Japanese employee, so what would happen when hiring a foreigner? In fact, in Japanese, a foreigner is called a *gaijin*, which really means "outsider." Traditional Japan is in fact not well prepared to deal with a diversified workforce.

Conclusion

Since the end of the bubble economy, Japanese society has clearly opened its doors for long-term residents, even though it has the reputation of being closed to foreigners. As we discussed briefly in this chapter, Japan is in desperate need of workers from overseas to support its aging population. During recent years, Japan has clearly adjusted its policies and welcomed more foreigners into its workforce. This has led to numerous changes and a more international atmosphere. But, although some experience this as a big change, the actual impact has been limited. The number of foreigners is not sufficient to support Japan's shrinking population. One person who might give outsiders the feeling that Westerners *do* bring about change in Japan is Carlos Ghosn, as he was able to turn around Nissan. In doing so, Ghosn presented a new role model for foreign managers in Japan, and he has opened many doors for them to enter Japanese firms. Consequently, many Japanese people are now expecting more from their foreign staff than just speaking English. Companies are now also recruiting mid-career foreigners to assist them in restructuring their operations. Obviously, however, Ghosn is still an exception. Our conclusion is that Japan is definitely changing, just like other nations, but we must concede that the contribution of foreign workers has until now been relatively small. The doors of Japan have started to open gradually, although only for the lucky or the well-educated. Japan definitely needs a strong labor force from abroad, and it is clear that diversity is the key to help the nation. Now is the time for Japan to break with its long history of being a group of isolated islands and to become a real international player.

Bibliography

Alston, J. P. (1986): *The American Samurai: blending American and Japanese managerial practices.* Walter De Gruyter.

Asahi Shimbun (2007): *More firms recruiting foreign graduates.* Asahi Shimbun, July 25, 2007.

Ballon, R. J. (1990): *Management careers in Japan and the foreign firm.* Institute of Comparative Culture Business Series Bulletin 130. Tokyo: Sophia University.

Bungeishunju (2003): *Waga nihongata keiei no sinzui wo katarô.* Bungei shunju, August 2003.

Byham, W. C. (1993): *Shogun Management: How North Americans can thrive in Japanese companies.* Harper Business.

CNN News (2005): *Carlos Ghosn: Nissan's turnaround artist.* Downloaded from http://edition.cnn.com/2005/BUSINESS/04/20/boardroom.ghosn/ CNN.com on January 28, 2008.

Debroux, Ph. (1993): *The foreign employer in Japan.* Sophia University.

The Nikkei Weekly (2006): *Foreigners play greater role in Japan.* The Nikkei Weekly, March 6, 2006.

The Nikkei Weekly (2007a): *Foreign students gets look.* The Nikkei Weekly, May 14, 2007.

The Nikkei Weekly (2007b): *Locals see language learning as critical.* Nikkei Weekly, December 12, 2007

Fucini, J. J. and Fucini, S. (1990): *Working for the Japanese: Inside Mazda's American auto plant.* The Free Press.

Honyama, S. (2003): *Atarashii jôshi wa americajin.* Tokyo: Basilico.

Inoue, Y. (2005): *Shain ni Story o.* Nikkei Business, April 4, 2005.

Japanese Trade Union Confederation (2008): *Aratana gaikokujin kenshû jitsunô jisshû seido no tsuika seikaku nit suite.* Downloaded from http://www.jtuc-rengo.or.jp/roudou/gaikokujin/seisaku.html on January 27, 2008.

The Japan Institute of Labor (2003): *Gaikokujin 200 nin o honsha saiyô e / matsushita denki ga chûkoku o chûshin ni.* Downloaded from http://www.jil.go.jp/mm/kigyo/20030404b.html on January 30, 2008.

The Nikkei Sunday (2007): *Keidanren to propose relaxing visa requirements for engineers.* The Nikkei Sunday, March 18, 2007.

Japan Times Jobs (2007): Downloaded from http://job.japantimes.com/cl_f_index.php on January 8, 2008.

Kogi, K. (2002): *Communication no gokui.* Diamondo September 21, 2002.

Khan, S. and Yoshihara, H. (1994): *Strategy and performance of foreign companies in Japan.* Quorum Books.

Leppert, P. (2001): Doing business with Japan. Jain Publishing Company.

March, R. M. (1992): *Working for a Japanese company: Insights into the multicultural workplace.* Kodansha International, 1992.

Napier, N. K, and S. Taylor (2002): *Experiences of women professionals abroad: Comparisons across Japan, China and Turkey.* International Journal of Human Resource Management 13(5), p. 837–851.

Rutledge, B. (2001): *Working in Japan.* Asuku Publishing.

Trevor, M. (1983): *Japan's reluctant multinationals: Japanese management at home and abroad.* St. Martin's Press.

Uniqlo Company Homepage (2008): *Gaikokujin ryûgakusei saiyô.* Downloaded from http://www.uniqlo.com/jp/employment/students/foreigner/ on January 28, 2008.

The Yomiuri Shimbun (2006): *Shigoto jihô fueru gaikokujin ryûgakusei no teiki saiyô.* The Yomiuri Shimbun August 21, 2006.

Yuzawa, T. and M. Udagawa (1990): *Foreign business in Japan before World War II.* University of Tokyo Press.

15. Glossary

aidoru	idol
anime	animation
ba	place
bunkatsu hôshiki	divided production system
bûmu	fad
burando ryoku	brand power
bushido	the way of the samurai
datsu-sara	corporate dropout
freeter	job-hopping, part-time worker
furyo saiken	nonperforming loan
gai(koku)jin	foreigner
gambaru	do one's best

haken	dispatch worker
hikikomori	social dropout who stays constantly at home
hitori hôshiki	one-man production system
ippanshoku	career in administration of a Japanese company
jidôka	automation
jinmyaku	personal relationships
jisedaihô	law of the next generation
jukensei	student preparing for examination
junkai hôshiki	chase production system
kabushiki kaisha	stock company
kaisha	Japanese firm
kaizen	improvement
kanai	inside the house
kanban	card (used in manufacturing)
keiretsu	Japanese conglomerate
kitto katsu	sure winner
kôgai	environmental pollution
kôhai	one's junior (somebody who entered the company at a later stage)
kyôran bukka	crazy price inflation

manga	comic book
naitei	letter of acceptance, acceptance notice
Neet	young person (Not in Education, Employment or Training)
nomikai	drinking party
okusan	full-time wife of an office worker
otaku	fanatic
salarymen	office worker
seiketsu	systematize
seiri	sort
seishain	regular employees
seiso	clean
seiton	setting in order
sekuhara	sexual harassment (abbr.)
sempai	one's senior (somebody who entered the company at an earlier stage)
senmon gakkô	vocational school
shain ryokô	company outing
shinhatsubai	new release, new on sale
shinkaishahô	new company law
shinshôhin	new product
shitsuke	standardize
shujin	master (lit.), husband

shukkô	being transferred
sôgô shôsha	general trading company
sôgôshoku	career track in a Japanese company (non-administrative work)
taishokukin	allowance for retirement
tenshoku	job change
tenshokusha	one who has changed jobs
wakon yôsai	Western talent with Japanese spirit
yokonarabi	going along with the crowd
yûgen kaisha	limited company
zaibatsu	financial combine
zaiteku	financial management technique

16. About the Authors

All authors can be reached at japanesemanagement@gmail.com.

Megumi Aoki is a student at the Faculty of Comparative Culture at Sophia University, majoring in International Business and Economics.

Matthew Cabuloy is a business student at the University of San Francisco's McClaren School of Business, with a minor in Japanese Studies. In 2007, Matt was an exchange student at the Faculty of Liberal Arts at Sophia University.

Parissa Haghirian is an Associate Professor of International Management at Sophia University in Tokyo, Japan. Her research interests include knowledge management and transfer within multinational corporations, Japanese market entry, and cross-cultural management.

Natsuki Hayakawa is currently studying at Sophia University in Tokyo. She is majoring in International Business and will be graduating in 2009. She lived in the United States for nine years and plans to work for a Japanese trading company (*sôgô shôsha*) in the future.

Jeffrey Honma is a fourth year student at Sophia University planning to graduate in International Business and Economics from the Comparative Culture Department. He plans to not join a large corporation, but to learn more Japanese and find a job suitable for his future career, hopefully utilizing his international background. His hobby is ice hockey.

Yui Inada is a business student graduating from Sophia University in Tokyo, who is majoring in International Business and Economics. The focus of her studies includes human resource management and international marketing.

Hitoshi Kakishima is a student at Sophia University in the Faculty of Comparative Culture. He spent his high school life in Australia at Grace Lutheran College. He is currently majoring in International Business and Economics, and is expected to graduate in March 2009. As he has a strong interest in trading, he plans to get a job in a Japanese trading company (*sôgô shôsha*).

Pascal Kalbermatten was a graduate student at the University of St. Gallen in Switzerland at the time of writing this book chapter. His major was Information and Technology Management and during his studies he spent an exchange semester at Sophia University in Tokyo.

Hayaka Kawamura is an undergraduate in the Faculty of Comparative Culture at Sophia University in Tokyo, majoring in International Business and Economics. He studied at Pangbourne College in England from 1998 to 2003 before entering Sophia University. He is planning to graduate in March, 2009, and is hoping to get a job with a Japanese beer brewer and plans to make Japanese beer popular around the world.

Kotaro Kinoshita is a fourth year student at Sophia University planning to graduate in International Business and Economics from the Comparative Culture Department. He plans to join a large corporation and has visions of becoming a successful businessman. His hobbies are soccer and playing violin.

Nodoka Kobayashi graduated from Sophia University in Tokyo in 2008, majoring in Comparative Culture, with a focus on International Business. She spent one year at Loyola University in Chicago from 2006-2007, where she studied International Marketing Strategy in order to see the Japanese market from a different point of view. She also had an internship with Jetro (Japan External Trade Organization) in Chicago.

Saaya Konishi is currently a student at Sophia University in Tokyo majoring in International Business and Economics. She has lived in the United States, Canada, Indonesia, and Japan. She enjoys traveling, swimming, and watching movies. She is expected to graduate in March, 2009.

Manuel Lukas is student of economics at the University of St.Gallen, Switzerland. In autumn 2007, he was an exchange student at Sophia University in Tokyo.

RolfMadrid was an undergraduate student at Sophia University and majored in International Business and Economics. He transferred to Sophia University from Ateneo de Manila University in Manila after his year-long exchange program at Sophia University. He hopes to improve the plight of Filipinos someday through sharing what he has learned and experienced abroad.

Kaoru Miki is majoring in International Business and Economics at the Faculty of Liberal Arts at Sophia University. In 2006, during a 10 month internship in Poland, she supported the Polish Window Company with its Japanese market entry, and after that she worked at the Warsaw branch of a Japanese trading company where she researched the current situation and potential of the Eastern European market.

Baktash Muhammadi is a 4th year BA student in the Faculty of Comparative Cultures at Sophia University, majoring in International Business and Economics. He is especially interested in the field of economic development.

Jun Nishida is a student majoring in Social Studies from the Faculty of Comparative Culture at Sophia University in Tokyo. She has lived in Taiwan and is expected to graduate in 2009.

Mari Okachi is a student at the Faculty of Liberal Arts at Sophia University, majoring in International Business and Economics. After graduation, she plans a career with a multinational corporation in Tokyo

Alison Onishi graduated from Sophia University with a degree in International Business and Economics, and has returned to Hawaii to pursue her post graduate studies. Her academic interests include microeconomics and human resource development and management.

Delphine Pilate graduated from the University of Antwerp as a Commercial Engineer in 2009, with International Management as her major. For one semester, she studied at Sophia University in Tokyo, where she broadened her management perspectives. She intends to work in an international environment to further develop her skills and to learn more about diverse cultures from an economic point of view.

Miho Saito is a student in the Faculty of Comparative Culture at Sophia University, majoring in Political Science.

Ayano Sakuragi is a third-year student at Sophia University, studying Political Science in the English Department. She plans to join a large corporation, with the intention of finally taking over her father's clothing business.

Anna Sanga is majoring in Social Science from the Faculty of Comparative Culture at Sophia University. As a high school student, Anna lived in Australia. She is expected to graduate in 2009, and will work for a multinational Japanese corporation, putting what she has learnt about Japanese management into practice.

Aaron Schiffer was in the 2008 graduating class of Alber's School of Business at Seattle University. In 2007, he was an exchange student at the Faculty of Liberal Arts of Sophia University. Majoring in International Business, with a minor in Japanese language, he is striving for success in the business worlds of Japan and America.

Yuuko Shimizu is a student in the Faculty of Comparative Culture at Sophia University in Tokyo. She is majoring in International Business and Economics and plans to graduate in 2009.

Yuka Tanaka studied at Sophia University, majoring in International Business and Economics. After living in England and the U.S for 10 years in total, she became interested in how different cultures influence economies. She enjoys traveling, watching films, and playing badminton.

Greg Taylor is a graduate student in Sophia University's M.A. in International Business and Development Studies program. He received a B.S. in Computer Science and a minor in Theater from Cal Poly, San Luis Obispo. He worked professionally as a senior game programmer for seven years in Los Angeles. Greg enjoys social Lindy Hop dancing and listening to jazz music.

Michael Tiffany is a student at Sophia University`s Faculty of Liberal Arts majoring in International Business and Economics. He has a strong interest in the workings of Japanese business. It is not usual for him to roam around Tokyo taking pictures.

Asako Washizu is a student from the Faculty of Comparative Culture at Sophia University in Tokyo. She is majoring in

International Business and Economics and plans to graduate in 2009.

Aya Yoshida is a student at Sophia University in Tokyo in the Faculty of Comparative Culture and is majoring in International Business and Economy. She graduated from Toshimagaoka Girls' Private High School and studied abroad in the United States during her high school life. Her hobbies are classical ballet and playing the piano. She would like to work at a TV station in the future.

Index

F

G

H

I

J

K

L

R

S

T

U

V

W

Y

Z